BETWEEN POVERTY
AND THE PYRE

BETWEEN POVERTY AND THE PYRE

Moments in the history of
widowhood

*Edited by Jan Bremmer and
Lourens van den Bosch*

London and New York

First published 1995
by Routledge
11 New Fetter Lane, London EC4P 4EE

Simultaneously published in the USA and Canada
by Routledge
29 West 35th Street, New York, NY 10001

Typeset in Garamond by
Ponting–Green Publishing Services, Chesham, Bucks
Printed and bound in Great Britain by
TJ Press (Padstow) Ltd, Padstow, Cornwall

British Library Cataloguing in Publication Data
A catalogue record for this book is available from
the British Library

Library of Congress Cataloging in Publication Data
Between poverty and the pyre: moments in the history of
widowhood / edited by Jan Bremmer and
Lourens van den Bosch
p.   cm.
Includes bibliographical references and index.
1. Widowhood–History–Cross-cultural studies.
I. Bremmer, Jan N.   II. Bosch, Lourens P. van den
HQ1058.B48   1995
305.48'9654'09–dc20   94–27018

ISBN 0–415–08370–2

CONTENTS

CONTENTS

ILLUSTRATIONS

Between pp. 102–3

NOTES ON
CONTRIBUTORS

Lourens P. van den Bosch b. 1944, is Associate Professor of History of Religion at the Rijksuniversiteit Groningen. He is the author of *Atharvaveda-parisista: Chapters 21–29, Introduction, Translation and Notes* (1978) and *Inleiding in het hindoeïsme* (1990).

Jan N. Bremmer b. 1944, is Professor of History of Religion at the Rijksuniversiteit Groningen. He is the author of *The Early Greek Concept of the Soul* (1983) and *Greek Religion* (1994), co-author of *Roman Myth and Mythography* (1987), editor of *Interpretations of Greek Mythology* (1987), *From Sappho to de Sade: Moments in the History of Sexuality* (1989) and *A Dictionary of Ancient Religions* (1995), and co-editor of *A Cultural History of Gesture* (1991).

Rolf H. Bremmer Jr b. 1950, is Associate Professor of Medieval English at the Rijksuniversiteit Leiden. He is the author of *The Fyve Wyttes* (1987) and *A Bibliographical Guide to Old Frisian Studies* (1992), editor of *Franciscus Junius and His Circle* (1995), and co-editor of *Aspects of Old Frisian Philology* (1990), *P.J. Cosijn: Notes on Beowulf* (1991), *Zur Phonologie und Morphologie des Altniederländischen* (1992), *Current Trends in West Germanic Etymological Lexicography* (1993) and *Companion to Old English Poetry (1994).*

Marjo Buitelaar b. 1958, is Associate Professor of Cultural Anthropology at the Rijksuniversiteit Groningen. She is the author of *Fasting and Feasting in Morocco: Women's Participation in Ramadan* (1993), and co-editor of *De Koran: Ontstaan, interpretatie en praktijk* (1993).

Heleen C. Gall b. 1946, is Associate Professor of Legal History at the Rijksuniversiteit Leiden. She is the author of *Bronnen van de Nederlandse codificatie: Personen- en familierecht 1798–1820* (1980) and *Willem Bilderdijk en het privatissimum van Professor D.G. van* *der Keessel* (1986), and co-author of *Catalogue of Legal Codes Published Before 1800 at the National Library of Indonesia* (1992).

Dieneke Hempenius-van Dijk b. 1947, is Associate Professor of Legal History at the Rijksuniversiteit Groningen. She is the author of *De weeskamer van de stad Groningen 1613–1811* (1991).

Olwen Hufton b. 1938, is Professor of History at the European University Institute, Florence and formerly William Keenan Professor of History and of Women's History, Harvard University. She is the author of *Bayeux in the Late Eighteenth Century* (1967), *The Poor of Eighteenth-Century France* (1974), *Europe: Privilege and Protest* (1981) and *Women and the Limits of Citizenship in the French Revolution* (1992).

Willy Jansen b. 1950, is Professor of Women's Studies at the Katholieke Universiteit of Nijmegen. She is the author of *Women Without Men* (1987) and *Mythen van het fundament* (1993), editor of *Lokale Islam* (1985), and co-editor of *Islamitische Pelgrimstochten* (1991).

Yme Kuiper b. 1949, is Associate Professor of History of Religion and Cultural Anthropology at the Rijksuniversiteit Groningen. He is the author of *Adel in Friesland 1780–1880* (1993) and co-editor of *Feest en ritueel in Europa* (1983), *Struggles of Gods* (1984), *Antropologie tussen wetenschap en kunst: Essays over Clifford Geertz* (1987) and *Concepts of Person in Religion and Thought* (1990).

Geertje van Os b. 1964, is a member of the Amsterdam School for Social Science Research and is preparing a dissertation on widowhood in modern Spain. She is the author of 'Als de bisschop een priester wijdt, wijdt de duvel een pastoorsmeid', *Volkskundig Bulletin* 18 (1992).

Kirsten van der Ploeg b. 1963, was Assistant Librarian of the Faculty of Theology of the Rijksuniversiteit Groningen.

Karel van der Toorn b. 1956, is Professor of Ancient Religions at the Rijksuniversiteit Leiden. He is the author of *Sin and Sanction in Israel and Mesopotamia* (1985) and *Van haar wieg tot haar graf: De rol van de godsdienst in het leven van de Israëlitische en de Babylonische vrouw* (1987), and co-editor of *Dictionary of Demons and Deities in the Bible* (1995).

Frouke Veenstra b. 1953, is Librarian of the Faculty of Theology of the Rijksuniversiteit Groningen.

PREFACE

Since time immemorial widows have been associated with notions of ambiguity. They often represented a marginal group and, unlike widowers, their lives were controlled by many rules. This marginality may explain the small amount of attention which they receive in scholarly research. This lack of interest induced us to organize a colloquium on the position of widows throughout the centuries in the Mediterranean and western Europe and in those great religious traditions, Islam and Hinduism, which more and more are becoming a part of our own culture. We felt that the subject should be looked at from as many angles as possible and therefore invited historians, jurists, philologists, anthropologists, and theologians. The conference, which was held in Groningen in February 1992, was a great success and its proceedings will provide a basis for further historical and anthropological research into widowhood.

We thank all those who made the event possible. The Faculty of Theology of the Rijksuniversiteit Groningen and the Groninger Universiteits Fonds supported the conference with generous contributions. Mirjam Buigel-de Witte, secretary of the Centre for Religious Studies, proved to be of great assistance both before and during the conference. Ken Dowden was (as he so often is) very helpful and revised the English text of various contributions. We are grateful to Annemiek Boonstra for her assistance in compiling the index.

Finally, we thank the contributors for their enthusiasm and for their interest in the colloquium. Without them we would have been unable to offer the reader this volume with its various studies on widowhood past and present. These studies, we hope, may enable us to take a fresh look at the power relations between men and women, which are often at the basis of the many restrictions connected with widowhood.

Lourens P. van den Bosch, Jan N. Bremmer
Centre for Religious Studies, Groningen, The Netherlands

EDITORS' NOTE

In biblical quotations, the King James version is used unless indicated otherwise. A difference in verse sequence is indicated when the English sequence differs from the original Hebrew one.

A few quotations are taken from *The Living Bible*.

1

WIDOWS' WORLDS
Representations and realities
Marjo Buitelaar

What is a widow?[1] The shortest answer to this question seems to be 'a woman who has outlived her husband'. But this definition is not as straightforward as it may at first appear. How to describe, for instance, a woman who has outlived her spouse and subsequently remarries? Is she still a widow or has she left widowhood behind her? In social terms, a remarrying woman will usually no longer be considered a widow, but in legal terms she may still have rights pertaining to widowhood, such as a widow's pension. If the term 'widow' is restricted to women who do not remarry after their husband is deceased, it appears that although this definition may apply to contemporary western widows, historically and cross-culturally speaking it would be more correct to say that the death of her spouse is only one prerequisite for a woman to be called a 'widow'. In his contribution to this book Van der Toorn tells us that in Assyria the term widow was only associated with a woman 'if her husband and father-in-law were dead and she had no son' (see p. 23). A widow, therefore, was not just any woman who had outlived her husband. The term was reserved for formerly married women who had neither male protection nor means of financial support and who were thus in need of special legal protection, although this may have been a question of association rather than strict definition. Also, as Kuiper remarks in his discussion of widowhood in Dutch society of the eighteenth and nineteenth centuries, a small group of widows belonging to the nobility, *douarières*, were distinguished from the majority of widows.

The Latin term for 'widow', *vidua*, is related to a root meaning 'to place apart'.[2] As will become clear in the chapters which follow, in most cases widows are, in fact, placed apart from much more than just their husbands. In addressing the question 'what is a widow?'

1

the contributors to this book discuss various implications of the separations that occur upon the death of a husband. Sometimes they focus on the image of the widow that exists in a specific cultural and historical context. They may do so by discussing images of widows which serve as role models for other women, like the Hindu ideal of the *satī*, the 'widow' who, as Van den Bosch tells us, joins her deceased husband on his funeral pyre. There is Israel's 'ideal widow' Judith, who 'feared God with great devotion' and was praised for her wisdom and chastity. At other times the images of the widows that are presented are descriptive rather than prescriptive, as for example the widow-witch in Anglo-Saxon England discussed by Rolf Bremmer, or the changing image of the widow-in-mourning in Dutch society, whose black garments, as Van Os argues, expressed her dignity but could also have an erotic connotation. Most essays not only present us with different images of the widow, but also analyse the social reality of widows. Sometimes they are concerned with their economic situation, as in Hufton's sketch of the limited occupational options for most widows in eighteenth-century Britain and France. At other times they investigate legal aspects of widowhood, such as Gall's study of the legal positions of 'European' widows in the seventeenth-century Dutch East Indies, and Hempenius-van Dijk's description of the rights of seventeenth- and eighteenth-century widows from the Dutch provinces of Groningen and Friesland to widows' pensions, inheritance and guardianship over children. Other essays focus primarily on the social position of specific widows, such as Jansen's depiction of Amina, an Algerian widow who, despite her financial independence, lacked the power to guarantee her daughter respectable marriage arrangements. Closely related to the legal and social position of widows is the issue of the religious activities of widows, which is yet another focus of attention in several of the chapters that follow. It has been noted that widows are in general more involved in religious activities than widowers or married women. Jan Bremmer, for example, notes the great number of widows among the first followers of Jesus and discusses the changing views of early Christian societies on the issue of remarriage by widows. On the other hand, widows may be excluded from religious ceremonies, as the Brahmin widows in India were.

We meet a few famous widows in this book. Two early Muslim widows, Khadija and Aisha, are, indeed, exceptional. Khadija, first wife of the prophet Muhammed and his first convert to Islam, was a rich and powerful widow when she proposed to him; while Aisha, the youngest widow left behind by Muhammed after his death, played an important role in the transmission of religious knowledge and, as a consequence, the development of the Islamic doctrine. There is also, of course, the already-mentioned Jewish heroine Judith, who saved her people by using her charms and eloquence in order to enter the enemy's camp and behead General Holofernes. Unlike her Muslim counterparts, Judith is less a historical than a literary figure, and has been a source of inspiration to western artists through the centuries. In this respect she may be likened to other famous literary widows, such as Gertrude of Denmark, who traumatized her son Hamlet by marrying her deceased husband's brother; or Jocasta, who had an even more disruptive influence by unknowingly marrying her son Oedipus.[3] No one who has heard 'Penelope's Lament' by the Italian composer Monteverdi will ever forget the grief of this Homeric grass widow, whose faithfulness to her missing husband Odysseus was eventually rewarded by his return.

This volume is an interdisciplinary presentation of various ways in which widowhood is embedded in different historical and cultural contexts. It diverges from the vast body of scholarship on literary widows,[4] and from recent studies by social psychologists who focus on mourning processes of widows in western cultures.[5] In the field of anthropology, we find an ethnographic interest in the participation of widows in mortuary rituals. As might be expected, the literature on Brahmin 'widow-burning' or *sutti'ism* is over-represented. As Van den Bosch remarks in his contribution to this volume, this can partly be explained by the fact that in our confrontation with other cultures, we tend to become fascinated by the fanciful and the bizarre rather than the plain and ordinary. Activities of widows who on first appearance seem less extraordinary can also supply us with original insights, as is demonstrated convincingly in Danforth's poetic monograph on death rituals in rural Greece.[6] Strangely enough, widowhood, as distinct from the participation of widows in mortuary ritual, has so far received little attention from anthropologists. Two interesting exceptions are the studies by Lopata and Potash.[7] The essays in Potash's volume investigate the socioeconomic position of widows in Africa. They reveal that, contrary to commonly held views, most African widows do not enjoy communal support, but head their own households and are self-reliant, only to be supported by their children in old age. Lopata's cross-cultural survey focuses on the different 'support systems' that widows may or may not have at their disposal: economic, social, emotional and service systems that determine their

3

position as widows to a considerable extent. In the studies of Lopata and Potash we search in vain for more than incidental references to the meaning of widowhood as a cultural construction of female identity.

The contributors to this volume do not restrict themselves to interpretations of a specific aspect of widowhood. Rather, they are concerned with both representations and social realities of widows. Their chapters provide us with materials which offer suggestions and directions for a discussion on cultural constructions and meanings of widowhood. By way of a preliminary exploration, I will touch upon some of the recurrent themes that cross-culturally and cross-historically, in various combinations and with different degrees of emphasis, are the foci of attention in the construction of the widow as a separate(d) social category.

As no one category in patterns of gender classification can be fully understood without examining other categories of the system in which it is embedded,[8] a first step is to pose the question as to what other social categories the widow is compared to in the various chapters. Strikingly, in most texts widows are rarely compared to a seemingly obvious social category: widowers. Granted that the authors did not receive suggestions to do so, it must be noted that they did make comparisons between widows and other social categories. Indeed, the conspicuous absence of widowers indicates that, as a variation on a theme studied by Ortner, it is not true to say that 'widow is to woman as widower is to man'.[9] In fact, widowerhood as a social category seems to be a historical latecomer. In Latin and Greek there is no masculine form to match the term 'widow', while in the Anglo-Saxon language a masculine form only appeared in the late fourteenth century. Apparently, in most societies widowerhood affects male identity to a much lesser extent than widowhood affects female identity. In the remainder of this chapter the question will be addressed as to how this difference can be understood.

Comparison between absolute figures of widows and widowers suggests asymmetries in the two categories. In the United States there are four widows to every widower.[10] In this volume, it is noted that in nineteenth-century Dutch society there were three times as many widows as widowers, while in eighteenth-century France 80 per cent of the widowers between the ages of 20 and 29 remarried as compared to 60 per cent of the widows of the same age. This difference increased to 52 per cent remarrying widowers as compared to only

20 per cent of the widows between the ages of 40 and 49. It could be argued that the discrepancy between remarrying widowers and widows must be explained by the fact that women tend to marry at a younger age than men and tend to live longer, resulting in a surplus of widowed women. While this may be true for Asian and Middle Eastern societies, it should be noted that except for aristocratic circles, where girls were sometimes married off at very young ages, in western Europe discrepancies in age at the time of marriage have never been dramatic. Moreover, it is only since the beginning of the twentieth century that women in western Europe have tended to live longer than men.[11] Even where discrepancies between the numbers of widows and widowers are due to differences in age between marriage partners, ideas about female and male identity and the power relations that lie behind such age differences influence views on the propriety of remarriage after the death of one's spouse. Different kinds of dependencies that result from the sexual division of labour, for instance, may affect the occurrence of remarriage. As Stirling remarks about rural Turkey: 'The loss of a wife is a serious blow to a man. He cannot himself look after small children, or cook. He cannot even decently fetch himself water'.[12] In any event, the importance of discrepancies between figures of widows and widowers to this argument is that they reveal that widowerhood is less often a permanent position for men than widowhood is for women.

How this relates to notions of female and male identity can be assessed by examining the categories to which widows are in fact likened or opposed. In most of the chapters contained in this book we find comparisons of widows with orphans, on the one hand; and with virgins, nuns, spinsters and ascetics on the other. In one way or another, all these categories share the absence of an individual male's legitimate guardianship, although the implications of this lack of male control and protection vary for the different categories. A closer examination of instances where the various texts mention orphans and unmarried women reveals two different concerns: in comparisons with orphans the problem is the widow's socioeconomic position, while with unmarried women it is her sexuality.

There are references in several chapters to the vulnerability of widows and orphans, usually concerning religious admonishments and legal provisions that are made to protect them. For example, Job claimed 'that he freely gave food to the poor, the widow and the orphan'. Similarly, in the laws of the Anglo-Saxon King Æthelred the clergy were instructed 'not to vex the widows and orphans too often, but to gladden them eagerly'. Some seventeenth- and eighteenth-century Dutch widows received certain benefits because they were placed in the category of the so-called *personae miserabiles*, a status they shared with orphans, the chronically sick and other 'unfortunate persons'. These references suggest an image of the widow as a poor and helpless woman, emphasizing her vulnerability. In the world view of Near Eastern societies and early Judaism, for example, widows and orphans were considered prototypes of the socially underprivileged: to speak of a 'poor widow' was considered a tautology. Indeed, many of the widows mentioned in this study lived in circumstances of extreme poverty. Anglo-Saxon widows and their children could be bonded into slavery when unable to pay debts, while many widows in eighteenth-century France and Britain were found in judicial records concerning theft and prostitution. As the position of Dutch *douarières* demonstrates, however, poverty does not necessarily adhere to widowhood. Roman upper-class widows provide another example. They lived comfortably enough to uphold the status of *univira*, a woman who has had only one husband. Her status as a war-widow means that the Algerian woman Amina is financially better off than many of her fellow-countrywomen. It is interesting to note that in most public imagery of widows only the extremely poor and the lavishly rich are represented, whereas in reality we find widows among all social strata. Moreover, from the proverbial poor widow in the Ancient Near East, 'whose ass is fit (only) for breaking wind', to Franz Léhar's *Lustige Witwe* ('Merry Widow'), whose family worries that she will squander her late husband's fortune while enjoying herself in Paris, the views on these women are not without ridicule.

At the conceptual level, then, the category of the widow is characterized by contrasting extremes: she may be either lavishly rich or utterly poor and she appeals either to compassion or mockery, in some cases even to both. This dichotomous stereotyping is related to the fact that as a woman without direct male guardianship, the widow is an anomaly. As Van der Toorn characterizes it: 'On the one hand, she has neither male support nor protection, but on the other, she is free to live her life as it pleases her' (see p. 28). The dichotomous representations of widows can be just as compelling and stirring to the imagination as those of the orphan. Orphans can be both more vulnerable and more empowered than 'ordinary' children. Charles Dickens' *Oliver Twist* presents us with images of extreme pathos and vulnerability, juxtaposed against the accomplished pick-pocketing of the street 'toughs'. Likewise, widows are represented as both more vulnerable and more empowered than 'ordinary' women.

Where widows and orphans do part company, however, is with regard to sexuality. As becomes clear when widows are compared to other social categories, it is her potentially unfettered sexual longing that makes the widow a source of such cultural anxiety. In several chapters, we find comparisons or relations between widows and other adult women who (supposedly) have no sexual relations with men. In eighteenth-century French cities, for instance, widows and spinsters often lived together. Sharing the costs of rent, heating and lighting and household chores obviously had economic benefits for these women, but more affluent widows and spinsters could also be found living together, such groupings providing them with the only alternative to family life besides the convent. Widows and other women without men are also mentioned in Van Os's discussion of changing meanings of the mourning dress, when she notes a parallel between the attire of early Christian nuns and widows, neither of whom took an interest in elegant and stylish garments, both hiding their feminine figure underneath shapeless habits. In Anglo-Saxon England, King Æthelred's laws concerning the abduction of women for marriage mentioned widows and nuns in the same breath. Similarly, according to the rules of the Old English Penitential, rapists of either a virgin or a widow faced excommunication.

To understand why virgins – including nuns and spinsters – and widows may be mentioned in the same breath, Ardener's argument on sexual mismatches may be elucidating.[13] She observes that when the classificatory pair 'woman:man', as it features in the universe of 'adults', is compared with its occurrence in the universe of 'fecund persons', in most cultures the category of man tends to match in both universes, while the category of woman in the universe of adults meets with two mismatches in the universe of fecund persons, i.e. virgins and post-menopausal women. Following Douglas, Ardener goes on to argue that such mismatches or 'empty slots' on either side of a category, in this case the category of fecund persons, help to define it. Thus, attention may be concentrated upon virginity so that sexually experienced or fully adult women may be more clearly defined. Constituting the boundary area, the mismatches themselves are ambiguous categories, 'points of danger' in Douglas's terms, that can only be controlled by surrounding them with powerful symbolism.[14]

In view of this discussion of widowhood, it could be argued that the category 'woman' in the universe of adults meets in the universe of sexually active persons with virgins and widows as 'mismatches'. From the references to the texts mentioned above, it becomes clear that what is mainly at stake is the chastity of virgins and widows as opposed to the active sexuality of married women. In societies where social organization is based on marriage, women who fall outside the category of married women become anomalies that give rise to tensions. The position of widows is not necessarily anomalous in societies where marriage plays a less crucial role in the social organization. In rural Luo society, for instance, marriage is perceived as a transitional phase and all women past menopause live separately from their husbands.[15] In many Polynesian cultures widows are not set apart in sexual terms from married women. In these societies, one's spouse is often not the only legitimate sexual partner: widows, divorced women and most unmarried girls engage in sexual relations as well.[16] In societies where sex-regulations differ, widows may be regarded differently. Where marriage is the exclusive domain for sexual relations and for male control over female sexuality, virgins and widows are anomalies *par excellence*. Their sexuality is a particular focus of symbolic attention, and chastity becomes the dominant, if not the overruling (prescriptive) trait of their female identity.

And yet, a widow is no virgin. While both are 'empty slots' that flank the category of the sexually active woman, the crucial difference between the two is that they do so from exactly opposite sides: a virgin is sexually ignorant and inexperienced, whereas a widow is a sexually experienced woman. While both may be the objects of chastity cults, the symbolism connected to virginity is of a different nature from the symbolism linked to widowhood. Because of her sexual ignorance, the virgin may come to represent highly positive values like purity and integrity. As she is sexually inexperienced, the virgin is not yet fully a woman, but neither can she be compared with a pre-pubescent girl. Her sexuality is dormant, waiting to be awoken through intercourse with a man, who will thus help her enter the category of 'real woman'. This ambiguous classification of virgins places them in a powerful and creative, yet vulnerable position, as the fate of Joan of Arc illustrates.[17]

The sexual experience of widows, on the contrary, renders them suspicious. While as a sexually experienced and therefore 'real' woman the widow is less ambivalent than the virgin, in her case it is predominantly her unleashed sexuality that makes her an anomaly.

The symbolism that surrounds the ambiguous position of widows is imbued with fear of uncontrolled female sexuality. This makes the widow a powerful symbol of disorder and destructive potential. The meaning of the Arabic term *fitna*, although not only restricted to references to widows, may illustrate this tension that uncontrolled female sexuality creates. *Fitna* means chaos or destruction, but the term is also used to refer to women's power of fatal sexual attraction over men, which, if not controlled, causes sexual disorder.[18] The same fear of uncontrolled female sexuality has been documented in South Asia, where the ritual exclusion of a widow is implicitly associated with the threat posed by her as a potentially sexually active woman who is no longer under external control.[19]

A Moroccan proverb says: 'A woman without a man is like a public bath (*hammâm*) without water', meaning that she will get hotter and hotter while there is no sperm to cool her off.[20] This proverb aptly illustrates the image of the widow found in different societies as a woman who, having tasted the sweetness of sexual pleasure, is not willing to resign herself to chastity, but develops powerful sexual propensities and needs. In this volume the case of a Dutch widow in the Dutch East Indies is cited, about whom it was said that 'in the fourth week of her widowhood, [she had] a fourth lover, and, at the end of three months, she married again, and would have done it sooner, if the laws had allowed it'. Elsewhere Brandes describes a preoccupation with sexually demanding widows among men in a contemporary small Andalusian town:

> In one instance, a fifty-nine-year-old widower eloped with a forty-year-old widow, who, it was said, had been trying to seduce him for months. Within days of the elopement, word was out that the man had left her, with the complaint that she had a voracious sexual appetite. Every time he would turn over to sleep, she would try to arouse him into another encounter. It was more than he could take, and all the men I knew seemed to sympathize with the man's lot.[21]

The men in Brandes's study even suspected that women aimed for widowhood as the ultimate goal in marriage: they claimed that widows immediately gain weight and acquire a lustrous glow after their husbands die and that they are likely to become sexually promiscuous.[22] Similar examples of the image of the widow as a potential seductress can be found in several chapters in this volume. In ancient Israel, for instance, the ideal image of the widow was that of a solitary and chaste woman, but in more popular imagery widows may have been viewed as women of easy morals. In the same vein, the life-story of the Anglo-Saxon woman Judith, daughter of Charles the Bald, twice widowed before she married a third time at the age of 19, may have fed popular conceptions in the later Middle Ages of the overdeveloped sexual interest of widows. A preoccupation with the sexuality of widows may also explain Van Os's observation that the mourning woman-in-black in Romantic painting displays an air of danger and fatal attraction.

As a result of her previously active sexual life, the chastity of a widow is less impressive and more precarious than that of the inexperienced virgin. In competition with virgins to become the role model for women, famous widows are therefore defeated. Aisha, for instance, the favourite wife of the prophet Muhammed, was given the honorary name 'mother of the believers'. Tellingly, as a widow, particularly as one who even took pride in the fact that Muhammed had preferred making love to her over sleeping with his other wives, she was not as fit to become the role model for Muslim women as was Fatima, Muhammed's only daughter. The cultural image of Fatima is devoid of sexuality. Although she was married and had two children, it is noteworthy that in popular Shi'a imagery, Fatima is depicted as a virgin mother, much like the Christian virgin Mary. Of the two most important women in Jesus's life, his virgin mother Mary became the role model for Christian women rather than Mary Magdalen, whose sexuality, like that of widows, was beyond male control.[23] Similarly, the reason that the Hebrew widow Judith was able to become a heroine and role model for chastity in Ancient Israel may well have been that Hellenistic Judaism had no virginity cult. Indeed, when we meet Judith again in an Anglo-Saxon poem centuries later, by which time a virginity cult had, in fact, been developed in Christianity, she has been transformed into a virgin.

The ambiguous classification of widows, however, cannot solely be attributed to their suspect sexuality. As the fear of Andalusian men indicates, the very fact that widows have outlived their husbands may as such cause anxiety. Having looked death in the eye, widows are situated on the indefinite threshold between life and death. To borrow from an argument about the elderly, widows are liminars *par excellence*.[24] They are often associated with the power, awe or dread of the already dead.[25] While the same may be said about widowers, in the case of widows the situation tends to be more anomalous and acute; especially in societies where the identity of women is defined largely in terms of their relation to a husband, the association of the widow with a spouse who is no longer in this world may result in a conception of her as someone who, by extension, is more closely associated with death.[26] In the present volume, this view is illustrated by the description of the black mourning dress as a means to disguise widows and set them apart from other persons. The liminality of widows who remain closely associated with their deceased spouse is also illustrated in the description of the mortuary rituals of high caste Hindu widows. Discarding previous identity-markers like the mirror that her husband gave her at marriage to look at the reflection of her own soul, a widow remains in a liminal situation for the rest of her life.

The cultural anxiety that a widow may cause is also linked to the fact that by surviving her husband she defies his male authority. By outliving him, she in a way outwits him. Widows often have freedom and power at their disposal that they did not have as wives. Although political widows who replace their husbands in powerful political positions like Corazon Aquino and Eva Peron are rare, formerly dependent women often surprise their family and friends in widowhood by revealing themselves as strong persons proving capable of fending for themselves and their children. The need to survive may lead widows to seek employment that causes marginalization, either because it concerns illegal practices, such as the opium-smuggling of the Dutch widows Neeltje Koek and Helena Kakelaar in the Dutch East Indies, or because they take on jobs that are conceived of as typical male occupations. Poor widows in Bangladesh, for example, are obliged to break the rules of *purdah* or seclusion and work in the construction industry, previously defined as an exclusively male domain of labour.[27] In nineteenth-century Bristol, widows could likewise be found on building sites.[28] Some guilds in eighteenth-century France in certain circumstances allowed widows to run their late husband's business. By flouting cultural conceptions of women's place in the social order, these widows may indeed gain more freedom of movement and independence, yet this also enhances their anomalous position. Women who take on such masculine behaviour are neither feminine nor masculine; they become 'women in between'.[29] Such 'women in between' are suitable persons to become mediators in the crossing of boundaries between other cultural categories. Thus in a sex-segregated society like Algeria, many widows work as professional mediators between male and female domains, and as professional attendants in the rites of passage of birth, puberty, marriage and death.[30]

But why should the power that widows in these 'extra-ordinary' positions possess be perceived as dangerous? Douglas contends:

[W]here the social system explicitly recognises positions of authority, those holding such positions are endowed with explicit spiritual power, controlled, conscious, external and approved – powers to bless or curse. Where the social system requires people to hold dangerously ambiguous roles, these persons are credited with uncontrolled, unconscious, danger-ous, disapproved powers – such as witchcraft.[31]

In other words, the power that widows may possess *de facto* is not rightfully theirs but belongs *de jure* to men. This explains why in western Europe, where gender relations are rapidly developing towards a more balanced distribution of power, the symbolism connected with widowhood has now lost most of its meaning, as is illustrated by the disappearance of mourning dress in the Nether-lands.[32]

Having assessed some dimensions of the ambiguous classification of the widow, much of the symbolism that surrounds widowhood can be interpreted in the light of the solutions that people may seek when confronted with anomalous situations which seem to defy their basic cultural assumptions. Again, turning to Douglas may help to elucidate matters. Douglas mentions four provisions for dealing with ambiguous or anomalous events:[33] (i) reinterpretation; (ii) avoidance; (iii) physical control; and (iv) attribution of danger. In the various contributions to this book, examples of ways in which a widow or the people around her may settle the ambiguity of her widowhood by reinterpreting her anomalous position occur most frequently. The most obvious solution to reduce the ambiguity of her uncontrolled sexuality, for instance, is a reinterpretation of her position through remarriage. In societies where even within the holy bonds of marriage sexuality is conceived of as sinful, views on remarriage are not without ambivalence. While the remarriage of widows is actually encouraged by Islam,[34] in the Hebrew and early Christian societies it was considered the lesser of two evils. Although this reflected the general view on marriage, the pressure to abstain from remarriage was stronger than that on first marriage. For young widows who feared the temptations of the flesh it was considered better to remarry, but widows who were strong enough to resist such temp-tations and lead a chaste life gained more respect.

In the case of chaste widows, reinterpretation may take place through desexualization. Early Christian mourning dress customs had a defeminizing effect on women, while Hindu widows in some Brahmin castes took leave of femininity by shaving their heads. Widows despecified in this way were no longer referred to as 'she' but as 'it'.[35] Albeit on a different level, we can interpret the situation of widows who replaced their deceased husband in business in seventeenth- and eighteenth-century France and England as a re-classification of these women into 'honorary men'.

No longer having a husband to care for, many widows shift to religion as the focus of their attention. In this case, reinterpretation takes place by the transformation from a devoted wife into a devout believer. Much like the widows among the early followers of Christ, many contemporary Christian widows who become active in church life have found a new goal in life as well as a means to protect their reputation.[36] As the struggle of widows to survive often reveals, however, in reality there may be a large discrepancy between widows' own wishes to reinterpret their precarious position and the limited number of options open to them given the actual circumstances. The ideal of the chaste widow, for example, is often a luxury open only to the élite. In fact, upholding a specific image of the widow may be an expression of class difference, as widowhood in China may illustrate. In the Ch'ing period (1644–1912) élite women who had been widowed before the age of 30 and succeeded in remaining chaste until the age of 50 were honoured as 'exemplary women' and were rewarded with a testimonial of merit from shrines in which they would henceforth be commemorated among other virtuous persons. During the eighteenth century the ideal of the chaste widow was propagated to the lower classes as part of a moral education campaign. But just when this ideal became more attainable for widows of the lower strata, members of the élite grew increasingly disdainful of the chaste widow cult.[37] Similarly, the Roman ideal of the *univira*, the woman who had only been married once, was a typical upper-class phenomenon.

Regardless of whether a widow does or does not remain chaste, the death of a husband is often followed by a period of time during which a widow observes certain taboos. The imposition of taboos on widows can be seen as an example of the avoidance of anomalies so as to affirm the categories which they transgress.[38] Encompassing widows with rituals and symbols that set them apart from others reinforces the boundaries of the social category of married women. In Morocco, for instance, personal law is based on prescriptions from

Islamic law and Moroccan widows have to observe the '*idda*, a waiting period of three menstrual cycles or, in the case of pregnancy, until delivery, before they can marry again.[39] Besides this legal measure which, like the 'weeping period' of seventeenth-century widows in the Dutch East Indies, was intended to establish whether a newborn child is a descendant of the deceased, many widows also observe a voluntary mourning period during which they dress in white, do not pay visits to friends or the public bath and avoid physical contacts by eating apart and not lending out any of their possessions to others. To conclude her mourning period, the widow performs a major ablution in the public bath, puts on her ordinary clothes again and burns her mourning clothes.[40] Contrary to their Moroccan counterparts, high caste Hindu widows were not reincorporated into society. A widow remained in mourning dress until her death, and she had to observe many rules of avoidance for the rest of her life since she was considered impure. Her presence was regarded as a bad omen and she was therefore excluded from important public ceremonies.

The fate of Brahmin widows also offers an extreme example of how the existence of an anomaly may be physically controlled: through the practice of *sutti'ism* or 'widow-burning' the anomalous position of a widow is permanently eliminated. Preceding her 'last journey' to the pyre, a reinterpretation of her ambiguous classification takes place. The rituals connected to the cremation of a *satī* have more resemblances to marriage ceremonies than to funerary rites. In this manner the widow is reclassified as a bride who performs the sacrament of marriage for the second time.

Last of all, the anomalous position of the widow may be controlled by attributing danger to her. Rather than taking steps to reduce her ambiguity, the labelling of a widow as a dangerous person acknowledges and reinforces her ambiguous classification. The dangers that may be ascribed to widows such as her fatal sexual attractiveness to men, her association with black magic and her 'working relationship' with death have already been commented on. As the recurring images of the widow as a witch or seductress in several of the chapters in this book reveal, the attribution of dangerous powers to widows usually occurs in combination with a reinterpretation of their position, and measures to avoid them. Because of their supernatural powers, witches do not belong entirely to this earth and are not considered completely human. Even in modern Dutch society, where much of the symbolism linked to widowhood has fallen into disuse, a woman whose husband has died may suddenly be confronted with avoidance behaviour from couples who were previously friends, because she is seen as a rival by her female friends.

Having explored the different social categories to which widows may be compared, as well as the various consequences that the death of a spouse may have for the social identity of women, I will, by way of conclusion, again consider the statement: the relationship 'widow is to woman' is not the same as 'widower is to man'. It is clear that asymmetries between these pairs can largely be attributed to the fact that in many societies, and certainly in most cultures under discussion in this book, a widow derives her social identity from the fact that she no longer lives under male control and protection. As women tend to be more dependent on their husbands for their social identity than husbands are on their wives, women appear to lose more in terms of social identity when this partner dies. As women are often more strongly defined by their partner when he is alive ('wife of . . .'), so they are also more strongly defined by the death of a spouse. Men's social identity lives on after the death of a spouse, but a woman generally needs something to compensate for her 'greater' loss. There is considerable agreement in the way the ambiguity that this loss entails is expressed by and controlled through the symbolism that is connected to widowhood. Nevertheless, even though we may recognise certain cross-historical and cross-cultural parallels in the representations of widows, a 'universal' category of the widow does not exist, nor can different conceptions of widows within a particular society be reduced to a single 'typical' image only. The chapters which follow should help us to begin to perceive the rich cultural variation in the representations and realities of the widows' worlds.

NOTES

A superscript number after a date indicates the edition of the work cited

1 I would like to thank Debbi Long for helping to clarify both my argument and my English, and Ton Zwaan for his comments on an earlier draft of this paper.

2 R.S.P. Beekes, 'Widow', *Historische Sprachforschung* 105 (1992) 171–87.

3 Cf. J. Bremmer, 'Oedipus and the Greek Oedipus Complex', in J. Bremmer (ed.), *Interpretations of Greek Mythology* (London, 1988²) 41–59.

4 See, for example, J. Bacon, 'Wives, Widows and Writings in Restoration Comedy', *Studies in English Literature* 31 (1991) 427–43; C. Carlton,

'The Widow's Tale: Male Myths and Female Reality in 16th and 17th Century England', *Albion* 10 (1978) 118–29; L. Mirrer (ed.), *Upon my Husband's Death: Widows in the Literature and Histories of Medieval Europe* (Ann Arbor, 1992).

5 See A. Lewis, *Widowhood in America* (New York, 1975); J. Peterson and M. Briley, *Widows and Widowhood: A Creative Approach to Being Alone* (New York, 1977); N. Stevens, *Well-Being in Widowhood: A Question of Balance* (Nijmegen, 1989). For review works on widows see: C. Balkwell, 'Transition Widowhood: A Review of the Literature', *Family Relations* 30 (1981) 117–27; C. Barrett, 'Review Essay: Women in Widowhood', *Signs* 2 (1977) 856–68; C. Strugnell, *Adjustment to Widowhood and Some Related Problems: A Selected Bibliography* (New York, 1974).

6 L. Danforth, *The Death Rituals of Rural Greece* (Princeton, 1982).

7 H. Lopata, *Widows*, 2 vols (Durham, 1987); B. Potash, *Widows in African Societies: Choices and Constraints* (Stanford, 1986).

8 Cf. K. Hastrup, 'The Semantics of Biology: Virginity', in S. Ardener (ed.), *Defining Females: The Nature of Women in Society* (London, 1978) 49–65.

9 See S. Ortner, 'Is Female to Male as Nature to Culture?', in M. Rosaldo and L. Lamphere (eds), *Women, Culture & Society* (Stanford, 1974) 67–87.

10 Barrett, 'Women in Widowhood', 861.

11 See G. Hajnal, 'European Marriage Patterns in Perspective', in D. Glass and D. Eversley (eds), *Population in History: Essays in Historical Demography* (London, 1965) 101–43; P. Laslett, *The World We Have Lost* (London, 1973).

12 P. Stirling, *Turkish Village* (London, 1965) 195.

13 S. Ardener, 'Introduction: The Nature of Women in Society', in Ardener, *Defining Females*, 36–40.

14 See M. Douglas, *Purity and Danger* (London, 1966).

15 B. Potash, 'Wives of the Grave: Widows in a Rural Luo Community', in Potash, *Widows in African Societies*, 44–65.

16 S. Ortner, 'Gender and Sexuality in Hierarchical Societies: The Case of Polynesia and Some Comparative Implications', in S. Ortner and H. Whitehead (eds), *Sexual Meanings: The Cultural Construction of Gender and Sexuality* (Cambridge, 1981) 387.

17 See Hastrup, 'The Semantics of Biology', 59, who also argues that the unspecified virgin may be conceived of as 'a third sex' or have aspects of both sexes, as in the cosmology of Tewa Indians, where the founder of the female moiety is the White Corn Woman, while the founder of the male moiety is the Blue Corn Maiden.

18 See A. Bouhdiba, *Sexuality in Islam*, 1975[1] (London, 1985). For the role of *fitna* in male fear of female sexuality see also F. Mernissi, *Beyond the Veil: Male–Female Dynamics in a Modern Muslim Society* (Cambridge, 1975).

19 S. Vatuk, 'Sexuality and the Middle-Aged Woman in South Asia', in V. Kerns and J. Brown (eds), *In Her Prime: New Views of Middle-Aged Women* (Urbana and Chicago, 1992) 162–3.

20 Although women subscribe to this general image when talking about their self-image, individual women often claim to have more self-control over their sexual desires than men; see M. Buitelaar, *Fasting and Feasting in Morocco: Women's Participation in Ramadan* (Oxford, 1993).

21 S. Brandes, 'Like Wounded Stags: Male Sexual Ideology in an Andalusian Town', in Ortner and Whitehead, *Sexual Meanings*, 226.

22 Ibid.

23 See M. Combs-Schilling, *Sacred Performances: Islam, Sexuality, and Sacrifice* (New York, 1989) 88.

24 Liminars are persons who find themselves in a state of so-called liminality, a concept that was first used by Van Gennep and later elaborated on by Turner. Liminality comes from the Latin word *limen* or 'threshold', and refers to the transitional phase in rites of passage between one stage of life and the next. During this liminal phase, the characteristics of the ritual subjects are ambiguous; they pass through a cultural realm that has few or none of the attributes of the past or coming state. Cf. A. van Gennep, *The Rites of Passage*, 1909[1] (London, 1960); V. Turner, *The Ritual Process: Structure and Anti-Structure* (New York, 1969).

25 See B. Meyerhoff, 'Rites and Signs of Ripening: The Intertwining of Ritual, Time and Growing Older', in D. Keitzer and J. Keith (eds), *Age and Anthropological Theory* (Ithaca, 1984) 316. See also N. Foner, *Ages in Conflict: A Cross-Cultural Perspective on Inequality between Old and Young* (New York, 1984) 24.

26 Again, reference to a contrasting example may illustrate this point. In his study on death rituals among the Tiwi in Australia, E. Venbrux (*Under the Mango Tree: A Case of Homicide in an Australian Aboriginal Society*, Dissertation, Nijmegen, 1993) notes that a person's position within the agnatic kinship system is more important to his or her identity than marital relations. Losing a spouse therefore does not affect one's identity as strongly, and the ambiguity of widowhood is identical to that of widowerhood.

27 E. Fernea, 'Women and Family in Development Plans in the Arab East', *Journal of Asian and African Studies* 21 (1986) 84.

28 C. Power, 'Widows and Others on Bristol Building Sites: Some Women in Nineteenth-Century Construction', *Local Historian* 20 (1990) 84–7.

29 See V. Turner, *Dramas, Fields, and Metaphors: Symbolic Action in Human Society* (Ithaca, 1974) 232–3, who speaks of the 'betwixt and between' state of liminality and liminars.

30 W. Jansen, *Women without Men: Gender and Marginality in an Algerian Town* (Leiden, 1987) 12.

31 Douglas, *Purity and Danger*, 99.

32 Leaving, as it is, many women empty-handed when they are faced with the death of their spouse (see Van Os, notes 12 and 13 [this vol., p.241]). Without the aid of ritual, ceremonies or symbols to express their grief, many people create their own private rituals to express different stages in their mourning process, cf. Meyerhoff, 'Rites and Signs of Ripening'.

33 It must be noted that she actually mentions five provisions, the fifth being that ambiguous symbols can be used in ritual to call attention to

other levels of existence. In my view, however, this last provision is less a device to control ambiguity than a way to make profitable use of it; see Douglas, *Purity and Danger*, 39–40.

34 For example, most of the women to whom the prophet Muhammed was married were widows. Because of their special status as 'mothers of the believers' they were inhibited from remarrying after Muhammed's death, but Muhammed's initial marriage choices offer an example (*sunna*, the tradition of the Prophet, exemplary behaviour) to other men. See L. Ahmed, *Women and Gender in Islam* (New York, 1992) 52.

35 Hastrup, 'The Semantics of Biology', 59.

36 See W. Christian, *Person and God in a Spanish Valley* (Princeton, 1989²); Danforth, *The Death Rituals of Rural Greece*.

37 S. Mann, 'Widows in Kinship, Class and Community Structure of Qing Dynasty China', *Journal of Asian Studies* 46 (1987) 37–56.

38 Douglas, *Purity and Danger*, 39.

39 Cf. L. Buskens, *Islamitisch recht en familiebetrekkingen in Marokko: Aspecten van wet en werkelijkheid, in het bijzonder in de steden Rabat en Salé en het omliggende platteland* (Dissertation, Leiden, 1993) 106.

40 Personal observation during my fieldwork in Morocco in 1985.

7 For the sources, milieu and intentions of the gospels see the balanced survey by H. Koester, *Ancient Christian Gospels: Their History and Development* (London and Philadelphia, 1990).

8 Cf. M. Fander, *Die Stellung der Frau im Markusevangelium* (Altenberge, 1989).

9 Cf. F. Bovon, *Das Evangelium nach Lukas* I (Zürich and Neukirchen, 1989) 13f. Koester, *Ancient Christian Gospels*, 337 dates Luke even after the turn of the first century.

10 Cf. B. Witherington III, *Women in the Ministry of Jesus* (Cambridge, 1984) 117.

11 As is rightly stressed by M. de Baar, '"En onder 't hennerot het haantje zoekt te blijven." De betrokkenheid van vrouwen bij het huisgezin van Jean de Labadie (1669–1732)', *Jaarboek voor Vrouwengeschiedenis* 8 (1987, 11–43) 15.

12 Cf. J.N. Bremmer, 'Why did Early Christianity Attract Upper-Class Women?', in A.A.R. Bastiaensen, A. Hilhorst and C.H. Kneepkens (eds), *Fructus centesimus: Mélanges G.J.M. Bartelink* (Steenbrugge and Dordrecht, 1989) 37–47.

13 Witherington, *Women in the Ministry of Jesus*, 125–31.

14 As is argued by B. Witherington III, *Women in the Earliest Churches* (Cambridge, 1988) 157.

15 Cf. M. Hengel, *Between Jesus and Paul* (London, 1983) 1–29. For the complicated issue of the language situation in Palestine in Jesus's time, see M. Hengel, *The 'Hellenization' of Judaea in the First Century after Christ* (London and Philadelphia, 1989); G. Horsley, *New Documents Illustrating Early Christianity* 4 (Macquarie, 1989) 5–40.

16 Cf. Hengel, *Between Jesus and Paul*, 16.

17 Stählin (note 6 above) 440 wrongly concludes from Peter's calling of 'the saints and widows' (9:41) after his resurrection of Tabitha that the widows in Joppa already constituted a separate order.

18 H.G. Kippenberg, 'The Role of Christianity in the Depolitization of the Roman Empire', in S.N. Eisenstadt (ed.), *The Origins and Diversity of Axial Age Civilizations* (Albany, 1986) 261–79, 527–32, considers the organization of the weak an important factor in the rise of the Christian bishop.

19 Greeks: B. Kötting, *Die Bewertung der Wiederverheiratung (der zweiten Ehe) in der Antike und in der frühen Kirche* (Opladen, 1988) does not even discuss Ancient Greece. See in general also I. Weiler, 'Witwen und Waisen im griechischen Altertum: Bemerkungen zu antiken Randgruppen', in H. Kloft (ed.), *Sozialmassnahmen und Fürsorge: Zur Eigenart antiker Sozialpolitik* (Graz and Horn, 1988) 15–33 (not very informative); better, L.-M. Günther, 'Witwen in der griechischen Antike – zwischen Oikos und Polis', *Historia* 42 (1993) 308–25.

20 The exception confirming the rule was that the bride of the highest Athenian magistrate, the *archon basileus*, had to enter marriage as a virgin (Demosthenes 59.75).

21 Athens: W.E. Thompson, 'Athenian Marriage Pattern: Remarriage', *Calif. Stud. Class. Ant.* 5 (1972) 211–25. Number of widows: T. Gallant, *Risk and Survival in Ancient Greece* (Cambridge, 1991) 27. For the age

of marriage see R. Sallares, *The Ecology of the Ancient Greek World* (London, 1991) 148–51.

22 Cf. D. Gill, 'Corinth: A Roman Colony in Achaea', *Biblische Zeitschrift* 37 (1993) 259–64.

23 Upper-class Greek women: see most recently R.A. Kearsley, 'Women in Public Life', in S.R. Llewelyn (ed.), *New Documents Illustrating Early Christianity*, vol. 6 (1992) 24–7. Jewish women: see the bibliography in Bremmer, 'Why did Early Christianity', 41 n.11. Pagan philosophers: S. Treggiari, *Roman Marriage*: Iusti Coniuges *from the Time of Cicero to the Time of Ulpian* (Oxford, 1991) 185–97.

24 In ancient Athens the famous lawgiver Solon only considered 60-year-old women as really old: Demosthenes 43.62. We find the same age limit also in the apocryphal *Acts of John* 30.

25 This has often been postulated; see most recently the surveys by Thurston, *The Widows*, 44–55; W. Venter, 'The Position of the Widow in the Early Church according to the Writings of the Apostolic Fathers', *Ekklesiastikos Pharos* (published in Johannesburg) 72 (1990, 11–29) 13–5.

26 Cf. R. Metz, *La consécration des vierges dans l'église romaine* (Dissertation, Strasbourg, 1954) 43–8.

27 J.-D. Kaestli, 'Fiction littéraire et réalité sociale: que peut-on savoir de la place des femmes dans le milieu de production des Actes apocryphes des apôtres?', *Apocrypha* 1 (1990, 279–302) 300 persuasively argues that the *seniores* in *Pet.* 19–21 are not 'old men' but 'older widows'. Date: P. Lampe, *Die stadtrömischen Christen in den ersten beiden Jahrhunderten* (Tübingen, 1989²) 99.

28 S.L. Davies, *The Revolt of the Widows: The Social World of the Apocryphal Acts* (Carbondale, 1980) 70–94, implausibly concludes from the prominence of widows that they were the authors of the apocryphal *Acts*.

29 Cf. E. Junod and J.D. Kaestli, *Acta Iohannis* I (Turnhout, 1983) 114f.

30 *Univira*: M. Lightman and W. Zeisel, '*Univira*: an Example of Continuity and Change in Roman Society', *Church History* 46 (1977) 19–32; Kötting (note 19 above), 15–9; idem, *Ecclesia peregrinans* I (Münster, 1988) 245–55; P.W. van der Horst, *Ancient Jewish Epitaphs* (Kampen, 1991) 103–5; Treggiari, *Roman Marriage*, 232–7.

31 Cf. J.F. Gardner, *Women in Roman Law & Society* (London, 1986) 50–6; K.R. Bradley, *Discovering the Roman Family* (New York and Oxford, 1991) 156–76; Treggiari, *Roman Marriage*, 500f.

32 M. Penta, 'La viduitas nella condizione della donna romana', *Atti della Academia di Scienze Morali e Politiche di Napoli* 91 (1980) 341–51; Treggiari, *Roman Marriage*, 500–2; J.-U. Krause, 'Die gesellschaftliche Stellung von Witwen im Römischen Reich', *Saeculum* 45 (1994) 71–104.

33 For the most recent dating of Hermas see N. Brox, *Der Hirt des Hermas* (Göttingen, 1991) 23f. The mention of widows in Clement (1 *Clemens* 8.4), a bishop of Rome who lived at the end of the first century, is clearly derived from the Old Testament and cannot be used as an indication for the position of widows in the church of that time.

34 Cf. *Vis.* II.4.3; *Mand.* IV.4 (remarriage), VIII.10; *Sim.* I.8, V.3.7, IX.26.2

(deacons) and 27.2 (bishops); Justin Martyr, *Apology* I.67.7 (deacons); M. Leutzsch, *Die Wahrnehmung sozialer Wirklichkeit im 'Hirten des Hermas'* (Göttingen, 1987) 73f., 135, 161.

35 Cf. Eusebius, *Historia Ecclesiastica* IV.23.10. Leutzsch, *Die Wahrnehmung*, 246–51 rightly stresses that these data are unfortunately insufficient to reconstruct the size of the Christian congregation in the city of Rome.

36 Recently serious objections have been raised against both the accepted time and place of origin of the church order. I still follow the traditional ascription but the matter deserves further investigation, cf. M. Metzger, 'A propos des réglements ecclesiastiques et de la prétendue *Tradition Apostolique*', *Revue des Sciences Religieuses* 66 (1992) 249–61 (with further bibliography); see also P. Bradshaw, *The Search for the Origins of Christian Worship* (London, 1992) 80–110.

37 Eusebius, *Historia Ecclesiastica* VI.43. For the importance of charity for the development of the Christian church in Late Antiquity, see P. Brown, *Power and Persuasion in Late Antiquity: Towards a Christian Empire* (Madison, 1992) 78–103.

38 Cf. B.D. Shaw, 'African Christianity: Disputes, Definitions, and "Donatists"', in M.R. Greenshields and T.A. Robinson (eds), *Orthodoxy and Heresy in Religious Movements: Discipline and Dissent* (Lewiston, Queenston and Lampeter, 1992, 5–34) 25f.

39 Tertullian, *De virginibus velandis* 9f.; *Ad uxorem* 1.4.4; *De exhortatione castitatis* 11; *De pudicitia* 13, cf. G. Schöllgen, *Ecclesia sordida? Zur Frage der sozialen Schichtung frühchristlicher Gemeinden am Beispiel Karthagos zur Zeit Tertullians* (Münster, 1984) 305–7. P. Brown: *The Body and Society: Man, Women and Sexual Renunciation in Early Christianity* (New York, 1988) 147.

40 Cf. M. Metzger, *Les Constitutions Apostoliques* I–III (Paris, 1985–7) I, 15 (bibliography). For important observations on the original shape of this church order see G. Schöllgen, 'Die Kapiteleinteilung der syrischen Didaskalie', in *Tesserae: Festschrift für Josef Engeman*: *Jahrbuch für Antike und Christentum*, Suppl. 18 (1991) 373–9.

41 Cf. C. Osiek, 'The Widow as Altar: The Rise and Fall of a Symbol', *The Second Century* 3 (1983) 159–69.

42 For a first discussion of gossip in antiquity see V. Hunter, 'Gossip and the Politics of Reputation in Classical Athens', *Phoenix* 44 (1990) 299–325.

43 For an interesting sociolinguistic approach see D. Tanner, *You Just Don't Understand: Women and Men in Conversation* (New York, 1991[2]) 96–122.

44 Muslims: E. Evers Rosander, *Women in Borderland: Managing Muslim Identity where Morocco meets Spain* (Stockholm, 1991) 211–27 (with thanks to Marjo Buitelaar). The classic study of gossip is M. Gluckman, 'Gossip and Scandal', *Current Anthropology* 4 (1963) 307–16. See also Pia Holenstein and Norbert Schindler, 'Geschwätzgeschichte(n): Ein kulturhistorisches Plädoyer für die Rehabilitierung der unkontrollierten Rede', in R. von Dülmen (ed.), *Dynamik der Tradition* (Frankfurt, 1992) 41–108, 271–81.

45 Reports, though, about the influence of aristocratic women on the conversion of their husbands have to be carefully scrutinised, cf. K. Cooper, 'Insinuations of Womanly Influence: An Aspect of the Christianization of the Roman Aristocracy', *Journal of Roman Studies* 82 (1992) 150–64; H. Sivan, 'Anician Women, the Cento of Proba, and Aristocratic Conversion in the Fourth Century', *Vigiliae Christianae* 47 (1993) 140–57.

46 Cf. R. MacMullen, *Christianizing the Roman Empire* (New Haven and London, 1984) 25–42.

47 Cf. A. Henrichs and L. Koenen, *Zeitschrift für Papyrologie und Epigraphik* 44 (1981) 308.

48 J.A. Beckford, 'Socialization in Small Religious Movements', in L. Laeyendecker *et al.* (eds), *Experiences and Explanations: Historical and Sociological Essays on Religion in Everyday Life* (Leeuwarden, 1990, 139–59) 144. There is a growing interest in social networks in Early Christianity; see the studies collected in *Semeia*, no. 56 (1992).

49 For widows in the *Didascalia* see R. Gryson, *Le ministère des femmes dans l'Eglise ancienne* (Gembloux, 1972) 65–75; A. Faivre, *Naissance d'une hiérarchie: Les premières étapes du cursus clerical* (Paris, 1977) 131–5. For preaching women see also Gregory of Nazianze, *Ep.* 5.4; *Patrologia Graeca* 37.1546.

50 Origen: Gryson, ibid., 53–64, but note the convincing objections of Thurston, *The Widows*, 96 against Gryson's all too sceptical approach. *Canones Hippolyti*: R.-G. Coquin, *Les canons d'Hippolyte* (Paris, 1966); Faivre, *Naissance d'une hiérarchie*, 73.

51 In the *Testamentum Domini*, a Syrian church order of the second half of the fifth century, widows still occupy a very important position; see Faivre, *Naissance d'une hiérarchie*, 106–10.

52 A.G. Martimort, *Les diaconesses* (Rome, 1982); J. Ysebaert, 'The Deaconesses in the Western Church of Late Antiquity', in G.J.M. Bartelink *et al.* (eds), *Eulogia: Mélanges Antoon A.R. Bastiaensen* (Steenbrugge and The Hague, 1991) 421–36.

53 John Chrysostom, *Patrologia Graeca* 51, 323D.

54 See G. Clark, *Women in Late Antiquity* (Oxford, 1993).

55 In the fourth century the influence of the emperor on conversions increased dramatically: M.R. Salzman, 'Aristocratic Women: Conductors of Christianity in the Fourth Century', *Helios* 16 (1989) 207–20.

56 Brown, *The Body and Society*; add to his bibliography H. Cancik, 'Zur Entstehung der christlichen Sexualmoral', in A.K. Siems (ed.), *Sexualität und Erotik in der Antike* (Darmstadt, 1988) 347–74. Important reviews are A. Cameron, *The Tablet*, 22 April 1989; F. Naerebout, *Leidschrift* (Leiden) 7 (1989) 85–99; F.E. Consolino *et al.*, 'Sessualità, castità, ascesi nella società tardoantic. Una discussione a proposito del libro di Peter Brown', *Riv. di Storia e Lett. Rel.* 28 (1992) 105–25; C. Kannengiesser, *Religious Studies Review* 19 (1993) 126–9 (with additional bibliography).

57 See also J.N. Bremmer, 'Symbols of Marginality from Early Pythagoreans to Late Antique Monks', *Greece & Rome* 39 (1992) 205–14.

58 P. Veyne, *La société romaine* (Paris, 1991) 88–130 ('La famille et l'amour sous le Haut-Empire romain', *Annales ESC* 33, 1978, 35–63).

59 See the innovative study by B. Shaw, 'The Cultural Meaning of Death: Age and Gender in the Roman Family', in D.I. Kertzer and R.P. Saller (eds), *The Family in Italy from Antiquity to the Present* (New Haven and London, 1991) 66–90.

60 For Veyne and the development towards asceticism see also my observations in Bremmer, 'Why did Early Christianity', 44f.

61 For a list of all fourth-century treatises on virginity see Th. Camelot, 'Les traités "De virginitate" au IVe siècle', *Etudes carmélitaines* 31 (1952) 189–97. The literature on the problem is immense, but see in addition to Brown especially A. Cameron, *Christianity and the Rhetoric of Empire* (Berkeley, Los Angeles and Oxford, 1991) 165–81; M. van Uytfanghe, 'Encratisme en verdrongen erotiek in de apocriefe "apostelromans": Omtrent de christelijke problematisering van de sexualiteit', *Handelingen der Koninklijke Zuidnederlandse Maatschappij voor Taal- en Letterkunde en Geschiedenis* 45 (1991) 175–94 (with an excellent bibliography).

62 Ambrose, *De viduis*, cf. A.V. Nazarro, 'Il *De viduis* di Ambrogio', *Vichiana* 13 (1984) 274–98 and 'Metafore e immagini agricole del De Viduis di Ambrogio', *Vetera Christianorum* 28 (1991) 277–89.

63 John Chrysostom, *Oratio ad viduam juniorem*, cf. the modern edition with translation and commentary: Jean Chrysostome, *A une jeune veuve: Sur le mariage unique*, (eds) B. Grillet and G.H. Ettlinger (*Sources Chrétiennes* 138 (Paris, 1968)); the sermon *Vidua eligatur* (*Patrologia Graeca* 51, 321–38) on 1 *Tim.* 5:9, and the fifteenth sermon on 1 *Tim.* 5:11. For Chrysostom's ideas about sexuality see also E.A. Clark, *Ascetic Piety and Women's Faith: Essays on Late Ancient Christianity* (Lewiston and Queenston, 1986) 229–64.

64 Jerome, *Epp.* 54, 123; E.A. Clark, *Jerome, Chrysostom, and Friends* (New York and Toronto, 1979) 1–34.

65 Augustine, *De bono viduitatis*. It is distressing to note that this treatise was still being reprinted in 1951 to offer comfort to German war-widows, cf. A. Maxsein, *Aurelius Augustinus: Das Gut der Witwenschaft* (Würzburg, 1952) vii.

66 For a detailed discussion of these allusions see A. Quacquarelli, *Il triplice frutto della vita cristiana: 100, 60 e 30 (Matteo XIII – 8, nelle diverse interpretazioni* (Rome, 1953); P.F. Beatrice, 'Il sermone "De centesima, sexagesima, tricesima" dello Ps. Cipriano e la teologia del martirio', *Augustinianum* 19 (1979) 215–43; N. Adkin, 'Athanasius' *Letter to Virgins* and Jerome's *Libellus de virginitate servanda*', *Rivista di filologia e di istruzione classica* 120 (1992) 185–203.

67 For the later Augustine's views about sexuality see R. Markus, *The End of Ancient Christianity* (Cambridge, 1990) 57–62; see also K. Thraede, 'Zwischen Eva und Maria: das Bild der Frau bei Ambrosius und Augustin auf dem Hintergrund der Zeit', in W. Affeldt (ed.), *Frauen in Spätantike und Frühmittelalter* (Sigmaringen, 1990) 129–39.

68 Augustine, *Ep.* 3*, tr. R.B. Eno, *St. Augustine: Letters Volume VI (1* – 29*)* (Washington, 1990) 31–7.

69 On the (lack of) effectiveness of this legislation see Treggiari, *Roman Marriage*, 294–8; see also E. Fantham, '*Stuprum*: Public Attitudes and

Penalties for Sexual Offences in Republican Rome', *Echos du Monde Classique* 10 (1991) 267–91.

70 *Codex Theodosianus* (*CTh*) 8.16.1 (marriage), 9.21.4 (counterfeit money).

71 Cf. *CTh* 3.11.1 (380), 9.25.1 (354), 2 (364, also mentioned by Sozomen, *Historia Ecclesiastica* 6.3), 3 (420); J. Evans-Grubbs, 'Abduction Marriage in Antiquity: A Law of Constantine (*CTh* 9.24.1) and its Social Context', *Journal of Roman Studies* 79 (1989, 59–102) 76f. Basil: Gregory of Nazianze, *Or.* 43.56f.

72 Note also his advice in *Ep.* 130.13 on which eunuchs to take on as servants.

73 For the liberty which Christianity offered to women see also L. Cracco Ruggini, 'La donna e il sacro, tra paganesimo e cristianesimo', in Uglione (note 1 above), 243–75.

74 I note in passing that an 'order of widows' is no longer mentioned. We may therefore conclude that the order had apparently also disappeared in the West, the region probably aimed at in this edict.

75 *CTh* 16.2.20 (370), 16.2.27, 28 (390); see also R. Lizzi, 'Una società esortata all' ascetismo: misure legislative e motivazioni economiche nel IV-V secolo d. C.', *Studi Storici* 30 (1989) 129–53.

76 For these women see J.N.D. Kelly, *Jerome* (London, 1975) 91–9 (Marcella and Paula), 191 (Furia), 210–2 (Fabiola); more recently, E.A. Clark, *The Origenist Controversy* (Princeton, 1992) 26–30; S. Rebenich, *Hieronymus und sein Kreis: prosopographische und sozialgeschichtliche Untersuchungen* (Stuttgart, 1992); C. Krumeich, *Hieronymus und die christliche feminae clarissimae* (Bonn, 1993).

77 John Chrysostom, *Life of Olympias* 4.

78 Male euergetism: P. Veyne, *Bread and Circuses: Historical Sociology and Political Pluralism* (London, 1990). Female: Ch. Pietri, 'Evergétisme et richesses ecclésiastiques dans l'Italie du IVe à la fin du Ve s.: l'exemple romain', *Ktema* 3 (1978) 317ff.; F.E. Consolino, 'Santo o patrone? Le aristocratiche tardo antiche e il potere della carità', *Studi Storici* 31 (1990) 969–91; K.J. Torjesen, 'In Praise of Noble Women: Asceticism, Patronage and Honor', *Semeia*, no. 57 (1992) 41–64.

79 Cf. the important study by J.W. Drijvers, 'Virginity and Asceticism in Late Roman Western Elites', in Blok and Mason (note 2 above), 241–73; A. Giardina, 'Carità eversiva: le donazioni di Melania la giovane e gli equilibri della società tardoromana', *Studi Storici* 29 (1988) 127–42.

80 Jerome himself also opposed these teachings but had no objections to women teaching each other. For a balanced appraisal of Jerome's attitude towards women see A. Arjava, 'Jerome and Women', *Arctos* 23 (1989) 5–18.

81 Cf. A. Arjava, 'Divorce in Later Roman Law', *Arctos* 22 (1988) 5–21; D.G. Hunter, 'The Paradise of Patriarchy: Ambrosiaster on Woman as (not) God's Image', *Journal of Theological Studies* 43 (1992) 447–69.

82 Palladius, *Dialogus de vita s. Joannis Chrysostomi* 5, cf. A.-M. Malingrey, 'Vierges et veuves dans la communauté chrétienne d'Antioche', *Roczniki Humanistyczne* [Lublin] 27 (1979).

83 Versions of this chapter were given in the spring of 1992 to the Groningen Ancient History Seminar, which was organized by Wim

Jongman, and on 31 August 1993 to the Belle van Zuylen Institute, Amsterdam. I thank Jan den Boeft, Theo Korteweg and Hans Roldanus for their observations on various versions of this text, and Ken Dowden for his skilful revision of my English.

4

WIDOWS IN
ANGLO-SAXON
ENGLAND

Rolf H. Bremmer Jr

For the early Middle Ages, no country in Western Europe can boast of such wide documentation as Anglo-Saxon England.* One of the interesting aspects of its cultural history, which started with the Germanic invasions in the course of the fifth century and ended with the Norman Conquest in AD 1066, is that it passed from a pagan Germanic into a Christian society. Studying the position of widows in this period, therefore, implies an awareness of two traditions which have often blended to a degree where it is impossible to distinguish them. Moreover, the nature of the available sources, varying from epic to sermon and law, and composed in different periods and places, should alert us to the danger of making a monolith picture of the Anglo-Saxon widow. We should also bear in mind that most of the extant documents were produced by and intended for the upper crust of a mainly illiterate society. Because of these restrictions, what we discover of the image of widows will necessarily be of a mixed nature.[1]

TERMINOLOGY

The Anglo-Saxons had two specific words for designating a woman whose husband had died. The more common one was *widuwe* and variants, a word with cognates in most of the other Germanic languages (but not in Scandinavian), in Slavonic, Prussian, Latin or Sanskrit – in other words, it belongs to the common lexicon of Indo-European.[2] Like most other earlier stages of these languages, the Anglo-Saxon had no masculine form of widow, 'widower' in English being a neologism of the late fourteenth century. The absence of masculine forms in earlier times undoubtedly reveals that the woman as the one who had lost a partner was the marked person in society, whereas the widower was in a less vulnerable situation and freer to choose a new partner. His was not a recognized and permanent position. The other word used with some frequency for designating a widow is *laf*, literally 'what has been left behind'.[3] It always occurs in the combination 'X's *laf*' and never in the generic sense. This term defines the widow in relation to her deceased husband. Thirdly, in certain contexts *wif*, 'woman who is not a virgin', can also mean 'widow', a conclusion which is corroborated by its being used to translate Latin *vidua*.[4] A variety of words for designating a widow suggests that such a woman occupied a place of some conspicuousness in the social relations of the Anglo-Saxons. For a proper insight into the nature of that place, we will first turn to the laws.

WIDOWS AND LEGISLATION

Owing to a fairly large number of mainly vernacular codes of law that have survived, we are in a position to see at least how in legislation the position of women in general, but also of widows in particular, was defined. Notwithstanding these texts, we must bear in mind that what has come down to us in written law reveals perhaps only a fraction of the regulations that prevailed in daily life. Law was customary law, and on the whole only such rules as had actually resulted from jurisprudence were laid down in codes of law.[5] As time passed, we can observe two main developments in the course of five centuries of legislative activities, often going hand in hand. The one is the growing importance of the king at the expense of the kindred, the other is the increasing influence of the church, apparent in the assimilation of, especially, canon law.[6]

The pillar of Germanic society was the kindred, and it was this form of social organization which the Anglo-Saxon tribes brought with them to Britain. In the *cynn*, or kindred, the males were formally responsible for the underaged and women. However much reality may have differed from theory, no woman could officially act without a legal guardian. Until her marriage, a woman remained under the protection (*mund*) of her father (or brothers); at her wedding she passed into that of her husband. Only as a widow would she be fairly independent, but her husband's kinsmen would still be legally responsible for the rights of her children. The laws of King Ine of Wessex (*c.* AD 690) state that a widow was to 'have her child and raise it'. She was to be given 'six shillings for its maintenance' as well as 'a cow in summer, an ox in winter' (Ine 38). Ine added to this provision that her husband's kinsmen were to act as the child's protector, 'to look after the parental home until he is grown up'. The contemporaneous laws of the Kentish Kings Hlothhere and Eadric specify the age of adulthood here as 10 years old.[7] Remarkably, under the *wergeld*-system, which regulated financial compensation for injuries or death, she would still come under the responsibility of her paternal kin.[8] Within this complicated division of legal obligations and regulations, a woman retained a certain amount of independence as a wife, resting on the material transactions that went along with a marriage. On his daughter's marriage, the father gave her property, usually land, as was agreed in the negotiations with the prospective husband. This was the dowry, which could alternatively be called *wedd* ,'pledge' (the origin of the word 'wedding'); *wituma*, 'dowry'; *gifu*, 'present'; or *fæderenfeoh*, 'paternal fee'. The husband himself provided her with the *morgengyfu*, 'morning-gift', a substantial present of land and goods, the morning after the marriage had been consummated.[9] *Be Wifmannes Beweddunge*, a document of the late tenth century describing the various steps leading to a legally contracted marriage, required the groom to declare before the bride's kinsmen, among other things, 'what he grants her in return for the acceptance of his suit, and what he grants her if she should live longer than he' (Wif 3). In other words, right from the outset of her marriage it had to be clear what the bride's dower amounted to.[10]

Occasionally, we are given a chance to see how such legal regulations were given shape in practice. Two marriage contracts survive, both from the early eleventh century, of which the contents make clear that the parties involved belonged to the élite. It is well worth quoting one of them:

> Here in this document is stated the agreement which Wulfric and the archbishop [of York and Worcester] made when he obtained the archbishop's sister as his wife, namely he promised her the estates at Orleton and Ribbesford for her lifetime, and promised her that he would obtain the estate at Knightwick for her for three lives from the community at Winchcombe, and gave her the estate at Alton to grant and bestow upon whomsoever she pleased during her lifetime or at her death, as she preferred, and promised her 50 mancuses [1 mancus = 30 silver pennies] of gold and 30 men and 30 horses.[11]

With such a start, the newly wedded wife would be certain to have considerable independence from her husband. She could freely spend the income of her morning-gift, while the dowry was added to her husband's property, albeit not always for good. If she became a widow, and had no children, the dowry would return to her paternal kin, to whom she would often move as well, while she remained still in control of the morning-gift herself. Several wills make clear that the husband could not bequeath property which had been given to her as her morning-gift, or they enumerate the estates that were given as such so as to prevent inheritance disputes. Ælfhelm's will, for example, contains such a clause:[12]

> ... and I declare what I gave to my wife as a morning-gift, namely, Buddow and Burstead and Stratford and the three hides[13] at Enhale. And when we first came together, I gave her the two hides at Wilbraham, and Rayne and whatever pertains to it.

This will is exceptional because it mentions besides a morning-(after)-gift a night-before present to encourage his designated wife to accept his suit. Frequently, too, the wills promise wives a substantial dower, or at least the usufruct of one or more estates.[14] An instance of marital trust is found in the will of Ealdorman Ælfheah, which includes the provision: 'to my wife Ælfswith, if she live longer than I and maintains the property in accordance with the confidence I have in her, I grant all the other estates which I leave'.[15] Such wives, once widowed, would not end up in the margin of society, but could continue to play a role of importance.

THE ROYAL WIDOW

Influential widows are indeed known to us, usually belonging to royalty, even though they sometimes receive nothing more than the barest mention in a chronicle, such as Queen Sexburh of whom it is said that she 'ruled for a year' after her husband, King Cenwalh of Wessex, had died.[16] For a long time, the king's wife played a restricted role in Anglo-Saxon England, especially in the kingdom of Wessex. Bishop Asser, King Alfred the Great's (AD 852–99) biographer, suggested that the modest role assigned to them originated in the reputedly outrageous behaviour of King Beorhtric's wife, Eadburh.[17] As soon as this Mercian princess had been married to Beorhtric of Wessex (c. AD 800), according to Asser, she began to reveal a behaviour similar to that of her father, King Offa, by plotting and scheming and disposing of those who did not obey her wishes. Eventually, Eadburh poisoned her husband, who accidentally drank from the wrong cup. Forced into exile to France, the royal widow visited Charlemagne, who presented her with a nunnery. But even as an abbess in such holy surroundings, she could not hide her true character. Caught in bed with a compatriot, she had to end her life as a beggar in Pavia.

More successful was the career of Æthelfled, King Alfred's daughter. Married to Ealdorman Æthelred of Mercia, in an attempt to tighten the bonds between Wessex and Mercia, she proved an able wife. During her twenty-year marriage, she actively participated in the administration of Mercia and helped her husband in recovering land from the Scandinavian invaders. Contemporary chroniclers refer to them as 'Lord and Lady of the Mercians', even as 'Lords' (hlafordas), the male term. After her husband's death in AD 910, Æthelfled ruled Mercia single-handedly for another nine years. In effect, she had practically done so even before her widowhood, as her husband had been sickly for a good many years. Æthelfled ordered fortresses to be built, organized punitive expeditions into Wales and recaptured Derby from the Vikings. Upon her death, an Irish annalist reported that 'her fame spread abroad in every direction', an indication of the exceptional position she had held in the political constellation of England at the time.[18]

Royal widows seem to have been coveted partners more than once and for more than one reason. Such a marriage would enable the new king to buy off the lady's faction. If she were a foreign princess, the new marriage would continue the links with her home country. Marrying the dowager queen would also contain an element of legitimation.[19] One could add to these arguments that such a union would secure a continuance factor in the passing on of royal authority. Several examples of such marriages from the Germanic world are known to us. Paul the Deacon reports two of them:[20] Agilulf marries Theudelinda, widow of Authari, his maternal kinsman (mother's brother?) and becomes king. Interestingly, Paul has Theudelinda take the initiative for this marriage (Bk III, ch. 35). A gruesome story is Queen Rosemund's: a captive of war, she is married by the victorious Lombard King Alboin, who had killed her father, King of the Gepidae, and whose skull he had made into a goblet. Scarcely has she avenged her father, when she intends to marry Alboin's murderer Helmigis. When she wants to dispose of the latter in favour of yet another man, she offers him a poisoned drink. Helmigis drinks it, but then perceives her intentions and forces Rosemund to swallow the dregs, so that the two die together (Bk II, ch. 29). For the Suevi, chroniclers report that Audeca usurped the throne and took Siseguntia, the former King Miro's widow and his own mother-in-law, to wife, as he had already married Miro's daughter![21] The daughter apparently was only a stepping stone on his way to the Suevian throne. Especially famous through Shakespeare's *Hamlet* is the episode in Saxo Grammaticus's *History of The Danes*,[22] in which Fengi kills his brother King Orvendil and marries the latter's widow Gerutha – 'adding incest to fratricide' is Saxo's clerical comment (Bk III, ch. 77).

This type of marriage seems to have been concluded also in pagan Anglo-Saxon England. When Eadbald, son of the first Christian king of Kent, Æthelbert, ascended to the throne in AD 616, the *Anglo-Saxon Chronicle* drily recorded that 'he abandoned his baptismal faith and lived by heathen customs, so that he had his father's widow as wife'. The phraseology 'heathen custom', used by the chronicler around AD 900, suggests an intimate knowledge of Anglo-Saxon pagan mores of three centuries earlier, which is not very likely. He may have had in mind the practice of his contemporary Germanic pagans, more precisely, those of the Scandinavian settlers in England. More probably, we need not interpret 'heathen custom' as Germanic, but rather as the traditional terminology, adopted from the church fathers, to condemn any practice which was not Christian. Bede's was a more emotional reaction, when he wrote in his *Historia Ecclesiastica* (*HE*) that Eadbald 'was guilty of such fornication as the Apostle Paul [1 *Cor.* 5:1] mentions as being unheard of even among the heathen, in that he took his father's wife as his own' (Bk II, ch. 5).[23] We are not told whether the queen approved of her new husband, who would have been her stepson. Nor did Eadbald take much pleasure from the union, as Bede hastens to inform his readers: 'This apostate king did not escape the scourge of God's punishment, for he was subject to frequent fits of insanity and possessed by an evil spirit.'

Was the practice of marrying one's father's widow really pagan only, as the chronicler would like us to believe? Almost 250 years after Eadbald, Charles the Bald gave his 12-year-old daughter Judith in marriage to King Æthelwulf of Wessex. Æthelwulf did not enjoy this marriage very long, for he died two years later, leaving behind a widow of 14.[24] When his son Æthelbald succeeded him, Asser shows his abhorrence in saying:

> contrary to God's prohibition and Christian dignity, and also contrary to the practice of all pagans, [Æthelwulf] took over his father's marriage-bed, and married Judith, daughter of Charles, king of the Franks, incurring great disgrace from all who heard it.[25]

The tone of indignation is paramount, and Asser was right in his condemnation of the liaison from a Christian point of view, as we shall see later. But his remark about the pagan practices in this respect is Pauline, flatly contradicting, as we have seen, the chronicler's opinion that such a practice was heathen. Judith may have played an active role in this marriage, judging by her later career. Again a widow, now at 17, she returned to Francia, to elope with Baldwin, Count of Flanders, when she was about 19, and married for a third time.[26] Twice a widow, and three weddings before her 21st year might in Judith's case suggest something of the overdeveloped sexual appetite that widows were reputed to have, and feared for, especially in the later Middle Ages.[27]

Being twice the king's consort was also the lot of Emma of Normandy. First married to Æthelred the Unready, Emma later became the wife of Æthelred's fierce opponent and strategic superior, the first Danish king of all England, Cnut. Barely a year after Æthelred's death, 'the king [Cnut] ordered the widow of King Æthelred, Richard's daughter, to be fetched as his wife' (ASC s.a. 1017). Both marriages proved fruitful. From her marriage with Æthelred, her son Edward became king, from that with Cnut her son Harthacnut ascended the throne. The latter ruled from AD 1040–42, the former from AD 1042–66. Contemporary opinions of Emma are mixed, and certainly the sons bore few sentimental feelings towards their mother. When after Cnut's death in AD 1035, his son (by another woman) Harald Harefoot ascended to the throne, he 'had all the best treasures taken from her, which she could not keep back, which King Cnut had possessed (ASC C, s.a. 1035), and banished her to Bruges in AD 1037. Upon his coronation in AD 1040 her son Harthacnut allowed her to come back, but only for a short time was she allowed to live in relative peace. Harthacnut ruled for just two years and was succeeded by his half-brother Edward the Confessor. One of Edward's first actions as king was the dispossession of his mother:

> [He] deprived her of all the treasures which she owned, and which were beyond counting, because she had formerly been

very hard to the king, her son, in that she did less for him than he wished both before he became king and afterwards as well. (*ASC* D, s.a. 1043)[28]

However, Emma was allowed to live in Winchester, and she remained active there, as appears for example from her attesting to charters and wills until her death in 1051.[29]

Dowager queens naturally had a great interest in securing their position at the court. The lustre of that status is reflected, for example, by the signing habits of Queen Eadgyfu, widow of King Edward (AD 901–27). She proudly signed charters during the successive rules of her sons Edmund and Edred as 'mother of the king' (*mater regis*), and having outlived them, she added 'grand-mother of the king' (*ava regis*) to her name when her grandsons had ascended to the throne. The position of the dowager queen was nevertheless precarious, as we have seen in Emma's case. Also Eadgyfu had to suffer being stripped of all her possessions by her grandson Edwig, but they were restored to her after Edwig's death by her other grandson, King Edgar.[30] King Edgar's widow, Ælfthryth, earlier widow of Æthelwold, Ealdorman of East Anglia, was reputed to have killed her stepson Edward ('The Martyr') to clear the way for her own son Æthelred ('The Unready').[31] To her credit, her grandson Æthelstan the Ætheling on more than one occasion refers to her as 'my grandmother, who brought me up'.[32] Incidentally, this is the only indication we have for the period that grannies were employed (and appreciated) as babushkas!

For the epic *Beowulf*, it has been suggested that Beowulf married Queen Hygd, after her husband had died during a raiding campaign in Frisia, but the poem is not explicit on this matter. In fact the young Hygd offers Beowulf 'the hoard and the kingdom, rings and the royal throne; she did not feel her child [Heardred] could defend the ancestral seats of the kingdom against the peoples of other lands after the death of Hygelac' (*Beow* 2369–2372). Remarkably, the poet sees no problem in assigning to Hygd the active part of settling the question of succession to the throne. Hygd's solution comes tantaliz-ingly close to offering her hand as well. Beowulf, however, declines the offer but is content to assume the role of Heardred's regent. Only after Heardred's fall in battle does Beowulf ascend to the throne. When violent death has overtaken Beowulf himself, the poem pictures his funeral obsequies, which include an old woman mourn-ing with unbound hair at the funeral pyre. Some critics have identified her with Queen Hygd and made her into Beowulf's widow. The relevant passage in the manuscript, though, is badly damaged and as many emendations have been suggested as there are critical opinions.[33] Should the old woman really have been Beowulf's widow, the scene would be the only description we have of a widow performing the funeral rites in an Anglo-Saxon, Germanic setting.

WIDOWS OF LOWER RANK

Quite naturally, the fortunes and misfortunes of widows at the top attracted due attention from the society reporters of the day, the chroniclers. It is mainly wills and charters that allow us to glimpse their sisters of lower ranks and how they strove to maintain their positions. When injured in their material interest, they would appeal to court, and sometimes, if needs be, they had recourse to violence, sometimes to fraud. A certain estate at Snodland in Kent had been bequeathed to the bishop of Rochester by a woman called Æscwyn. Her son Ælfric begrudged this pious act and paid a priest to steal the title deeds from the bishop. When the bishop discovered the theft, Ælfric had died in the meantime. His widow, apparently accomplice to the crime, was forced to appear at a court meeting in the presence of King Edgar (c. AD 975) to deliver the stolen deeds. She saw her property – estates at Bromley and Fawkham – forfeited which thereby legally fell to the king. The widow also gave up the title deeds of these estates, which were then bought by the bishop, who generously allowed her the usufructs of them, thereby showing his Christian concern for her as a widow.[34]

The events as described in a charter drafted during Æthelred the Unready's reign (AD 978–1016) are quite complicated. After his father's death, a certain Wulfbold had gone to his stepmother's estate, and 'took everything he could find there, inside and out, small and great'. He was repeatedly ordered by the king to give up what he had seized, but failed to appear, and each time he was condemned to pay his *wergeld*[35] to the king. Finally, a great assembly, consisting of both ecclesiastic dignitaries and noblemen, was held at London, and Wulfbold's property was declared forfeit. Whatever he did, Wulfbold did not pay his fines until he died. And after his death, 'over and above all this', the charter indignantly continues, his widow together with her son went and killed Eadmer, her husband's brother's son, together with Eadmer's fifteen companions on an estate which Wulfbold had seized from his brother Brihtmær.[36] The charter vividly illustrates the precarious situation a widow could find herself in when her dower was seized from her and also to what extremes she would go to regain possession of it.

Not always would a widowed mother and her son close ranks. A remarkable case is given by an account of a shire-meeting held at Aylton, Herefordshire, during Cnut's reign. There Edwin, Enneawn's son, sued his own mother to gain the possession of two estates. When the bishop asked who would represent her – and from this question we may conclude that the nameless mother is a widow – her kinsman Thorkil took it upon himself to defend her. Three men were sent to her to enquire about her defence. When she heard what was going on, she replied that she had no land to which her son had a proper claim. And then she grew so angry with her son that she called her kinswoman Leofflæd, Thorkil's wife, to her and made the following public statement:

> Here sits Leofflæd, my kinswoman, to whom I grant both my land and my gold, and my raiment and my clothing and all that I own after my death.

She did not leave it at that but told the messengers in an authoritative tone:

> Behave as noblemen and do well; convey my message to the meeting before all the good men, and tell them to whom I have granted my land and all my possessions, and never one thing to my son; and ask them all to be witness to this.

Her request was indeed carried out, and Thorkil had her declaration confirmed by the meeting, and subsequently recorded in a gospel book in Hereford Cathedral, where it rests until the present day.[37]

As we have seen, the legal provisions were such that a widow could maintain a reasonably independent life. From documentary evidence like charters and wills, it becomes clear that we are dealing with widows belonging to the class of land-owning freemen. Rich widows were obviously popular candidates for spouses, and as often as not a widow may have longed for a man in the house. Remarriage was common, but there were certain restrictions imposed by the church. All later sources are unanimous in forbidding a widow to remarry within twelve months, an understandable measure as it had to be unambiguous that children born within this period were heirs to the property of her deceased husband. Ignoring the regulation resulted in her losing her morning-gift and all the goods which she had acquired through her former husband (II Cn 73). The new husband had to pay his *wergeld* as a fine to the king. If the proper period of twelve months had passed and she wanted to remarry, her paternal kinsmen were again involved in the negotiations (Wif 1). Having eligible women could be advantageous for a family, but several laws expressly state that a woman, whether a virgin or a widow, could not be forced to marry against her will (e.g. II Cn 74). Cnut also provided for abductions of widows with an eye to a marriage. Such an act would cost the abductor his *wergeld* (II Cn 52, 73–73.3), although the marriage could be allowed to stand. But even if a widow had been abducted and forced to marry, she would lose her properties if she refused to leave the new husband and return home. King Æthelred mentions the abduction of nuns and widows in one breath, and adds that the culprit should atone deeply for it 'both before God and the world' (VI Atr 39). An abducted nun who outlived her unwanted husband received nothing from the inheritance nor indeed did her children. If any of her children were killed, her share of the *wergeld* was to be paid to the king (Alf 8.1–3). Such severe provisions were no doubt intended for the nun to facilitate the choice between staying with her abductor or returning to the nunnery. A protecting influence may also have come from one of Cnut's codes which stated that the fine for raping or abducting a virgin was the same as that of raping a widow, viz. one *wergeld* (II Cn 52). The church was equally strict in such a case: rape or abduction of either a virgin or a widow, according to the *Old English Penitential*, resulted in excommunication.[38]

Sometimes women were treated merely as pawns in men's games. The *Beowulf* poet tells of the sad career of the Danish princess Hildeburh who was married to Finn, King of the Frisians, in an attempt to establish peace between the two tribes. When her brother Hnaef came to visit Frisia the old feud was stirred up again, and after two fights interrupted by the winter, Hildeburh was brought back to Denmark, leaving behind the ashes of her husband, her brother and her son (*Beow* 1063–1159). 'That was a pitiful lady!' is how the poet summed up her fate. But the hard reality was also that widows could be pushed around. A Kentish charter of the late tenth century tells the fate of a number of estates, belonging to a certain Ælfheah, but granted, first to his brother Ælfric, and after the latter's death to Ælfric's son Eadric. Eadric also died during Ælfheah's lifetime, 'leaving a widow and no children'. Ælfheah then resumed possession of his former estates, allowing the widow, however, to keep the estate

Eadric had given her as morning-gift. Before long, she had remarried a certain Leofsunu, who, 'on the strength of having married Eadric's widow', disregarded Ælfheah's will, and 'with his wife took possession of the estates'.[39] Clearly, Leofsunu saw the widow as an opportunity to further his own interests. Also in national politics, widows were being taken advantage of for similar reasons. In the turbulent days of Æthelred the Unready, the chief thegns of the Five Boroughs, Morcar and Sigeferth, were treacherously killed by the king's party. The goods of these noblemen were confiscated and the king ordered Sigeferth's widow Ealdgyth to be caught and placed in a nunnery in Malmesbury. From there, Æthelred's obnoxious son Edmund Ironside abducted her and married her against the king's will. Love, though, was the last thing on Edmund's mind: late in August, he marched to the Five Boroughs and 'at once took possession of all of Sigeferth's estates and Morcar's, and the people all submitted to him' (ASC E, s.a. 1015). With Sigeferth's widow at his side, Edmund undoubtedly meant to emphasize his position as the new leader of the Five Boroughs.

THE WIDOW-WITCH

Occasionally, a widow's measures against those that threatened her were less directly violent, but by no means less malevolent. In a charter from the second half of the tenth century, the exchange of a number of estates is recorded between Wulfstan Uccea and Bishop Æthelwold. With respect to the estate at Ailsworth, the charter informs us how Wulfstan had acquired it:

> A widow and her son had forfeited it, because they had driven iron pins into [an image of] Ælfsige, Wulfstan's father. And that was discovered, and the death-bringing instrument was dragged from her chamber. Then the woman was taken and drowned at London Bridge, and her son broke away and became an outlaw.

The king confiscated her land, and donated it to her intended victim, who later bequeathed it to his son.[40] We are not told why the widow had murder on her mind, but I think we are not far from the truth if we assume that she practised black magic to further her interests as a widow. Yet, one instance of a widow-witch from the period under investigation would be too slender for us to suppose that Anglo-Saxons associated widows with witchcraft.

There are some indications, though, that such an association was in the air. Two sources from the generation immediately after the Norman Conquest, but dealing with the Anglo-Saxon period, provide further examples of widow-witches. William the Conqueror's occupation of the English throne did not go unopposed. Perhaps most famous was the resistance offered by the semi-legendary Hereward the Wake, who held the Isle of Ely in East Anglia from spring 1070 to autum 1071 against William. Driven to despair by Hereward's valiant defence, according to the early twelfth-century *Gesta Herewardi*,[41] William even employs an old woman skilled in the art of black magic. As it happens, Hereward, having a scout around behind the enemy's lines disguised as a potter, spends the night at the house of a widow, who apparently provided bed and breakfast for her livelihood. Quite coincidentally, the other guest there is the witch who was hired by William. The two women converse in French, thinking that Hereward is unable to understand it. That night Hereward follows the witch and the widow, who proves to be an accomplice, to a spring where they seek advice of the spirit of the spring. Unfortunately, Hereward cannot hear what they are talking about. In the end, the witch pronounces her curses against Hereward and his men, bolstering her art by turning her bared arse (a very evil eye, indeed!) towards the island. Barely has she ended her act, when Hereward and his men set fire to the reeds that surround her, and she miserably ends her life there.[42] Remarkably, the one witch in the story is old,[43] while the other is explicitly referred to as a widow. Is it surprising to find the two together?

Supplied with fascinating details is William of Malmesbury's account of the witch of Berkely, to be found in his *De Gestis Regum Anglorum*, written in 1125.[44] William describes her as a woman 'well-versed in witchcraft, not ignorant of ancient auguries, a patroness of gluttony, an arbiter of lasciviousness, not setting a limit to her debauches'. One day, her jackdaw forbodes great disaster, and indeed the news comes that her sons and other relatives have suddenly perished. She falls ill, and makes preparations for her imminent death. She asks her remaining children, a monk and a nun, to see to her burial as follows: they must sew her corpse up in a stag-skin, put it into a sarcophagus, sealed with lead and iron, and chained with three heavy chains. Her children are to sing psalms and masses for fifty days on end to secure her a safe conduct to the hereafter. But all these precautions are of no avail. The first two nights fierce devils appear, and snap a chain each time. The third night an even fiercer devil bursts in, breaks the last chain, pushes aside the stone lid, and takes the widow's corpse to where she belonged. In view of her adult children, it is clear that here, too, we are dealing with a woman who is well advanced in age, and as such fits in to a familiar pattern.[45] Anthony Davies, in his interesting analysis of witches in Anglo-Saxon England, does much to play down the veracity of the witches in the *Gesta Herewardi* and William of Malmesbury's *Gesta Regum*. In particular, he considers William's witch to be an instance of 'fabrication'.[46] If this were indeed the case, it would still leave us with the fact that three out of five known cases of witches in Anglo-Saxon England involve widows. That two of these three date from early post-Conquest sources may point to a growing marginalization of widows in English society.

CHANGING PERSPECTIVES: THE CHURCH'S VIEW OF WIDOWS

What we have seen so far concerns mostly the legal and social position of widows from a secular point of view. An important factor that would gradually change the way people looked at widows was the teaching of the church. Right from the early years of the conversion, the church saw itself confronted with customs that it could not tolerate. One of these was marrying spouses within certain degrees of kinship so as to avoid the risk of incest.[47] In a long letter to Augustine, the first missionary from Rome, Pope Gregory the Great answered a number of questions which Augustine had presented him with (*c.* AD 600). One of his questions, according to Bede (*HE* Bk I, ch. 27), was: 'Is it lawful for a man to marry his stepmother or sister-in-law?' Gregory's answer on this matter was firm. Marrying one's stepmother he considered a great sin, for Moses's law said that 'Thou shalt not uncover the nakedness of thy father' (*Lev.* 18:8). Gregory must have realized that at first sight the logic of this precept was somewhat shaky. Therefore he added that married people had become one flesh, so that anyone who would marry his father's wife would uncover his nakedness, as he had been one flesh with her. Gregory's argument for prohibiting a marriage with a sister-in-law is based on other grounds. He might likewise have referred to Moses (*Lev.* 18:16), but instead Gregory mentions the fate of John the Baptist, who was beheaded for denouncing Herod's having married his brother's wife. John was a confessor of Christ, and Christ had said 'I am the Truth'. John died for the truth, *ergo* marrying one's sister-in-law was out of the question. While Gregory was lenient towards marrying relatives of the fourth degree onwards, in later times the church and, following its example, legislating kings likewise forbade marriage within the sixth degree (e.g. VI Atr 12; 1 Cn 7). Injunctions on trespassing were of the most drastic kind. The *Old English Penitential* (in the second half of the tenth century), a handbook assisting priests to define sins and to assign the appropriate penance, states that any man 'who marries his next of kin or his godmother or his brother's widow or his step-mother, let him be excommunicated from all Christian men'. If such a man shows remorse, he must do penance for the rest of his life by the bishop's judgement.[48] Some manuscripts containing a version of the *Old English Penitential* also include a report of a synod convened by Pope Gregory II at Rome in AD 721. In it, Gregory is reported to have said, among other things:[49]

> 'If any one has his own relative as a spouse or the widow of his next of kin, let him be excommunicated.' And all the bishops answered and said three times: 'Let him be excommunicated.'

We have seen in the cases of Kings Eadbald and Æthelbald that English royalty (then as now) tended to consider themselves above the law. Yet, both Bede's and Asser's strong reactions against these marriages show that the church's doctrine concerning the impermiss-ibility of marrying widows of one's next of kin was embraced wholeheartedly by the clergy.[50]

COMMISERATION WITH WIDOWS

In secular legislation, the Christian angle with respect to widows first becomes conspicuously clear in the long preamble to the laws of King Alfred the Great. Based particularly upon *Exodus* 20–22 and *Matthew* 5, Alfred includes the following statement on widows (Af El 34), merging the 'I' referring to God with his own:

> Do not oppress the widows and the orphans, nor injure them. If you do nonetheless otherwise, they will call to me, and I will hear them, and I will strike you with my sword, and I will bring about that your wives will become widows and your children orphans.[51]

A similar admonition, this time directed specifically to the clergy, is found in the laws of Æthelred (VI Atr 46–8) to comfort and feed the poor, 'not to vex the widows and orphans too often, but to gladden them eagerly', and to desist from hurting strangers and those that have come from afar. The passage stems from Archbishop Wulfstan's pen and is also found almost verbatim in one of his sermons.[52] In his sermon 'De Virginitate', Abbot Ælfric of Eynsham, the most prolific homilist of the period, tells his audience to give a third of the tithes to 'the poor, and widows, and orphans and foreigners', an instruction which also found its way into the laws of King Æthelred (VIII Atr 6).[53] Another homilist, in a sermon on the Christian life, admonishes his audience to give alms daily, even as little as a quarter loaf 'in gratitude to God to beggars or widows or orphans or servants or foreigners'.[54] Obeying this precept was given the prospect of heavenly blessings, as could be illustrated by the examples of various pious men. Anglo-Saxon homilists could find an excellent case in the apocryphal *Gospel of Matthew*. In it, Ioachim, Anna's husband and Mary's father, serves as an exemplary house father: each year he divided the increase of his flock into three. One third he gave to 'the poor, and widows, and orphans and foreigners', a third to God's servants and one third he kept for his own household. God increased his possessions to such an extent that there was no man in Jerusalem as rich as him.[55] In his sermons, Ælfric recurrently highlights alms-giving by biblical persons, and points out that Job was not boasting, but set an example to all men when he said: 'I delivered the crying poor, and I helped the orphan that was without support and I comforted the heart of the widow.'[56] Elsewhere, in a sermon on the Greater Litany, he adduces the witness of Isaiah, who exhorted the judges as follows: 'Help the oppressed, and judge orphans; defend the widow against cruel oppression, and rebuke me afterwards.'[57] In the epilogue to his sermon on the Maccabees, Ælfric includes an account of the High Priest Onias, who employed the gifts sent by King Seleucus 'to protect widows and orphans from hunger'.[58]

In Old English saints' lives, too, we recurrently meet the act of alms-giving to widows and other vulnerable members of society as an essential part of Christian life. On their missionary tour through Persia the apostles Simon and Jude had just converted a general, who very enthusiastically suggested burning all idolaters, who had plotted against the apostles, on a pyre. But no, said the apostles, we have come to preach life, not death. Christ taught us to love our enemies. Simon and Jude also declined the general's present of vast treasures, and urged instead 'if you want to make this money useful to your soul, distribute it to the poor and the sick, to widows and orphans and to destitute taxpayers[!]'.[59] The apostle Thomas, too, entreated Gondophorus, King of the Indians: 'Let now your goods profit the widows, the poor and the sick, and know for sure that they will be kept for you a hundredfold.'[60] St Lucy convinced her mother, herself a widow who for nine years had successfully managed her late husband's property, to sell her 'shining gems and even her landed property for ready money' in order to distribute it to 'the poor and to strangers, to widows and exiles and to the wise servants of God'. And to her wooer, 'an impious idolater', she retorted upon his invitation to sacrifice to his idols, that 'a pure offering, and acceptable to God, is that one should visit widows, comfort exiles and help orphans in their afflictions'.[61] St Lawrence, at his bishop's command, distributed his church's treasures 'to priests, and poor strangers, and widows, to each according to his need'.[62] Indeed, the faithful are told they will gain the glory of heaven by prayers and vigils and alms-giving, 'if you want to abandon all evil, both of manslaughter and perjury, and help widows and fatherless and motherless children, so that you may be called "God's children" with your brothers'.[63] By such virtuous examples and alluring prospects the clergy sought to influence the behaviour of their audience.

Kings, too, would hear how to behave properly, as in Ælfric's treatise *De Duodecim Abusivis*, where he advised the king: 'not to oppress with violence either the poor or the humble, but to judge each one justly. He must be a protector to the widows and orphans, suppress robbery, punish fornicators and expel the wicked from his realm.'[64] Note how the widows take preference in this enumeration of a king's moral duties. Occasionally, we are told of a king's concern for widows, as when Abbo of Fleury in his martyrdom of Edmund, the last king of the East Anglians, remarks that Edmund 'was generous towards the weak and the widows like a father'.[65] Queen Eormenburh, widow of King Ecgfrith of Northumbria, 'was in all respects virtuous', because she honoured widows, orphans, the poor and crippled, 'unlike many people of noble birth today,' the author added in reproof, suggesting a cooling of the first love of the early years of Christianity in England.[66]

A genuine concern for widows also occupied Archbishop Wulfstan of York – who served as a legislator to both King Æthelred and his successor Cnut. In a thundering sermon composed and delivered in AD 1014, he pulls out all the stops of his rhetorical skills in painting a graphic picture of the social disintegration of the English people due to the continuing Viking raids. It is the English themselves who pile sin upon sin, and sacrilege upon sacrilege. Also 'widows have wrongfully been forced to marry, too many of them have been impoverished and greatly humiliated'.[67] The precarious state of widows in social life was slightly earlier observed by a chronicler deprecatingly recording Ealdorman Ælfhere's opposition to the Benedictine Revival of the late tenth century. Ælfhere 'broke God's law and hindered the monastic life, and destroyed monasteries and dispersed the monks . . . and they plundered widows time and again' (*ASC* D 975). Elsewhere, Wulfstan complained about reeves, i.e. manorial officers, robbing widows over and over again.[68]

Now Archbishop Wulfstan may inveigh against such abominable deeds committed by laymen, but even bishops themselves were liable to neglect their pastoral duties towards widows. The tenth-century *Blickling Homilies* include a sermon which draws on the apocryphal *Visio St Pauli*. In that vision, an angel guides St Paul through Hell, explaining to him what sins the tormented souls have committed. Paul suddenly sees four angels leading a man with great cruelty to a fiery river into which he is sunk up to his knees and then bound with fiery chains. Upon his enquiring who this man is, the angel replies: 'He is a bishop who did more evil than good. Before the world he had a great name, but he disregarded all his duties as well as his Creator who had given him that office.' Paul inferred from this that the bishop had shown no mercy to either widows or orphans or any of God's poor, and commented that the bishop was rightly requited according to his deeds.[69]

Christian charity had probably been shown by prince Æthelstan, King Æthelred the Unready's son, for in his will he mentions the money which Æthelwold's widow owed him and which he had paid 'for her help'. However much she will have been pleased at the time of the gesture, now she had to pay back the considerable amount of twelve pounds, as Æthelstan needed them for buying posthumous masses. Slavery was a hard reality in those days, a state into which people could transfer themselves if, for example, they were unable to pay their debts or if compelled by hunger.[70] Paradoxically, slave-owning clergymen also had to propagate the church's preference for freeing slaves. A number of acts of manumission have come down to us, some of which mention widows. Godwig 'the Buck' redeemed Leofgife, a breadmaker, with her children for half a pound from her owner, Abbot Æilsige. Æilsige, in his turn, bought off Ongynethel and her son Gythiccael for a similar price. Marh freed his own slave Lethelt and her children by swearing on his private relics. Also widows spent money on freeing their less fortunate congeners. Edivu, Sæwgele's widow, bought Gladu for half a pound. Liueger, 'the female baker of Exeter', redeemed Edith and her children for thirty (silver) pennies from Bishop Gosfreige. Occasionally, we read of widows redeeming themselves, such as Edith, daughter of Leofric 'Curly-head' who paid four pounds and twenty pennies for her freedom and that of her children. Apparently on the occasion of a visit to Bath, paid for by King Eadred and Archbishop Æthelgar, two widows and their children as well as a man called Wurgustel and his children were set free.[71]

THE CHASTE AND PIOUS WIDOW

If some widows were poorly off – now an easy prey to plunder or bargained away to slave-traders, now a coveted candidate for a forced marriage – it is remarkable that the church did not encourage remarriage for pastoral reasons. Here, however, we see the high regard – some would say obsession – the church had for chastity. In fact, church fathers like Augustine, Jerome and Ambrose had divided the believers into three states or degrees of perfection: virgins, widows and the married,[72] a division also taken up by the Anglo-Saxon theologian Aldhelm (c. AD 700) in his treatise *De Virginitate*.[73] Ælfric repeatedly mentions these three states in his sermons and letters, frequently in connection with the parable of the sower and the seed (*Matt.* 13:23). Virginity bears fruit a hundredfold, widowhood sixtyfold and wedded life thirtyfold.[74] In his sermon on the wedding at Cana, Ælfric refers to an expositor who said that the wedding-house was three-storied, 'because in God's church there are three degrees of chosen men', whereupon he enumerates the degrees.[75]

Seen in the light of this concern for chastity, admonitions not to remarry become understandable. Whereas secular law knows of no limit to the number of marriages, the church discouraged remarriage. Ælfric does not tire of reminding his audience of this restriction, sometimes by appealing to St Paul.[76] The *Old English Penitential* states that no Christian is allowed to marry more than twice, likewise with reference to Paul (although the apostle is not as explicit as medieval theologians would have it, cf. 1 *Cor.* 7:8–9).[77] Moreover, the widow should be young when she remarries. According to the Canons, a remarriage should not receive the church's blessings, 'so as to make clear to them that it had been better for them to have remained chaste'.[78] Archbishop Wulfstan wholeheartedly agreed with Abbot Ælfric: a priest should be absent from a second marriage to make the spouses feel that it was not quite right to remarry. But apparently, even Anglo-Saxon blood was thicker than water, for Wulfstan continues his argument by saying that it is 'certainly too much should it happen a third time, and completely wrong should it happen more often'.[79] The underlying thought is that marriage was the proper institute for sexual intercourse, and intercourse was only tolerated for procreation. So the older the candidate for a second marriage was, the more likely he or she was driven by other motives than procreation. In the words of Ælfric, 'it is very improper and shameful that worn out and impotent men desire marriage, because marriage is ordained for nothing but the procreation of children'.[80] Not only men were thus reproached by Ælfric. 'It is a shame and disgrace,' he wrote to Sigefyrth, 'that old women should have sex with men when they are worn out and too old for getting children, and a sign of inconstancy, for the sexes have been ordained for nothing else but for getting children only, as holy books teach us.'[81] The call for chastity had some appeal to the reeve Abba. In his will, he promises his land to his wife should he die childless 'as long as she wants to keep it with chastity'. His brother Alchere is to be her guardian, in that case. If, however, 'she does not want to keep it with chastity, but prefers to conclude a second marriage', Abba's land is to go to his kinsmen while she can keep her own, that is, her morning-gift. Yet Abba allows us to see that there are more options open to a widow than permanent widowhood or remarriage. He also foresees that his (nameless) wife might want to enter a monastery or even go on a pilgrimage to Rome. In that case his two brothers should pay her 2000 pence and get the land in return.[82]

Widows were therefore urged to follow the example of such biblical widows as Judith or Anna. An anonymous poet recast the *Book of Judith* into an epic and, although the poem is open to more than one interpretation, chastity certainly plays a prominent role in it. Despite her being a widow, the poem calls Judith several times a 'virgin'.[83] To Ælfric, Judith's story had more than one meaning. Her example should rouse the English to defend themselves courageously against the Scandinavian invaders, as he explained in an expository letter on the Old and New Testament to Sigwerd.[84] Elsewhere, in the epilogue to his sermon on Judith, addressed to 'my sister', Ælfric interprets Judith tropologically as a figure of Ecclesia, Christ's sole pure bride, who successfully defeated the devil (Holofernes). Moreover, many nuns should take example of this chaste widow of the old dispensation, Ælfric urged, while there are too many nuns, brides of Christ, who have not the slightest problem with fornicating here, there and everywhere.[85] Wulfstan exhorts widows to follow the example of Anna in a way which is well worth quoting:

> She was in the temple day and night diligently serving. She fasted greatly and attended prayers and called on Christ with mourning spirit, and distributed alms over and again, and ever propitiated God as far as she could by word and deed, and has now heavenly bliss for a reward. So shall a good widow obey her Lord.[86]

For the Anglo-Saxon homilist, the Bible provided more exemplary widows besides Anna. Best known is perhaps the hospitable widow of Zarephath who boarded Elijah (1 *Kings* 17), and who was also selected for praise by Jesus Christ (*Luke* 4:26). Men of God supported believing widows: Elijah restored the widow of Zarephath's son to life,[87] Elisha saved a widow from her creditors (2 *Kings* 4), Jesus Christ resurrected the son of the widow of Nain (*Luke* 7:11–16), while Peter brought back to life Dorcas (a widow herself?) who had provided numerous widows of Joppa with garments (*Acts* 9:36–42).[88] Such examples are reflected in the many saints' lives that circulated in Anglo-Saxon England. St John is reputed to have raised Drusiana in Ephesus, a widow 'of great faith, [who] gave much in alms, and the poor, whom she had bountifully fed, sad, with weeping, followed the corpse'.[89] St Lawrence healed a widow, called Quiriaca, of a troublesome migraine. During times of persecution under the emperor Decius, 'she had hidden in her dwelling priests and many lay Christians'.[90] Both St Maur and St Martin restored a widow's son to life,[91] while through the intercession of St Clement a widow's son regained his life twelve months after drowning![92]

Such miracles are not recorded for Anglo-Saxon widows or their sons, as far as I know. They had to make do with the sermons and saints' lives they would hear. Yet one should not get the impression that all widows occurring in such edifying texts behaved in an exemplary way. Occasionally we meet the exception to the rule such as the widow of a noble family from Cappadocia who had seven children. Raising those children appeared to be a burdensome task, and one day one of her children so infuriated her that she was driven to curse it. On her way to church she was persuaded by a devil in disguise not to curse just the one child but all seven of them. 'She then went to the baptismal font, unbound her hair, dipped it into the water, and with great fury sinfully cursed all her children.' Back home she came to her senses, and, conscience-stricken, hanged herself 'in the halter that she had spun with her feet'.[93] Less sensational and more romantic was the plight of St Eugenia. As a young girl, she converted to Christianity, dressed as a man and, accompanied by two converted eunuchs, joined a monastery. She quickly made a career there and was elected abbot. Eugenia proved especially skilful as a physician, and on one occasion healed a woman called Melantia of a long-lasting fever. The woman – a widow, it appeared – was much charmed by the abbot's looks and qualities, and tried to win his favours, thinking all the time that the object of her affection was a young man. She called Eugenia home to her, feigning sickness, and then plainly made a proposal, telling her that she had been a widow for a year (so no restrictions in that respect!) and that her husband had endowed her well with land, cattle and servants. As her final trump card, she added that she and her husband had never had sex. So what would prevent the abbot from becoming her husband and lord? However much Melantia pleaded, Eugenia firmly resisted the temptation, until the widow in her frustration falsely accused the abbot of having assaulted her. To plead innocence Eugenia had to reveal her true identity and sex by baring her breasts before the judge.[94] Luckily, the judge appeared to be her father(!), who had long been searching for his daughter. Melantia was spared on Eugenia's request, but Christ sent fire from heaven, which destroyed her house and all her property. In Eugenia's *vita*, then, a calculating widow is used to portray 'undisguised woman at her worst', contrasting with the 'de-sexed' Eugenia, the ideal woman as Ælfric saw her.[95]

Equally calculating, though perhaps taking a less frontal approach, was Earl Dolfin's widow. She fell in love with the previously mentioned Hereward the Wake, the rebel who withstood William the Conqueror, and openly sent messages to Hereward asking him to marry her, disregarding the fact that he was married already. Hereward was not averse to her overtures, nor did he remain cold under her charms. After all, 'there was nobody more lovely nor more beautiful in the realm, and scarcely anybody more eminent in their wealth'. Moreover, King William had promised her that if Hereward pledged faith with him he would not withhold his royal consent to the marriage. Beauty, wealth and peace made Hereward succumb to the deal, much to the disappointment of his wife, who thereupon 'chose the better life' and became a nun. Hereward's selfish choice did not turn out to be a success, as from this point onwards his career would be increasingly beset by misfortune.[96]

PIOUS WIDOWS: SOME EXAMPLES

The problem, one feels, with the picture of widows presented in homiletic discourse is that the ideal was too far removed from what was practically attainable. Were there no widows, then, in Anglo-Saxon England who lived a virtuous and pious life? Certainly, many widows took the veil, and especially noble widows often became abbesses of either nunneries or twin-monasteries. Cynethryth, King Offa of Mercia's widow, became Abbess of Cookham, her namesake Cynethryth, King Wiglaf of Mercia's widow, Abbess of Winch-combe.[97] Eafe, King Æthelwealh of Sussex's widow, was in charge of a monastery, as was Werburh, once Queen of the Mercians, according to the twelfth-century chronicler Simeon of Durham.[98] Widows of lesser or unspecified rank, too, rose to the highest office: Ceolburg, widow of Ealdorman Æthelmund of the Hwicce, became Abbess of Berkeley; Dunne governed a monastery together with her daughter Bucge.[99] St Mildreth joined the monastery which was headed by her mother, Queen Eormenburh.[100] Ælfflæd assisted her mother Eanfled in governing the famous monastery of Whitby (Bede, *HE* Bk III, ch. 24 and Bk IV, ch. 26). Abbess Heriburg governed Watton, near Beverley, and counted her own daughter Coenburg among the nuns (Bede, *HE* Bk V, ch. 3); Wulfthryth (Wlfrid) was in charge of Wilton, outliving her saintly daughter Edith (Edgitha) in that monastery.[101]

The list no doubt can be augmented with many examples. Even married women could and did retire from wedded life and, as grass widows, entered the monastery. As Ælfric wrote in a passage on matrimony: 'Separation is allowed to those who love exalted chastity more than anxious lust'.[102] The most notorious case is Æthelthryth, who managed to preserve her virginity through two marriages, and finally received permission from her second husband, King Ecgfrith of Northumbria, to become Christ's bride (Bede, *HE* Bk IV, chs 19–20). She was first married to Tondberht, Ealdorman of the South-Gyrwas, who had given her the Isle of Ely as a dowry. The marriage lasted five years, after which she was a widow for an equal number of years. She must have been considerably older than Ecgfrith, whom she married when he was 15. No matter how much land and money he offered her to get her into bed, Æthelthryth managed to resist his passes for twelve years, after which she took the veil. I myself am inclined to sympathize with Ecgfrith upon whom his wife forced celibacy from his 15th to his 27th year, but Bede exulted over the fact that she remained in *'virginitatis integritate gloriosa'*. Æthelthryth later became Abbess of Ely which she had founded on her own property: the Isle of Ely had been given to her as her dowry by her first husband.[103]

Other pious widows, outside the walls of the monastery, are harder to trace, but we may assume that they were around. The Old English translation of Theodulf of Orleans's capitulary takes for a fact that there are 'widows of such holy, pious life', that they can take the Eucharist daily, thus putting them on a par with monks.[104] One such woman takes flesh and blood in Oswyn, a widow who frequented St Edmund's burial place with prayers and fasts. She was in the habit of trimming the saint's hair and nails each year 'with pure love'.[105]

RETROSPECT

During the entire period, widows were an everyday phenomenon in society. The rate of mortality was high, not just for reasons of health, but also on account of violence.[106] Legal provisions saw to it that the widow of the land-owning ranks had sufficient security to carry on living after her husband's death without anxiety for her livelihood or that of her children. In the Germanic tradition there were no restrictions on remarriage barring the commonsensical term of one year to prevent hereditary complications should the woman prove pregnant. However, in a pre-centralized society like that of Anglo-Saxon England, maintenance of the law still very much depended on the local community and the right of the strongest. Hence, the frequent cases we have seen of widows being deprived of their lands. Christianity brought a new order to marital life, and consequently, to that of widows. If limiting a widow's possibilities in choice and number of successive spouses, the church also opened up for her the road to a new career in the monastery. The church's emphasis on alms-giving to widows and the picture of widows as social underdogs undoubtedly stems from the Bible. Whether it tallied with everyday reality in Anglo-Saxon England is something for which I have found precious little corroborative evidence. The examples of pious widows we meet in the devotional writings of, especially, Ælfric and Wulfstan are rarer to find in the reality of their day than those widows who opted for a less secluded, but more eventful life. As always, the distance between life and doctrine is hard to bridge.

NOTES

* My thanks are due to Christine Fell, Robin Smith, Derek Pearsall and Jan Bremmer for stylistic improvements and valuable suggestions.
1 A very informative introduction to women in general is C. Fell, *Women in Anglo-Saxon England and the Impact of 1066* (London, 1984). Also relevant is a collection of new and older articles edited by H. Damico and A.H. Olsen, *New Readings on Women in Old English Literature* (Bloomington and Indianapolis, 1990), and J.T. Rosenthal, 'Anglo-Saxon Attitudes: Men's Sources, Women's History', in idem (ed.), *Medieval Women and the Sources of Medieval History* (Athens, Ga. and London, 1990) 259–84, with a useful bibliography.
2 Cf. R.S.P. Beekes, 'Widow', *Historische Sprachforschung* 105 (1992) 171–87; for a more traditional view see, for example, W.P. Lehmann, *A Gothic Etymological Dictionary* (Leiden, 1986) s.v. *widuwo*.
3 Nineteenth-century scholars would often use the now obsolescent word 'relict' as a translation of *laf*.
4 For example: *Raptores . . . viduarum vel virginum* is translated as *Beþ ðpam men e wif oððe mæden ofernimþ . . .* , see J. Raith (ed.), *Die altenglischen Version des Halitgar'schen Bussbuches (sog. Poenitentiale Pseudo-Ecgberti)* (Darmstadt, 1964²) II, 13. Most of my research for this chapter is based on vernacular texts. I have greatly profited by A. diPaolo Healy and R.L. Venezky, *A Microfiche Concordance to Old English* (Toronto, 1980).
5 An outstanding introduction to Anglo-Saxon law is P. Wormald, '*Lex Scripta* and *Verbum Regis*: Legislation and Germanic Kingship, from Euric to Cnut', in P.H. Sawyer and I.N. Wood (eds), *Early Medieval Kingship* (Leeds, 1977) 105–38; also informative is M.P. Richards and B.J. Stanfield, 'Concepts of Anglo-Saxon Women in the Laws', in Damico and Olsen, *New Readings*, 89–99. The classic edition of the Anglo-Saxon laws is F. Lieberman, *Die Gesetze der Angelsachsen*, 3 vols (Halle, 1903–16; repr. Aalen, 1960). All subsequent references to the laws are from this edition, with the usual abbreviations.
6 On the influence of the Church on secular legislation, see A.J. Franzen, *The Literature of Penance in Anglo-Saxon England* (New Brunswick, 1983) especially 125–7 and 146–8.
7 Cf. F. and J. Gies, *Marriage and the Family in the Middle Ages* (New York, 1987) 110f.
8 The Laws of King Æthelbert of Kent, issued *c.* AD 603, assigned special fines for trespasses against noble widows: 'The wergeld for widows of the highest rank, 50 shillings, that of the second rank, 20 shillings, that of the third, 12 shillings, that of the fourth, 7 shillings' (Abt 75).
9 This was common Germanic practice, cf., for example, K.F. Drew (tr.), *The Lombard Laws* (Philadelphia, 1973) 85 (Rothair 182), 147 (Liutprant 7); A.M. Lucas, *Women in the Middle Ages: Religion, Marriage and*

1 A very informative introduction to women in general is C. Fell, *Women in Anglo-Saxon England and the Impact of 1066* (London, 1984). Also relevant is a collection of new and older articles edited by H. Damico and A.H. Olsen, *New Readings on Women in Old English Literature* (Bloomington and Indianapolis, 1990), and J.T. Rosenthal, 'Anglo-Saxon Attitudes: Men's Sources, Women's History', in idem (ed.), *Medieval Women and the Sources of Medieval History* (Athens, Ga. and London, 1990) 259–84, with a useful bibliography.

2 Cf. R.S.P. Beekes, 'Widow', *Historische Sprachforschung* 105 (1992) 171–87; for a more traditional view see, for example, W.P. Lehmann, *A Gothic Etymological Dictionary* (Leiden, 1986) s.v. *widuwo*.

3 Nineteenth-century scholars would often use the now obsolescent word 'relict' as a translation of *laf*.

4 For example: *Raptores ... viduarum vel virginum* is translated as *Beþ ðþam men e wif oððe mæden ofernimþ ...*, see J. Raith (ed.), *Die altenglischen Version des Halitgar'schen Bussbuches (sog. Poenitentiale Pseudo-Ecgberti)* (Darmstadt, 1964²) II, 13. Most of my research for this chapter is based on vernacular texts. I have greatly profited by A. diPaolo Healy and R.L. Venezky, *A Microfiche Concordance to Old English* (Toronto, 1980).

5 An outstanding introduction to Anglo-Saxon law is P. Wormald, '*Lex Scripta* and *Verbum Regis*: Legislation and Germanic Kingship, from Euric to Cnut', in P.H. Sawyer and I.N. Wood (eds), *Early Medieval Kingship* (Leeds, 1977) 105–38; also informative is M.P. Richards and B.J. Stanfield, 'Concepts of Anglo-Saxon Women in the Laws', in Damico and Olsen, *New Readings*, 89–99. The classic edition of the Anglo-Saxon laws is F. Lieberman, *Die Gesetze der Angelsachsen*, 3 vols (Halle, 1903–16; repr. Aalen, 1960). All subsequent references to the laws are from this edition, with the usual abbreviations.

6 On the influence of the Church on secular legislation, see A.J. Franzen, *The Literature of Penance in Anglo-Saxon England* (New Brunswick, 1983) especially 125–7 and 146–8.

7 Cf. F. and J. Gies, *Marriage and the Family in the Middle Ages* (New York, 1987) 110f.

8 The Laws of King Æthelbert of Kent, issued c. AD 603, assigned special fines for trespasses against noble widows: 'The wergeld for widows of the highest rank, 50 shillings, that of the second rank, 20 shillings, that of the third, 12 shillings, that of the fourth, 7 shillings' (Abt 75).

9 This was common Germanic practice, cf., for example, K.F. Drew (tr.), *The Lombard Laws* (Philadelphia, 1973) 85 (Rothair 182), 147 (Liutprant 7); A.M. Lucas, *Women in the Middle Ages: Religion, Marriage and*

Letters (Brighton, 1983) 62f. For particulars concerning Anglo-Saxon England, see especially the index in Lieberman, *Gesetze*, vol. 2, s.v. Aussteuer, Eheschliessung, Frau, Vormund, Wittum, Witwe.

10 Cf. Gies, *Marriage and the Family*, 106.

11 A.J. Robertson, *Anglo-Saxon Charters* (Cambridge, 1939) no. LXXVI. The other marriage contract is Robertson, no. LXXVII.

12 D. Whitelock, *Anglo-Saxon Wills* (Cambridge, 1935) no. XIII; cf. her note on 135.

13 A 'hide' is an Anglo-Saxon surface measure, roughly a field large enough to maintain one family.

14 See, e.g., Robertson, *Charters*, nos III, VI, IX, XXVI and XXVII.

15 Whitelock, *Wills*, no. IX.

16 C. Plummer (ed.), *Two of the Saxon Chronicles Parallel*, 2 vols (1892), reissued with a bibliographical note by D. Whitelock (Oxford, 1952); D. Whitelock, D.C. Douglas and S.I. Tucker (trs), *The Anglo-Saxon Chronicle* (London, 1961). The quotation, *ASC* s.a. 672, is quoted from Whitelock *et al.*, as are all further quotations from the *ASC*.

17 Asser's *Life of Alfred*, chs 13–15, in S. Keynes and M. Lapidge (eds), *Alfred the Great* (Harmondsworth, 1983); cf. their note on 235f. On the position of the queen in Wessex, see P. Stafford, 'The King's Wife in Wessex, 800–1000', *Past and Present* 91 (1981) 3–27, repr. in Damico and Olsen, *New Readings*, 56–78. Unfortunately, Stafford's *Queens, Concubines and Dowagers: The King's Wife in the Early Middle Ages* (Athens, Ga., 1983) was not available to me.

18 On Æthelfled, see F.T. Wainwright, 'Æthelfled, Lady of the Mercians', in H.P.R. Finberg (ed.), *Scandinavian England* (Chichester, 1975) 305–24, repr. in Damico and Olsen, *New Readings*, 44–55; cf. R. Smith, 'Glimpses of Some Anglo-Saxon Women', in J. Dor (ed.), *A Wyf there Was: Essays in Honour of Paule Mertens-Fonck* (Liège, 1992, 256–63) 261–3.

19 P. Stafford, 'Sons and Mothers: Family Politics in the Early Middle Ages', in D. Baker (ed.), *Medieval Women* (Oxford, 1978, 79–100) 86.

20 W.D. Foulke (tr.), E. Peters (ed.), *History of the Lombards* (Philadelphia, 1977²).

21 Johannes Biclar, *Chronica*, J. Campos (ed.) (Madrid, 1960) s.a. 584; cf. Gregory of Tours, *The History of the Franks*, L. Thorpe (tr.) (Harmondsworth, 1974) Bk VI, ch. 43.

22 P. Fisher (tr.), H. Ellis Davidson (ed.), 2 vols (Cambridge and Totowa, N.J., 1979).

23 J.M. Wallace-Hadrill, *Bede's 'Ecclesiasical History of the English People': A Historical Commentary* (Oxford, 1988) 61, firmly states 'To marry one's father's widow was sound Germanic practice', but fails to give any supportive evidence. I only know of Radiger, son of the King of the Varni, who marries his father's widow at the behest of the father himself, who meaningfully adds 'just as our ancestral laws permit us'; see Procopius, *De Bello Gothico*, 7.20.20. Less Germanic, but in a similar vein to establish who is the new boss is Absalom's 'going in unto his father's [ten!] concubines in the sight of all Israel' (2 *Sam.* 16:22).

24 *ASC* s.a. 855–8; Asser, *Life of Alfred*, ch. 13.

25 Asser, *Life of Alfred*, ch. 17.
26 Cf. Keynes and Lapidge, *Alfred the Great*, 238.
27 Cf. L.O. Vasvari, 'Why is Dona Endrina a Widow? Traditional Culture and Textuality in the *Libro de Buen Amor*', in L. Mirrer (ed.), *Upon My Husband's Death: Widows in the Literature and Histories of Medieval Europe* (Ann Arbor, 1992) 259–88; H.M. Arden, 'Grief, Widowhood and Women's Sexuality in Medieval French Literature', in Mirrer, *Upon My Husband's Death*, 305–20. The most notoriously nymphomaniac widow in later medieval English literature is, of course, Geoffrey Chaucer's Wife of Bath, who also married first when she was 12, outlived five husbands and was on the look-out for number six, cf. C. Wood, 'Three Chaucerian Widows: Tales of Innocence and Experience', in Dor, *A Wyf ther Was*, 282–90.
28 It seems that Emma had been involved in a plot against Edward, cf. Whitelock, *Chronicle*, 107 n. 8.
29 Cf. F.E. Harmer, *Anglo-Saxon Writs* (Manchester, 1952) 547.
30 Plummer, *Two Saxon Chronicles*, II, 134.
31 On this rumour, see especially C.E. Wright, *The Cultivation of Saga in Anglo-Saxon England* (Edinburgh, 1939) 146–53, 157–71.
32 Whitelock, *Wills*, nos IX, XV and XX; cf. Harmer, *Writs*, 551.
33 See most recently, H. Bennett, 'The Female Mourner at Beowulf's Funeral: Filling in the Blanks/Hearing the Spaces', *Exemplaria* 4 (1992) 35–50.
34 W. de Gray Bich, *Cartularium Saxonicum* (London, 1185–93) no. 1296, cf. Whitelock, *Wills*, 128f.
35 *Wergeld*, 'man-price', was the amount of money paid in compensation for killing a man. In Anglo-Saxon England one's *wergeld* depended on social rank.
36 The events are recorded in Robertson, *Charters*, no. LXIII and are discussed by H.R. Loyn, 'Kinship in Anglo-Saxon England', *Anglo-Saxon England* 3 (1974, 197–209) 201f. Internecine strife between paternal kinsmen was not uncommon in Anglo-Saxon England, particularly when property or the throne was involved, cf. R.H. Bremmer Jr, 'The Importance of Kinship: Uncle and Nephew in *Beowulf*', *Amsterdamer Beiträge zur älteren Germanistik* 15 (1980, 21–38) 36–8.
37 Robertson, *Charters*, no. LXXVIII; cf. Fell, *Anglo-Saxon Women*, 78.
38 Raith, *Bussbuch*, II, 13. Old English did not always clearly distinguish in terminology between 'rape' and 'forceful abduction (to be married)', cf. H.H. Munske, *Die germanische Rechtswortschatz im Bereich der Missetaten: I. Die Terminologie der älteren westgermanischen Rechtsquellen* (Berlin and New York, 1973); see also B. Colman, 'Abduction of Women in Barbaric Law', *Florilegium* 5 (1983) 62–75.
39 Robertson, no. XLI, ll. 24–7.
40 On the practice of sympathetic magic, see A. Davies, 'Witches in Anglo-Saxon England: Five Case Histories', in D.S. Scragg (ed.), *Superstition and Popular Medicine in Anglo-Saxon England* (Manchester, 1989) 41–56, at 49f.
41 Edited as *Gesta Herewardi Incliti Exulis et Militis*, appended to T.D. Hardy and C.T. Martin (eds), *Lestoire des Engleis solum la translacion*

Maistre Geffrei Gaimar, 2 vols (London, 1888–9) I, 339–404, at 385 and 389; part of the legend is to be found in another version in E.O. Blake (ed.), *Liber Eliensis* (London, 1962) Bk II, chs 102–7, at 183 and 186. The *Gesta Herewardi* are translated in M. Swanton (tr.), *Three Lives of the Last Englishmen* (New York and London, 1984).

42 The episode is well described by Davies, 'Witches', 41–3.

43 'anus illa venifica', *Liber Eliensis*, 183.

44 W. Stubbs (ed.), *Willelmi Malmesbiriensis Monachi: De Gestis Regum Anglorum*, 2 vols (London, 1887–9) I, 253–5.

45 On attributing witchcraft to old women, cf. J. Bremmer, 'The Old Women of Ancient Greece', in J. Blok and P. Mason (eds), *Sexual Asymmetry: Studies in Ancient Society* (Amsterdam, 1987, 191–215) 204–6.

46 Davies, 'Witches', 45.

47 On the problem of incest, see M. de Jong, 'To the Limits of Kinship: Anti-Incest Legislation in the Early Medieval West (500–900)', in J. Bremmer (ed.), *From Sappho to De Sade* (London, 1989) 36–59.

48 Raith, *Bussbuch*, II, 18.

49 Raith, *Bussbuch*, 72.

50 Other references to this illicit union: A. Napier (ed.), *Wulfstan: Sammlung der ihm zugeschriebenen Homilien nebst untersuchungen über ihre Echtheit* (Berlin, 1883) no. L, 271, ll. 8–12; no. LIX, 308, ll. 4–8. On this prohibition, cf. P.J. Payer, *Sex and the Penitentials: The Development of a Sexual Code: 550–1150* (Toronto, Buffalo and London, 1984) 32.

51 Cf. *Exod.* 22:22–4.

52 Napier, *Wulfstan*, no. LX, 309, ll. 1–5.

53 J.C. Pope (ed.), *Homilies of Ælfric: A Supplementary Collection*, 2 vols (EETS OS) 259f. (London, 1967–8) II, no. XXX, ll. 96–8.

54 Napier, *Wulfstan*, no. XLVI, 238, l. 25–239, l. 1. The sermon was wrongly attributed to Wulfstan.

55 *Pseudo-Matthaei Evangelium*, in B. Assmann (ed.), *Angelsächsische Homilien und Heiligenleben* (Kassel, 1889, repr. with a supplementary introduction by P. Clemoes, Darmstadt, 1964) no. X, ll. 45–60.

56 B. Thorpe (ed.), *The Homilies of the Anglo-Saxon Church: The First Part, Containing the Sermones Catholici or Homilies of Ælfric*, 2 vols (London, 1844–6) I, 'Dominica I. in Mense Septembri, Quando Legitur Job', 448, ll. 15–17.

57 Thorpe, *Sermones Catholici*, II, 'Letania Maiore, Feria Secunda', 322, ll. 7–9.

58 W.W. Skeat (ed.), *Ælfric's Lives of Saints* (EETS OS) 76, 82, 94, 114 (London, 1881–1900) III, no. XXV 'Passio Machabeorum', ll. 254–5.

59 Thorpe, *Sermones Catholici*, II, 'Passio SS Simonis et Iude', 484, ll. 32–4.

60 Skeat, *Ælfric's Lives*, IV, no. XXXVI, 'Passio Sancti Thomae Apostoli', ll. 192–4.

61 Skeat, *Ælfric's Lives*, I, no. IX, 'St Lucy, Virgin', ll. 53–6; 61–3.

62 Thorpe, *Sermones Catholici*, I, 'Passio Beati Laurentii Martyris', 418, ll. 16–18.

63 Napier, *Wulfstan*, no. XLV, 228, ll. 18–23.

64 R. Morris (ed.), *Old English Homilies* (EETS OS) 29, 34 (London, 1868) ll. 296–304.

65 Skeat, *Ælfric's Lives*, IV, no. XXXII, l. 22.

66 M. Förster, 'Die altenglischen Beigaben des Lambeth-Psalters', *Archiv für das Studium der neueren Sprachen und Literaturen* 132 (1914, 328–35) 333f. The text dates from the second half of the eleventh century.

67 D. Bethurum (ed.), *The Homilies of Wulfstan* (Oxford, 1957) no. XX, ll. 42f.; cf. D. Whitelock (ed.), *Sermo Lupi ad Anglos* (London, 1963³) 51 n. 42.

68 K. Jost, *Die 'Institutes of Polity, Civil and Ecclesiastical': Ein Werk Erzbischof Wulfstans von York* (Bern, 1959) no. 10. English translation in M. Swanton, *Anglo-Saxon Prose* (London, 1975) 125–38.

69 R. Morris (ed.), *The Blickling Homilies of the Tenth Century* (EETS OS) 58, 63, 73 (London, 1874–80, repr. in 1 vol., 1967) IV, 43–5.

70 D.A.E. Pelteret, 'Slavery in Anglo-Saxon England', in D.A.E. Pelteret and J.D. Woods (eds), *The Anglo-Saxons: Synthesis and Achievement* (Waterloo, Ont., 1985) 117–33.

71 All these examples to be found in J. Earle, *A Hand-Book to the Land-Charters, and Other Saxonic Documents* (Oxford, 1888) 263, 264, 268 (sec. 4), 272 (secs 23, 26), 273 (sec. 27).

72 On the historical development of the degrees of chastity, see M. Bernards, *Speculum Virginum: Geistigkeit und Seelenleben der Frau im Hochmittelalter* (Vienna, 1952, repr. 1982) 40–51.

73 Bernards, *Speculum Virginum*, 42.

74 Thorpe, *Sermones Catholici*, I, 'In Purificatione S. Mariae', 148, ll. 6–22; op. cit., I, 'De Assumptione Beatae Mariae', 446, ll. 30–448, l. 3; op. cit, II, 'Dominica in Sexagesima', 92, ll. 32–94, l. 17; Assmann, *Angelsächsische Homilien*, no. II, 'Letter to Sigefryth: Be þære halgan clænnysse', ll. 172–6.

75 Thorpe, *Sermones Catholici*, II, 'Dominica II: Post Aepiphania Domini', 70, ll. 16–24; the exegesis was quite common, cf. J. Hill, 'Ælfric and Smaragdus', *Anglo-Saxon England* 21 (1992, 203–37) 223.

76 As, e.g. in Pope, *Homilies of Ælfric*, II, no. XIX 'De Doctrina Apostolica', 70–89.

77 Raith, *Bussbuch*, II, 20; Jost, *Institutes of Polity*, no. 17.

78 Cf. B. Fehr (ed.), *Die Hirtenbriefe Ælfrics in altenglischer und lateinischer Fassung* (Hamburg, 1914); in Ælfric's letter to Bishop Wulfsige (nr. I, 26–7) and in Ælfric's Old English Letter to Archbishop Wulfstan (nr. II, 156). In the latter letter, Ælfric seems to allow a remarriage to be blessed should the bride be a virgin.

79 Jost, *Institutes of Polity*, no. 17.

80 Thorpe, *Sermones Catholici*, II, 'Dominica in Sexagesima', 94, ll. 11–13. On the church's concern for regulating the sexual life of the Anglo-Saxons, see two very informative articles, if presented somewhat contentiously, by A. Davies, 'Sexual Behaviour in Later Anglo-Saxon England', in E. Kooper (ed.), *This Noble Craft ... Proceedings of the Xth Research Symposium of the Dutch and Belgian University Teachers of Old and Middle English and Historical Linguistics* (Amsterdam and Atlanta, Ga., 1991) 83–105, and 'The Sexual Conversion of the Anglo-Saxons', in Dor, *A Wyf there Was*, 80–102.

81 Assmann, *Angelsächsische Homilien*, no. II, 'Letter to Sigefryth', ll. 157–61.

82 Earle, *Hand-Book*, 108–11.

83 B.J. Timmer (ed.), *Judith* (Exeter, 1978²).

84 S.J. Crawford (ed.), *The Old English Version of the Heptateuch, Ælfric's Treatise on the Old and New Testament and his Preface to Genesis* (EETS OS) 160 (London, 1922) 48, ll. 772–80.

85 The latter two interpretations in Assmann, *Angelsächsische Homilien*, no. IX, ll. 410–39.

86 Jost, *Institutes of Polity*, no. 18.

87 Cf. Skeat, *Ælfric's Lives*, I, no. XVIII, 'Sermo Excerptus de Librum Regum', ll. 65–71.

88 Cf. Skeat, *Ælfric's Lives*, I, no. X, 'Cathedra S. Petri', ll. 53–79. Though Luke in *Acts* nowhere states explicitly that Dorcas (alias Tabitha) was a widow, Ælfric does not hesitate to call her so in ll. 54 and 77.

89 Thorpe, *Sermones Catholici*, I, 'Assumptio S. Iohannis Apostoli', 60, ll. 11–14.

90 Thorpe, *Sermones Catholici*, I, 'Passio Beati Laurentii Martyris', 418, ll. 18–22.

91 Skeat, *Ælfric's Lives*, I, no. VI, 'Natale S. Mauri, Abbatis', 102–7; Thorpe, *Sermones Catholici*, II, 'Depositio S. Martini Episcopi', 508, ll. 8–13.

92 Thorpe, *Sermones Catholici*, I, 'Natale S. Clementis Martyris', 566, ll. 4–27.

93 Thorpe, *Sermones Catholici*, II, 'Natale S. Stephani Protomartyris', 30. Ælfric calls all fathers and mothers to take heed of her example and not to curse their children, at 34.

94 Skeat, *Ælfric's Lives*, I, no. II, 'Natale S. Eugenie Virginis', 133–235.

95 Cf. P. Szarmach, 'Ælfric's Women Saints: Eugenia', in Damico and Olsen, *New Readings*, 146–57, at 151.

96 *Gesta Herewardi*, 397f.

97 P. Sims-Williams, *Religion and Literature in Western England 600–800* (Cambridge, 1990) 160 and 166, respectively.

98 Sims-Williams, *Religion*, 223.

99 Sims-Williams, *Religion*, 131f.; 39, 174, respectively.

100 Förster, 'Die altenglische Beigaben', 328–35. The name Eormenburh is used erroneously here; see D.W. Rollason, *The Mildrith Legend: A Study in Early Medieval Hagiography in England* (Leicester, 1982) 39f.

101 N.E.S.A. Hamilton (ed.), *Willelmi Malmesbiriensis Monachi 'De Gestis Pontificum Anglorum'* (London, 1870) II, 87. I owe the precise reference to Elizabeth van Houts, cf. her 'Women and the Writing of History in the Early Middle Ages', *Early Medieval Europe* 1 (1992, 53–68) 68.

102 Thorpe, *Sermones Catholici*, II, 'Letania Maior. Feria Secunda', 324, ll. 3–5.

103 Cf. C. Plummer (ed.), *Bedae Venerabilis Historia Ecclesiastica Gentis Anglorum*, 2 vols (Oxford, 1896) II, 235.

104 H. Sauer (ed.), *Theodulfi Capitula in England: Die altenglischen Übersetzungen, zusammen mit dem lateinischen Text* (Munich, 1978), no. 44, 399, ll. 17–19.

105 Skeat, *Ælfric's Lives*, IV, no. XXXII, ll. 198–205.
106 Old Frisian law even provided for brides whose bridegrooms were killed during the wedding festivities! If the bride followed the corpse to the graveyard and next proceeded to the groom's homestead, she would receive everything that was agreed upon in the wedding contract. The young widow was then free to choose a new husband; see W.J. Buma and W. Ebel (eds), *Das Fivelgoer Recht* (Göttingen, 1972) XIV, 4.

5

WIDOWS AND THE LAW

The legal position of widows in the Dutch Republic during the seventeenth and eighteenth centuries

Dieneke Hempenius-van Dijk

On 9 May 1780 the Court of Friesland passed judgment in the case of Metdina Sijpkens vs. the Governors of the Widows' Pension Fund of the city of Leeuwarden.[1] The point of litigation that the Court had to decide was whether the plaintiff was a widow or not. For Metdina Sijpkens, who lived at Eexta in the province of Groningen, it was a very important decision, for if the Court decided she was a widow, the defendants would have to pay her an annuity proportionate to the five shares her late husband had taken out in the pension fund for her benefit. The defendants on the other hand argued that the plaintiff could not be a widow. They based their argument on the fact that at the moment her husband died in Batavia, Metdina Sijpkens was suing him for a divorce on account of his adultery. For this argument they referred to the *Praelectiones* by Ulric Huber (1636–93),[2] undoubtedly the most famous jurisconsult and professor at law Friesland ever had. In this work Huber had argued that adultery in itself dissolves a marriage.[3] On this ground the Governors were of the opinion that Metdina Sijpkens' marriage was already dissolved through the adultery of her husband. Therefore she was a divorcée and not a widow when her husband died, and consequently they were not obliged to pay her.[4] When the Court gave judgment on 9 May 1780, it decided in favour of the plaintiff. The defendants were obliged to recognize her as a widow and to pay her the annual endowment beginning from the moment her husband had died.[5]

Although the reasoning of the judges in this case was not made known – as was usual in continental Europe in those times – it is not very difficult to guess why they decided this way. To accept the point of view that the mere act of adultery dissolved a marriage would have created numerous legal problems and therefore it was much 'safer' to let the judicial pronouncement of a divorce dissolve a marriage. Therefore a marriage stands as long as this divorce is not pronounced and when a husband dies during the divorce suit his wife becomes a widow with all the rights and obligations connected with that position.

In this chapter I shall deal with the legal position of widows in the Low Countries during the seventeenth and eighteenth centuries. Because of the great differences between the various parts of the Republic of the seven United Provinces where the law is concerned, it will be impossible to discuss the legal position of widows in the whole of the Republic's territory.[6] Therefore I shall concentrate on the rules of law in the two northern provinces, Groningen and Friesland. Where necessary I shall touch upon the rules of law in other parts of the Republic.

Looking at the legal position of widows, whether it is in Groningen and Friesland or elsewhere in the Dutch Republic, one ought to keep in mind that not every rule that applied to widows applied to them because they were widows. In the first place every widow – obvious though it may be – is a woman without a husband, and as such she has the same legal position as any unmarried woman, that is any unmarried woman of age. This means she was entitled to perform all acts of law permitted to persons who had attained majority and were not under the custody of a guardian, even if she had not yet reached the age of 25 years.[7] An example will illustrate this point.

> In the provinces of Holland and Zealand, the death of stadt-holder William II (1626–50) sparked off a very serious dispute concerning the legal position of his widow Mary Stuart I, who was not yet 25 years old when she lost her husband. The most important question was whether she could be guardian to her little son, the later stadtholder (and King of England and Scotland) William III (1650–1702), who was born a week after his father died. The Court of Holland and Zealand as well as later on the Supreme Council of these provinces decided that despite her age, the Princess Royal as a widow was to be considered a person of age and therefore competent to be the legal guardian of her son.[8]

Observing the local rules of law any widow could buy and sell, hire and let, make grants, in short perform any act of law she might wish to. In some provinces, like Guelderland and Overijssel, being a woman she was not allowed to litigate in a court of law or have a deed drawn up by a public notary without the assistance of a male guardian, who would be chosen just for the occasion.[9] The provinces of Groningen and Friesland, however, were among those provinces where general guardianship as regards women was unknown. In these provinces widows and other unmarried women of age could in principle litigate or have deeds passed in their own name without any male assistance.

In Friesland widows who wanted to sue had the privilege to summon their opponents directly before the highest judicial body of this province, the Frisian Court.[10] Metdina Sijpkens too had exercised this privilege when she sued the Governors of the Widows' Pension Fund of the city of Leeuwarden. In all other provinces of the Dutch Republic that had a comparable court founded before 1581 by one of the dukes, counts or other lords who originally governed these provinces, widows had the same privilege.[11] Where such courts had not existed, as in Groningen and Drenthe, widows did not enjoy this privilege. Where they did, this was because since the Middle Ages widows had been considered a category of the so-called *personae miserabiles*. These were persons who because of their misfortunes were in a disadvantageous position and for that reason enjoyed the special protection initially of the church and later on also of the secular authorities. After 1581, the year in which the Low Countries officially broke off from their overlord Philip II,[12] each seignorial court had continued its activities as the court of its province, and the privilege of the *personae miserabiles* to summon their opponents directly before this court had remained unimpaired. This privilege was also enjoyed by orphans, the chronically sick and other unfortunate persons.[13]

Except for rules of law that were applicable to widows in their capacity as unmarried major women or *personae miserabiles*, there were of course also rules that applied to them because they were widows. To a great extent these were rules that also applied to widowers and concerned everyone who had lost her or his spouse through death. These rules included, for instance, all rules concerning the position of the surviving spouse in the law of succession *ab intestata*, i.e. the law of succession that is applicable when the deceased has died without a will.[14] Nowhere in the Republic was the surviving spouse entitled to succeed to the estate of the deceased together with the children. The children inherited everything their father or mother left. If there were no children, the estate of the deceased spouse went to any other descendants, to his or her ascendants, or to his or her relatives in the collateral line. In the province of Groningen the right of inheritance with respect to these collateral relatives was limited to those within the tenth degree.[15] If there were no blood relations within this degree, the surviving husband or wife inherited the estate. In the city of Groningen and in the surrounding region, the Gorecht, husband and wife also succeeded to each other's estates in the case that the children born from their marriage all predeceased their parents.[16]

In the province of Friesland husband and wife could only be each other's intestate heir if the deceased spouse had no blood relations at all.[17] However, here a widow or a widower who had no personal assets, while the deceased partner had been rich, could claim one-fourth of the estate on condition that the marriage had been childless or that there were no more than four living children from the marriage. In the first case the surviving spouse became owner of this portion, and in the second case the surviving spouse only was the usufructuary of this portion, while the ownership remained with the children.[18] Indeed the position of the widow or widower in the law of intestate succession in Groningen and Friesland was still quite favourable. In the province of Holland, for instance, the law of intestate succession never allowed husband and wife to succeed to any part of each other's estate.[19] However, in Holland as elsewhere in the Republic it was always possible to make the surviving spouse a (co-)heir or (co-)heiress by means of an antenuptial contract or a will.

In 1616 the Court of Friesland passed judgment in the case of Ulbe van Aylva vs. Barbara van Douma. The latter was the widow of Taco (Taecke) van Aylva, a brother of Ulbe van Aylva. In the antenuptial contract they made before their marriage in 1591, Taco van Aylva had made his future wife heiress to a certain part of his estate in case their marriage should remain childless. Later on, in 1598, he made a will in which he appointed his brother Ulbe van Aylva as heir to the whole of his estate, while his wife Barbara was to have the goods he had willed her in their antenuptial contract, as a legacy.

When Taco van Aylva died, his brother, being his heir according to the will, demanded from his sister-in-law an inventory of all the assets his brother had left. Barbara van Douma resisted this demand, because the antenuptial contract declared her to be heiress and not legatee of the goods her late husband had wanted her to have. Therefore she had been owner of these goods from the moment her husband died, and had no obligations towards her brother-in-law concerning these goods. During the legal proceedings before the Court of Friesland she supported her case with the argument that an antenuptial contract, unlike a testament, is irrevocable and therefore her position as an heiress could not have been altered by the last will of her late husband. Eventually the Court decided in her favour. Thus the position of a wife as her husband's heiress was more secure if she was made his heiress in an antenuptial contract than in a will.[20]

What a woman could call her own after the death of her husband depended largely on the matrimonial property system she and her husband had chosen. If they had not made other arrangements in an antenuptial contract, it would be decided by the system as laid down in the matrimonial property law of the province or the region where they had married. In Groningen, as well as in Holland, this meant universal community of property,[21] as a result of which the widow could claim half of the estate she and her deceased husband had owned together. In Friesland, on the other hand, the system of community of gain and loss prevailed,[22] which meant that husband and wife each had their own estate while they shared among other things the fruits of their assets, their earnings and the results of what they undertook together or separately during their marriage. In the latter system it was possible that a poor spouse surviving a rich one was left with no assets to live on. The regulation in respect of the rights of such a poor spouse to one-fourth of the deceased rich spouse's inheritance was therefore an important compensation. Apart from what she owned under the matrimonial property law of the place where she had married or the arrangements of her ante-nuptial contract, a widow was always entitled to the paraphernalia and the dower she was given at the beginning of her marriage.[23]

If a widow or widower was left behind with minor children, he or she would immediately become the guardian of these children simply by operation of law. This at any rate was the case in most parts of the Republic. In order to avoid any misunderstanding, it is necessary to explain that on the Continent guardianship covers both the person of the orphan and his property.[24] So a guardian – the surviving parent or somebody else – is equally responsible for the care and education of his or her wards and for the administration of their property. The guardian is also the legal representative of the wards in case of a lawsuit or when a contract is to be made in which the wards are a party. Unlike testamentary guardians and guardians who are appointed by judicial decree, legal guardians – as well as surviving parents these also could be the grandparents of orphaned children – were not required to obtain confirmation by the local authorities or to take an oath of fidelity. Nor did they need to provide security or to make an inventory of the children's assets. This was the case in the province of Groningen, as in many parts of continental Europe.[25] This province was one of the parts of the Dutch Republic where before 1809, the year in which the first Civil Code of the Netherlands was introduced,[26] no distinction was made between the father and the mother as legal guardians of their children. Either could take on the administration of the paternal or maternal portion of their children without any further ado. However, under the guardianship law of this province a tacit mortgage rested on all of the surviving parent's assets, as a security for the children.[27] If later on, at their majority, the children found they were financially prejudiced because of maladministration by their surviving parent, they could recover their losses from these assets. In fact most surviving parents and their minor children continued to live together in a joint estate. Division of this joint estate did not occur until the children had reached their majority and claimed their paternal or maternal portion, or until the surviving parent remarried.

In the neighbouring province of Friesland, the law contained somewhat different rules with respect to the guardianship of the surviving parent. This was because from the end of the fifteenth century Friesland by its own deliberate choice lived under the rules of Roman law as understood at the end of the Middle Ages.[28] Consequently these rules were more deeply embedded in the legal life of this province than elsewhere in the Republic. According to the rules of this Roman law, the father exercised paternal power over his children as long as he lived, unless the children married or he emancipated them.[29] The death of the mother did not make any difference to the exercise of this paternal power.

In the case that the marriage was dissolved by the death of the husband, and the wife was left with minor children, things were different. Which rules were applicable depended in the first place on the age of the children. According to the rules of Roman law in Friesland, a distinction was made between *impuberes* and *puberes*, i.e. children under the age of 12 or 14 and children above that age, depending on whether these children were girls or boys.[30] Fatherless girls above the age of 12 and fatherless boys above the age of 14 only needed a guardian when they wished to sue or were sued or when they wished to make an important contract and the other party desired that they would be assisted by a guardian.[31] If the children had not yet reached the age of 12 or 14, they needed a guardian to take care of their persons and their property. In order to distinguish these two kinds of guardianship, I will use the Latin terms customary in Roman law, which the Frisians also used to distinguish between these two kinds of guardianship.[32] The first kind of guardianship will therefore be called *cura* and the guardian a *curator* (*curatrix*), while the second kind will be called *tutela* and the guardian a *tutor* (*tutrix*). In the case that children under the age of 12 or 14 lost their father and were left behind with their mother, it would be she who became their *tutrix* simply by operation of law.[33] One of her first duties was to make up an inventory of her children's property.[34] Otherwise, she acted as the *tutrix* of her children in the same way that surviving parents in the province of Groningen acted as guardians of theirs.

As soon as the children reached the age of 12 or 14, the *tutela* of the mother officially ended as did the *tutela* of other persons. As I have said before, fatherless children above that age only needed a *curator* in special circumstances. Before 1765, the children were free in their choice. It was, however, customary that children whose mother was alive chose their mother for their *curatrix*. If their mother had already been their *tutrix*, she mostly continued to act as their *curatrix* unless the children made it clear they did not want her to.[35] In 1765 the Estates of Friesland issued an edict in which they made this custom a rule of law.[36] The children even were deprived of their say in this matter. Henceforth they had no choice but to accept their mother as their *curatrix*. However, the mother had the right to excuse herself from this burden for certain specified reasons within two months after her children had become *puberes*.[37]

Almost everything that was ordained in this edict in respect to the mother as *tutrix* or *curatrix* of her children also applied to the grandmother if it was she who had to take upon herself the *tutela* or the *cura* of her grandchildren. In the legal system of the Continent of those days a woman could only be the guardian (*tutrix* as well as *curatrix*) of her own children or grandchildren.[38] Naturally she had to be a widow in order to be able to act as such. In this respect there was no distinction between the law of Friesland and the law elsewhere in the Republic of the seven United Provinces. How this requirement worked can be seen in the case of Trientje Rotgers from Groningen, the grandmother of Gerlef and Geertje Jans.

> When their father Jan Gerlefs remarried in 1694, she could not become legal guardian of her grandchildren, because at that moment she was still married to her second husband and therefore lacked the legal capacity to manage her own or others' affairs. Hence Jan Gerlefs had no other choice than to appoint some other persons as guardians of his children. By 1701 the personal situation of Trientje Rotgers had changed. She had become a widow and because of that she had regained her legal capacity. Consequently she presented a petition to the council of the city of Groningen to be recognised as the legal guardian of her grandchildren. Her petition was granted and the guardians who had administered the estate of the two children after their father had died in 1697, had to hand over to her the administration of this estate. From then on she was to act as the legal guardian of her grandchildren until their coming of age.[39]

Legally there were no particular rules concerning the death of a widow. What happened to her estate depended on the question whether she had left a will or not. And if she was a guardian (or a *tutrix*) at the moment of her demise, measures had to be taken to provide the children (or grandchildren) with one or more guardians, depending on the rules of local guardianship law.[40] If the worst came to the worst, the children that were left behind could almost always be admitted to an orphanage in order to be educated and cared for as long as it was necessary and the house would keep them.

If a widow wanted to remarry she had in the first place to observe all the rules that applied to anyone who wanted to marry. These rules, which among others dealt with the publication of the banns, differed widely from province to province.[41] In the second place the re-marrying widow was subjected to a number of rules that were connected with the solemnization of second and subsequent marriages and therefore were also applicable to remarrying widowers. For instance the rules that dealt with prohibited degrees of consanguinity and affinity applied equally to a man or a woman. The prohibited degrees were the same for widowed men as for widowed women. To give an example, a widow could no more remarry the brother of her deceased husband than a widower the sister of his deceased wife.[42] The only impediment that was always applicable to remarrying widows, and only sometimes to remarrying widowers, was that of the so-called 'year of mourning', the period after her husband's death in which she was not allowed to remarry. About the background to this impediment there have been various ideas in the course of the centuries, as well as in ecclesiastical circles.[43] According to the jurisconsults in the Republic of the United Provinces, this year of mourning served especially to avoid the 'mixing of blood' (in Latin: *conturbatio* or *confusio sanguinis*).[44] This meant that the paternity of a posthumous child could not erroneously be attributed to the second husband. In this way a man could be protected from an heir that was not his offspring. Where a 'year of mourning' was to be observed by widowers, this was meant as a demonstration of respect for the deceased wife. Nowhere in the Republic was the prohibition on remarriage within a certain period after the death of a spouse so strict that a marriage that had been solemnized in spite of this impediment was null and void. All the same, offenders were punished in some other way, for instance with a fine.[45]

The length of this 'year of mourning' depended on the rules of the local marriage laws. In most regions of the province of Groningen this period was fixed at one year and six weeks and in the province of Friesland at nine months. Since the reform of the Frisian Ordinance in 1723 there also was a 'year of mourning' for widowers. This period lasted six months.[46] In Friesland there was yet another marriage impediment applicable particularly to widows who were not yet 25 years of age at the time of their new marriage. If the father of such a widow was still alive, she could not marry without his consent, even though she was considered to be of age. In this respect too, the Frisians followed the rules of Roman law.[47]

A remarrying widow who was the guardian (in Friesland *tutrix* or *curatrix*) of her minor children or grandchildren lost the right to be a guardian (*tutrix* or *curatrix*). She was therefore obliged to take measures to ensure the continuation of the guardianship (in Friesland the *tutela* or the *cura*) if that was necessary. The grandmother who married again simply took care of the appointment of one or more new guardians and handed over to him or them the administration of her grandchildren's property. The mother who married again usually had to fulfil a few extra duties. Her remarrying meant that the paternal portion of the children had to be worked out, in so far as this had not been done at an earlier point. What the mother had to do exactly depended of course on the situation and the local rules of law.

Most of these rules were also applicable to widowers. According to the rules laid down in the *New Constitutions of the City of Groningen* in 1689, for instance, widows as well as widowers were forbidden to remarry before they had made a contract with the children from their former marriage or their guardians with respect to the children's paternal or maternal portions.[48] Before this rule was enacted, widows and widowers who remarried were free to make such a contract, whether it was a contract of division of the estate or a contract of redemption of their obligation to give the children their paternal or maternal portions.

An example of such a contract or redemption is the contract that was negotiated by Titia Ennes, widow of Meinardus Meijer and mother of Meinardina, Enne and Copius Meijer, and the appointed guardians of these children in February 1725. The making of this contract was necessary because Titia Ennes planned to remarry, which she did on 9 March 1725. Titia Ennes and her first husband had been married in universal community of property. Hence she was entitled to half of the estate that she and Meinardus Meijer had owned together, whereas their children as their father's heirs were entitled to the other half. Confronted with the question whether to make a contract of division or a contract of redemption, Titia Ennes had decided to do the latter, so she would not be compelled to divide the estate in order to give her children their paternal portions. Instead of this she would pay them a sum of money equal to these portions. The amount of this payment was based on an inventory of the components of the estate. In this case the amount of the redemption was fixed at 9000 guilders, i.e. 3000 guilders for each of the children, which the mother promised to pay to the guardians as soon as the children reached the age of 18. In exchange for this promise the guardians as representatives of their wards transferred to her the possession and ownership of the whole of the estate. Further, Titia Ennes agreed to take care of the children and to educate them according to their social position up to the age of 18. In addition she agreed to give each of her sons and her daughter a generous and suitable set of linen and woollen clothes. All of these stipulations were very common in contracts like these between remarrying parents and (the guardians of) their minor children.[49]

From 1689 the city of Groningen had, in fact, the most extensive set of such regulations in the whole of the province of Groningen. In the so-called 'Ommelanden', the northern and western part of the province, and in the region known as 'Beide Oldambten', in the eastern part of the province, widowed fathers and mothers of minor children were obliged to provide their children with guardians only when they wanted to remarry.[50] In Friesland this duty fell to the remarrying mother only when she had been the *tutrix* or *curatrix* of her children. As I have said before, the solemnization of a second or subsequent marriage had no consequences for the father's exercise of paternal power. He was not even obliged to make an inventory of his children's maternal portion. Since the above-mentioned reform of the Frisian Ordinance in 1723 the mother even had to make an official ('judicial') inventory of the paternal portion of the children.[51]

From the moment she said 'I will', a widow once again became a married woman, with all the consequences of her change in civil status. Not only did she lose her legal capacity, she also lost her right to any allowance she had enjoyed for whatever reason in connection with her widowhood. We can imagine how pleased the Governors of the Widows' Pension Fund of Leeuwarden must have been when in 1783 they learned that Metdina Sijpkens, their opponent in the lawsuit before the Court of Friesland, had become the wife of Hendrik Joseph Gockinga.[52] One thing was perfectly clear now: Metdina Sijpkens was no longer a widow and the Governors could with a clear conscience discontinue payment of the annual pension that the decision of the Frisian Court had obliged them to grant her.[53]

NOTES

1 Public Record Office in the province of Friesland, at Leeuwarden (Rijksarchief in de provincie Friesland), Judicial Archives (Rechterlijke Archieven), Court of Friesland (Hof van Friesland) WW 169, Judgment 1 of 9 May 1780; see for the file of this case: Judicial Archives, Court of Friesland SS 992, Judgment 1 of 9 May 1780.

2 About Ulric Huber, the author of the *Praelectiones* (note 3 below) and the famous *Heedensdaegse Rechtsgeleertheyt* (note 10 below) see,

for instance, the introduction to Percival Gane's *The Jurisprudence of My Time*, Note on the Author, xix ff.

3 Ulric Huber, *Praelectiones juris civilis secundum Institutiones et Digesta Justiniani* (Trajecti ad Rhenum [Utrecht], 1711[3]) Liber XXIV, titulus II, no. 14 (vol. III, 232).

4 Public Record Office in the province of Friesland, Judicial Archives, Court of Friesland SS 992, Judgment 1 of 9 May 1780, answer (filed 13 April 1779) nos 9–12 and the conclusion.

5 See note 1 above.

6 That is, the territory of the Dutch Republic in Europe. This comprised not only the territories of the seven provinces which had a vote in the Assembly of the Estates-General (Staten-Generaal), but also the territories of State-Flanders, State-Brabant and State-Limburg (the so-called 'Generaliteitslanden') and that of the province of Drenthe which had no vote in the Assembly of the Estates-General.

7 See, for instance, Joannes a Sande, *Decisiones Frisicae sive Rerum in Suprema Frisiorum curia judicatarum*, Libri V (Leovardiae [Leeuwarden], 1638[2]) Liber II, titulus I, definitio 3.

8 This case is recounted in Simon van Leeuwen, *Het Rooms-Hollandsch Regt, waarin de Roomse wetten met het huydendaagse Neerlands Regt . . . over een gebragt werden* (Leiden and Rotterdam, 1664) Bk I, ch. XII, n. 4 (English translation by John G. Kotzé as *Simon van Leeuwen's Commentaries on Roman Dutch Law*, revised and edited with notes in 2 vols by C.W. Decker, London, 1921).

9 See A.S. de Blécourt, *Kort begrip van het oud-vaderlandsch burgerlijk recht* (Groningen and Batavia, 1939[5]) 83f.

10 Ulric Huber, *Heedensdaegse Rechtsgeleertheyt, soo elders als in Frieslandt gebruikelijk* (Leeuwarden, 1768[5]) Bk IV, ch. XXV, nn. 1 and 2 (English translation by Percival Gane as *The Jurisprudence of My Time* II [Durban, 1939] 108). See also note 11 below.

11 The provinces of Holland and Zealand shared such a court (the Court of Holland, Zealand and West-Friesland) which was founded in 1428. The Courts of Friesland, Utrecht and Guelderland were much younger. They were founded in 1499, 1530 and 1547 respectively. The Court of Friesland was founded by Albrecht, Duke of Saxony, who was made 'gubernator' (governor) of Friesland by the German Emperor Maximilian in 1499. These courts and their development out of the councils of the Count of Holland and Zealand and other overlords are described by J.Ph. De Monté verLoren, *Hoofdlijnen uit de ontwikkeling der rechterlijke organisatie in de Noordelijke Nederlanden tot de Bataafse Omwenteling*, rev. J.E. Spruit (Deventer, 1982[6]) 133–9.

12 About this so-called 'placard of dismissal' see P. Geyl, *The Revolt of the Netherlands 1555–1609* (London, 1970) 183–5.

13 See also Van Leeuwen, *Het Rooms-Hollandsch Regt*, Bk IV, ch. VI, n. 5 (Kotzé as in note 8 above).

14 On the law of succession *ab intestata* in the Netherlands before 1809 see De Blécourt, *Kort begrip*, 479–500.

15 [P. Laman], *Aanleiding tot de eerste beginselen der Groninger regtskennis* (Groningen, 1778[3]) Bk II, ch. IX, questions 32 and 41.

16 [Laman], ibid., Bk II, ch. IX, question 16.
17 Huber, *Heedensdaegse Rechtsgeleertheyt*, Bk II, ch. XXIII, n. 52 (Gane, *Jurisprudence* I, 231).
18 Huber, ibid., Bk II, ch. XXIII, nn. 53 and 54 (Gane, *ibid.*).
19 Hugo de Groot (Grotius), *Inleidinge tot de Hollandsche Rechts-geleerdheid* (The Hague, 1631[1]); the latest edition is that of F.D. Dovring, H.F.W.D. Fischer and E.M. Meyers (Leiden, 1952) Bk II, ch. XXX, n. 2 (English translation by R.W. Lee, *The Jurisprudence of Holland* [Oxford, 1926] 217).
20 See Sande, *Decisiones Frisicae*, Liber II, titulus II, definitio 3.
21 [Laman], *Aanleiding* Bk I, ch. VIII, question 3 (p. 76) and De Groot, *Inleidinge*, particularly Bk II, ch. XI, nn. 7 and 8 (Lee, *Jurisprudence of Holland*, 121).
22 See Huber, *Heedensdaegse Rechtsgeleertheyt*, Bk I, ch. XI, n. 3 ff. (Gane, *Jurisprudence* I, 56 ff.).
23 See De Blécourt, *Kort begrip*, 105.
24 As regards the power of guardianship, the difference between the English common law system and the legal system of the continent of western Europe, with regard to the conducting of power of guardianship, is very well explained in the *International Encyclopedia of Comparative Law*, published under the auspices of the International Association of Legal Science, vol. IV (M. Rheinstein and M.A. Glendon, 'Persons and Family', Tübingen and Alphen aan de Rijn, 1980, ch. IV ('Interspousal Relations') 23. One may find other important information in ch. VII (S.J. Stoljar, under the heading of 'Children, Parents and Guardians').
25 [Laman], *Aanleiding*, Bk I, ch. XI, question 8 (pp. 122 and 123).
26 This was the *Code Napoleon, adapted for the kingdom of Holland* (*Wetboek Napoleon ingerigt voor het koningrijk Holland*), which came into force on 1 May 1809.
27 [Laman], *Aanleiding*, Bk II, ch. XV, question 10 (p. 265).
28 See P. Gerbenzon, 'Enkele nieuwe gegevens over de receptie van het Romeinse recht in Friesland', *Tijdschrift voor Rechtsgeschiedenis (The Legal History Review)* 27 (1959) 133–57. About the reception of Roman law in the Middle Ages, see, for instance, O.F. Robinson, T.D. Fergus and W.M. Gordon, *An Introduction to European Legal History* (Trowbridge, 1987[2]) especially 115–20 and 318–26.
29 See Huber, *Heedensdaegse Rechtsgeleertheyt*, Bk I, ch. XII (Gane, *Jurisprudence* I, 64 ff.).
30 See Huber, ibid., Bk I, ch. XIV, nn. 1–6 (Gane, ibid. I, 73).
31 Huber, ibid., Bk I, ch. XV, n. 15 (Gane, ibid. I, 78).
32 See note 30 above.
33 Huber, *Heedensdaegse Rechtsgeleertheyt*, Bk I, ch. XIV, n. 23 and ch. XVI, nn. 5–8 (Gane, *Jurisprudence* I, 75, 82f.).
34 Huber, ibid., Bk I, ch. XVIII, n. 3 (Gane, ibid. I, 89).
35 Huber, ibid., Bk I, ch. XVI, nn. 10 and 11 (Gane, ibid. I, 83).
36 One can find this edict in S. Binckes, *Verklaaringe van de Statuten, ordonnantien, reglementen en costumen van rechte in Friesland, anders genaamd 's Lands Ordonnantie* I (Leeuwarden, 1785–86) 95ff.
37 See art. 2 of this edict and Binckes, ibid., 101–4.

38 See Huber, *Heedensdaegse Rechtsgeleertheyt*, Bk I, ch. XVI, nn. 5 and 8 (Gane, *Jurisprudence* I, 82 and 84) and De Groot, *Inleidinge*, Bk I, ch. 7, n. 11 (Lee, *Jurisprudence*, 37).

39 See B.S. Hempenius-van Dijk, *De weeskamer van de stad Groningen 1613–1811* (Groningen, 1991) 83f.

40 See for Groningen [Laman], *Aanleiding*, Bk I, chs XI and XII (pp. 118–131) and for Friesland Huber, *Heedensdaegse Rechtsgeleertheyt*, Bk I, chs XIV–XXII (Gane, *Jurispru dence* I, 73–9).

41 See L.J. van Apeldoorn, *Geschiedenis van het Nederlandsche huwelijksrecht* (Amsterdam, 1925) 84–123.

42 See De Groot, *Inleidinge*, Bk I, ch. V, n. 11 (Lee, *Jurisprudence*, 25).

43 See E. Schrage, 'La transformation des concepts. Un exemple: Le delai de viduité d'après Symon Vincentimus et quelques autres juristes medievaux', in G. van Dievoet, Ph. Godding and D. van den Auweele (eds), *Langage et droits à travers l'histoire, réalités et fictions* (Louvain and Paris, 1989) 185–200.

44 Van Apeldoorn, *Het Nederlandsche huwelijksrecht*, 169. See also Binckes, *Verklaaringe* I, 40 and Van Leeuwen, *Rooms-Hollandsch Regt*, Bk I, ch. XIV, n. 12 (Kotzé as in note 8 above).

45 See Van Apeldoorn, *Nederlandsche huwelijksrecht*, 170 and Huber, *Heedensdaegse Rechtsgeleertheyt*, Bk I, ch. VII, nn. 1–4 (Gane, *Jurisprudence* I, 39). In the city of Groningen a widow who remarried within the period of the 'year of mourning' could lose every financial benefit she might enjoy after her previous husband's death on the basis of their antenuptial contract, his will or otherwise according to the matrimonial property law of the city (Stads Nieuwe Constituties (New Constitutions of the city of Groningen (15 May 1689), art. 26 (I). This ordinance is included in the *Corpus der Groninger regten*, Groningen 1725, under n. 14).

46 Huber, *Heedensdaegse Rechtsgeleertheyt*. For the *Frisian Ordinance* of 1602, revised in 1723, see Gane, *Jurisprudence* I, xii.

47 Sande, *Decisiones Frisicae* (as in note 7 above).

48 See Hempenius-van Dijk, *De weeskamer van de stad Groningen*, 97.

49 Hempenius-van Dijk, ibid., 385–6, where the full text of the deed of this contract is quoted.

50 *Land-recht van Hunsingo, Fyvelingo, ende het Wester-quartier* (31 October 1601), Bk III, art. 21, and *Landt-recht des Gerichts van Selwerdt*, (28 August 1673), Bk III, art. 12.

51 *Frisian Ordinance* as revised in 1723 (see note 46 above) Bk I, Title VII, art. 5; see also Binckes, *Verklaaringe*, 81f.

52 Public Record Office in the province of Groningen, at Groningen (Rijksarchief in de provincie Groningen), Records of banns published at the village of Eexta (D.T.B. no. 60) 5 May 1783.

53 The author wishes to thank Ms Xandra Bardet for editing her English text.

Plates

1 Adriana ('Jeanne') Wilhelmina, Lady van Andringa de Kempenaer (1858–1926) always wore a black dress after the death of her husband Quirinus van Andringa de Kempenaer in 1888. Around 1900, mourning rituals and etiquette were still strictly observed by the Dutch (landed) nobility. (Photo: Family archives Van Andringa de Kempenaer, Rijksarchief Friesland, Leeuwarden, The Netherlands)

2 In 1903 Jeanne van Andringa de Kempenaer bought the castle of Wychen (near Nimwegen) from the Belgian noble family Osy; in the first half of the seventeenth century the castle was owned by the most famous noble house in Dutch history, Van Nassau. For Jeanne the most important motive for buying this castle was to increase the aristocratic grandeur of her own family. (Photo: Astrid Kuiper, 1993)

3 The Frisian nobleman, diplomat and poet Onno Zwier van Haren
(1713–79), painted by the French portraitist J. Fournier in 1752. The Van
Harens were one of the major families of the court aristocracy of the Dutch
Republic. Van Haren was accused by some relatives of incestuous behaviour
but his wife (and widow) Sara passionately defended the reputation of her
late husband and of her family. (Photo: Iconographisch Bureau, The Hague,
The Netherlands [City hall of Aachen, Germany])

Bramenes cum mortuus est . secundum eorum legem crematur uxor autem eius præ amore . sese vivam in ignem cum illo conijcit

De Bramene doot wesende wort nae haer wet verbrant . en̄ syn vrouwe uut liefde haers mans . verbrant haer levendich met hem

58 en 59

4 According to South Indian *satī* tradition the *satī* jumps onto the pyre joining the corpse of her husband. (Copperplate: Joannes à Doetechum, in J. H. van Linschoten, *Itenerario, Voyage ofte Schipvaert van Jan Huygen van Linschoten naer Oost ofte Portugaels Indien, 1579–1592* (Amsterdam, 1596), edited by H. Kern and revised by H. Terpstra, 3 vols (Amsterdam, 1956²) II, plate 58/59)

5 The funeral cortège of an Indian *rājā* according to western romantic imagination. The *satī* is flanked by two brahminical priests, musicians and flagellating ascetics. Behind her, the palanquin containing the corpse of her deceased royal husband is carried. (Litho: L. Benett, in J. Verne, *Le tour du monde en quatre-vingt jours* (Paris, 1872) 57)

6 A living *satī* ('widow'), village near Sitapur, Śekhavatī district, Rajasthan. In 1985 the woman tried to burn herself on the funeral pyre of her husband but was rescued by the local police. She has transformed her house into a temple for her husband in order to commemorate him in front of his ashes, and lives as a strict ascetic in accordance with the brahminical rules for the widow. (Photo: L.P. van den Bosch, 1991)

7 Interior of a local Rānī Satī temple with a 'fabricated' picture of Roop Kanwar, in Bombay. Roop sacrificed herself on the funeral pyre of her husband Maal Singh in September 1987. On the right side of the picture the queen of *satīs*, Narayanī Devī, the clan goddess of the Marwari Agrawalas from Jhunjhunu, is represented with a trident in her hand. (Photo: L.P. van den Bosch, 1990)

8 A poster on the wall of the *Śrī satījīkā pracīna mandiram* near the Manikarnikā *ghāt* (staircase to the Ganges) – the 'burning *ghāt*' – in Benares. The *satī* is represented with the corpse of her husband on the pyre, while the heavenly gods Brahma, Vishnu and Śiva eulogize her heroic deed. A ray from the sun seems to bestow on the widow the divine *sat* which makes her invulnerable to any pain. (Photo: L.P. van den Bosch, 1994).

9 *Satī caura* (mould) near Sanskrit University, Benares, near the intersection of three roads. The *caura* symbolizes the pile on which the *satī* sacrificed herself. It has a conical form and is about 130 cm in height with a base of lotus petals. In a niche in the shaft a black female figure is represented. A trident marks the place and connects it with modern *satī* iconography. Notions of fertility seem to have been fused with *satī* iconography. (Photo: L.P. van den Bosch, 1994)

10 This sketch in charcoal depicts a recently widowed woman stopping a typical Dutch clock. To the left we see Death departing with his scythe. To the right the ferryman of the dead, Charon, departs with his boat to transport the deceased husband to the underworld. 'The Widow' is by the Meuse and Walloon painter Antoon van Welie in 1912. (Photo: J. van Wijk, Tiel, The Netherlands)

11 French widows in various stages of fashionable mourning. (Drawing: Roger Boutet de Monvel, *Gazette du Bon Ton*, Paris, 1920)

6

'EUROPEAN' WIDOWS IN THE DUTCH EAST INDIES

Their legal and social position

Heleen C. Gall

After the establishment of the Dutch United East India Company (Verenigde Oost-Indische Compagnie, VOC) in 1602,[1] the Dutch began to settle in the East Indies. At first only men were settlers, but this changed in 1610 with the arrival of the first Governor-General Pieter Both (1610–14). On 30 January 1610 Both left the Netherlands with a fleet of eight ships. Aboard there were not only sailors, but also occupying forces for the forts in the East Indies, ministers and artisans with their families, and thirty-six spinsters, the last turning out to be mainly 'of ill repute'. After a journey full of deprivation the company arrived on 19 December 1610 at Banten on Java.[2]

With the appearance of settlements all sorts of problems arose, including legal ones. In the early days of the VOC these were largely solved according to the law used on VOC ships. This, though based on Dutch law, was mainly concerned with disciplinary matters and was soon found to be incapable of settling all the disputes which could arise in the settlements. There was an obvious need for clarification of the law being applied, and also for laws to be made to meet the special conditions. This is why in 1621 the VOC directors (a council of seventeen called the 'Gentlemen XVII' [Heren XVII] whose office was in the Netherlands, from where they exercised their limited legislative powers) instructed the government in the Dutch East Indies to enforce four laws applied in the province of Holland. The first one is the Political Ordinance of 1 April 1580, containing rules regarding marriage, intestate succession – the succession executed in the case of a person who has died without leaving a will – and immovable property. The second law is the Interpretation

Ordinance of 13 May 1594, in which the Political Ordinance's rules of intestate succession are explained more fully; and the third is the Edict of 18 December 1599, which also contains rules regarding intestate succession.[3] On the fourth one, the VOC directors also instructed the VOC government in the East Indies – the government formed by the Governor-General and his Council who were given limited legislative powers as well – to apply the Judicial Ordinance of 1 April 1580, containing rules of procedure in force in the province of Holland.[4]

In 1625 the Governor-General and his Council charged two institutions, set up in 1620 in Batavia (the present-day Jakarta), the capital of the East Indies, with the drafting of new rules of procedure. The first institution was the Council of Justice (Raad van Justitie), which was originally commissioned to undertake the trial of all simple cases, criminal or civil, concerning VOC soldiers and servants. Later it became the court with the highest judicial power in the East Indies. The second one was the College or Court of Aldermen (Schepenbank), which not only exercised judicial powers but also powers over local government and police in Batavia. This Court had jurisdiction over all persons who were not VOC soldiers or servants, viz. the free citizens and the foreigners.[5]

These two institutions finished their task soon and the rules, including the instruction for the body discussed below, the Orphan Chamber, were promulgated by the Governor-General and his Council in 1625. At the same time they declared that the four laws of the province of Holland, referred to above, had to be observed in the administration of justice in the Dutch East Indies. In so far as cases were not covered by these laws or by edicts issued by the Governor-General or his successors, judges had to observe the general civil laws as practised in the home country, the Republic of the United Netherlands.[6] However, a problem was that the Republic did not have a uniform system of law. The Republic, which came into being at the end of the sixteenth century in part of the region forming the modern Netherlands, was composed of a number of sovereign provinces, a federation. Its representatives formed the States-General, a governing body concerned with promoting the common interests of the Republic, among which foreign and overseas relations were important.

Regarding the system of law, the States-General had no part in legislation within the provinces; each region was responsible for creating its own laws. In contrast, it was the highest legislative body for the areas governed by the VOC and the West Indies Company (West-Indische Compagnie, WIC).

Throughout the entire duration of the Dutch Republic (until 1795), Holland was to a considerable extent the most dominant province within the federation, and also within the regions of VOC and WIC monopoly. Where these areas were concerned, the States-General made too little use of their legislative powers. Owing to the consequent lack of adequate laws within these overseas regions, the law of the province of Holland – Dutch law – began to be applied there. So, in practice, the order to the judges to observe the general civil laws as practised in the Republic of the United Netherlands, in cases where there was a lack of adequate laws, came down on the application of the laws of the province of Holland.

In 1642 all the instructions, edicts and resolutions in force in the East Indies at that moment were compiled and called the Statutes of Batavia (Statuten van Batavia). They dealt, *inter alia*, with orphans, commissioners of marriage affairs, universal community of property, and intestate succession. These Statutes were endorsed by the Governor-General and his Council, and were declared operative, albeit temporarily until the delivery of a definitive regulation.[7] The States-General, however, never formulated this. In 1766 the New Statutes of Batavia were completed, which absorbed all rules promulgated between 1642 and 1766.[8] This time they were not declared operative by the Governor-General and his Council, but sent to the Netherlands for endorsement by the States-General. However, this never happened, so that these Statutes never acquired formal legal force. Nevertheless, they were put into practice as though they did possess such legal force.

THE LEGAL POSITION OF WIDOWS

Above all, the intention of this contribution is to draw a picture of the legal position that widows of Europeans or of Eurasian men with European status had in the Dutch East Indies. To a lesser extent, their social position will also be discussed. Regarding the time frame, the emphasis falls on the VOC period (1602–1798), but sometimes remarks on the nineteenth century will be made as well. As regards their status, the widows' origin made little difference because, if the solemnization of the marriage had taken place according to Dutch law, the bride and her offspring were granted European status. So generally speaking, if their origin was European, Asian or Eurasian, no distinction was made between them. I have deliberately left out of consideration the position of other widows in the Dutch East Indies. This topic deserves some separate contributions because of the many population groups, each of which had its own rules. On the other hand I do bring to the reader's attention the position of the Asian concubine whose European partner had died. Although she cannot be considered as a widow in the legal sense, I do not want to leave her position unmentioned, especially not in connection with the offspring, if any, born out of the concubinage.

To the reader's attention I also bring the role of the Dutch Reformed Church in European daily life in the East Indies. The Dutch Reformed faith, so the Statutes of Batavia prescribed, was the only faith permitted to be practised among the European settlers.[9] What was more, the regulation of 1650 for the Governor-General and his Council dictated that the whole administrative organization especially should also be backed up by the Christian Reformed religion. This regulation also prescribed that some Commissioners of the Governor-General's Council had always to be members of the Church Council, to maintain harmony between religion and administration.[10]

THE SETTLEMENTS

The establishment of the settlements did not work out at all in the way Jan Pietersz. Coen, the fourth and sixth Governor-General (1619–23 and 1627–29), had in mind. Several times he made appeals to the VOC directors to send more settlers, especially husbands with their wives and children. He also requested, more than once, that the directors send out large numbers of boys and girls from the orphanages in the home country. Once on the spot the girls could be prepared for marriage. He also pointed out that adult women were needed immediately for the sailors and soldiers who wanted to settle as free citizens in the Dutch East Indies. Everybody knows, he wrote, that the human race cannot survive without women.[11]

The women sent by the VOC were the lowest of the low. They lived, according to the sources, such a scandalous, dirty and lawless life, that not only many honourable youngsters would become licentious and corrupt, and the reputation of Christians be defamed among the Heathens and the Moors as well, but also the judgment of God would strike the country, unless measures were taken. That is why a women's house of correction was set up.[12]

Coen was dismayed to discover that every shipload time and again consisted of unrighteous women. Once he remarked: 'It is almost as if they originate from the wilderness instead of having been brought up among people.'[13] Compared with his subordinates he was more critical in this respect, because François Valentijn, a minister, who was stationed in Amboina from 1685 to 1695 and again during the years 1707 to 1713, wrote that the men of the garrison welcomed the women like 'roast pears'.[14]

Disappointed as to the character of the women, once again Coen pointed out to the VOC directors the importance of sending respectable Dutch families; and if that was impossible, to send at least underage, young girls in the hope that their constitution would be better than that of the older women.[15] In 1621 the directors wrote Coen that three families would sail for Batavia bringing several young girls, who were called 'Company daughters', with them.[16] These families and girls arrived in 1622. They received a set of clothing from the Company; later it became customary to give each a dowry upon marriage.

At the end of 1622 Coen was informed of the departure of one wife whose husband had already left, and of seven married couples and thirty-one single girls.[17] In spite of these measures he was not satisfied. He continued to point out the need for honourable women and respectable, married people. Also, he let the VOC directors know that it would be better, and was much more urgently necessary, to send ships with young 'daughters' and respectable women to the Indies rather than ships full of soldiers.[18] On 15 December 1623 a ship with eighty-two young 'daughters' departed from Amsterdam to the Indies.[19] Upon their arrival the girls were placed in families or in a special Company-financed school where they were brought up and educated in good manners. Once ready for marriage a good, honest partner was sought, and the wedding took place. This, the VOC directors once again emphasized, had to take place according to the rules in force in the province of Holland, namely the rules rendered in the Political Ordinance of 1580 already mentioned.[20] This meant that the marriage was solemnized, on pain of nulli- fication, by confirmation of the promises of marriage either in the church by the minister or in public before the magistrate chosen for this task, but not until a few prescriptions had been satisfied, such as, for instance, the publication of the banns.

These marriages did not have the result Coen had in mind because, mainly due to climatic circumstances, many of the unions turned out to be barren. Miscarriages and infant deaths occurred very often. The Gentlemen XVII decided to halt the transport of Dutch girls to the Dutch Indies.[21] In 1632 the Company school was closed. At that time it had only eleven pupils; twenty-four other girls were staying with Dutch families.[22]

Soon after this decision the Gentlemen XVII wrote: 'We shall never again realize our plan to stabilize a Batavian colony with Dutch families. We must aim at attracting several Indian [read Asian] nations who may in course of time choose to settle on a permanent basis ... and Dutchmen (Company servants or free citizens) who want to marry Indian women instead of Dutch women.'[23] Experiences with mixed marriages were excellent, according to a letter from Governor-General Hendrik Brouwer (1632–6) to the Gentlemen XVII. He wrote: 'There are good households here where the men are married to Indian women, their children are healthier, the women have fewer demands, and our soldiers are much better off married to them.'[24]

The condition for these marriages was that the women had to be Christians or had to be converted. The solemnization of marriage had to accord with Dutch law. The bride and her offspring were granted European status, which meant that they were covered by the laws in force for the Europeans in the Dutch East Indies. These were, *inter alia*, the Statutes of Batavia mentioned in the introduction.

Asian women living in concubinage with European men did not obtain European status, but this was different for their children, if they were acknowledged by their European fathers. Then the child could use the father's surname and was recognized as the child of the father alone, with all the juridical consequences. These were settled in the Indian Civil Code, which came into force in 1848.[25] An example of these consequences is the case in which the government, if the father was the first to die and there were still underage children, ignored the existence of the Asian mother, who until then had taken care of her children as normally as a legitimate mother would have done. From the moment of the father's death the government regarded the underage children as orphans who had lost both parents, and placed them in the orphanage or under the guardianship of a member of the father's family in the home country, so that in the latter case these children had to exchange the country of their birth and upbringing for a totally unknown country, where they knew nobody. In his novel *This Earth of Mankind* (n.p. [Australia], 1982), the Indonesian novelist Pramoedya Ananta Toer deals with this subject around the turn of the nineteenth and twentieth centuries. He also describes how, although there is a joint estate, the concubine, the 'njai', has to relinquish the whole of it to the legitimate heirs. Indeed, just as in the time preceding the coming into force of the Indian Civil Code, only if her partner had made a will in which he had named her as his heir, could she claim the portion reserved for her in the will.

THE LEGAL CONSEQUENCES OF 'EUROPEAN' MARRIAGES AND OF THEIR DISSOLUTION BY DEATH

As we have already mentioned above, 'European' marriages included not only marriages between European partners but also marriages between European or Eurasian male partners with European status, and female partners of Asian or Eurasian origin. These marriages had consequences of two kinds. First, there were the personal consequences which were invariable for all marriages. Second, there were the proprietary consequences, which were mostly variable in that they depended on the choice of the parties before the marriage; they could not be altered afterwards.

Regarding the personal consequences, the most important were that the spouses had to stay together and support each other and that, if they were minors before marriage, they became majors on marriage. For the man, this meant that he obtained his full capacity to act; for the woman, this meant that she acquired a limited capacity to act, like every other woman marrying in her majority, because as a result of marriage, every wife came under the husband's marital power. The limited capacity to act entailed the fact that she could not, without his consent, enter into binding contracts and other legal transactions. However, there were two exceptions: firstly, the wife could enter into contracts for household necessities; and secondly, she could carry on a public trade or profession with his express or implied consent.

Regarding the proprietary consequences, there were in principle two matrimonial property regimes: that where the marriage was in universal community of property, and the other where such a community had been excluded by an antenuptial contract. Such a contract could contain virtually any stipulation as long as it was not illegal, immoral or contrary to the nature of marriage. If it were so, the contract was null and void. In so far as there was no such contract, or where there was an invalid one, the universal community of property was the matrimonial property regime. This meant that all the assets and liabilities of the spouses, whether acquired or incurred before or during the marriage, were merged in a joint estate, administered by the husband.

On dissolution of the marriage by death, if there was neither an antenuptial contract nor a will, half of the joint estate accrued to the surviving spouse, the other half being the inheritance of the deceased, to which his or her intestate heirs were entitled. Could the surviving spouse belong among the intestate heirs? This question only came up if all the blood relatives who could be intestate heirs were lacking. The rules regarding the intestate succession do not answer this question, but mention that unanswered questions have to be solved according to Roman law.[26] Indeed, in the event that there were no blood relatives as heirs, the Roman law permitted the surviving spouse to be the heir. However, this possibility was by no means admitted by all Dutch lawyers. Hugo Grotius is one of the group who refuted it.[27]

The question of whether the sole surviving parent could be one of the intestate successors of his deceased child was decided in 1661, when the States-General put an end to uncertainty on this point in the Dutch East Indies by enacting a Charter, which made this possible.[28]

In cases where there were underage children, the surviving spouse was obliged to submit to the rules of the Orphan Chamber. The first Orphan Chamber on VOC territory was formally established on 1 October 1624 in the Dutch Indies at Batavia. The Orphan Masters had to swear, *inter alia*, to maintain conscientiously the rights of widows and orphans and to promote their welfare to their utmost power. Above all, the purpose of the establishment of the Orphan Chamber was to protect the interests of minors, in cases where one or both parents had died. Its task was to prevent a situation arising in which the minor could lose part of the inheritance through the negligence of the surviving spouse or other guardians, or through insufficient evidence for the size of that inheritance. This is why the surviving parent was obliged to appear in the Orphan Chamber and cause his or her children's inheritance to be ascertained and entered in the books of the Orphan Chamber.

Apart from some exceptions, the surviving spouse could be the legal guardian of the minor children. With the permission of the Orphan Chamber, he or she could continue the joint estate, after having drawn up an inventory of all the property. All losses which the estate might sustain afterwards had to be exclusively borne by the surviving spouse.[29] If the husband was the first to die, the wife could free herself from personal liability for community debts by renouncing all rights stemming from the community. Such a renunciation was effected in symbolic form: at the funeral of her husband, the wife walked out of the house in front of the bier in her everyday clothing, laying the keys of the house upon the coffin. In those days, this was the only way the renunciation could be made. After the Indian Civil Code came into force, she could do this within a reasonable time after her husband's death, by putting a deed of renunciation on file.[30]

In cases where the husband serving the VOC was the first one to die, the salary was discontinued. In general, pensions did not as yet exist. This is why rules were enacted by which the widows of high-ranking VOC servants were entitled to food allowances until the departure of the fleet for Holland, or until they remarried. If they decided to stay in the East Indies, they were only entitled to water, bread and firewood after the departure of the fleet. Only widows of ministers received a small allowance and were allowed to continue receiving the emoluments.[31]

Widows who stayed in the East Indies and who were unable to support themselves could apply for aid to the Poor Relief Board of the Church (see below, p.116) or to the Governor-General. Widows who were in fact able to make their own living occupied themselves for instance with letting out mourning coats or undertaking funerals. Others obtained a job in or on behalf of the orphanage, or were running girls' schools.[32] These jobs were legal ones, but there were also wives and widows who did illegal work, such as Neeltje Koek and Helena Kakelaar.

Neeltje Koek was the well-to-do widow of the very rich Vice-President of the College of Aldermen at Batavia, Jan Lambertsz Radder, who died at the end of the seventeenth century. Neeltje then married Meynardt de Roy, Commissioner for Native Affairs, charged with the solution of small problems between native persons, as for instance problems of marriage and divorce. Once married to De Roy, Neeltje decided to go into private trading: opium smuggling. Very soon she was doing a large-scale trade, and she set up a clandestine depot. All went so well that she was no longer able to get through the work alone. This is the reason why she asked her sister-in-law Helena Kakelaar to form a company with her. Helena was the widow of Jacob Radder, a brother of Neeltje's first husband. She was leprous and was not left well provided for by her husband, so she certainly needed some extra money. With enthusiasm she undertook the administration of the business.

Meyndert de Roy shut his eyes to Neeltje's and Helena's activities. Trading on one's own account was illegal and, where wife and family were involved in it, the husband was held responsible.[33] Nevertheless he enjoyed the profits, although not for long, since he died in 1707. The two widows did a roaring trade together. However, in the 1720s it came to an end because the Bailiff (the public prosecutor in the Court of Aldermen) Godefridus Bogaard raided the clandestine depot. At that moment there was a great quantity of opium available to the value of 23,600 rix-dollars ('rijksdaalders': one 'rijksdaalder' was two and a half guilders). The whole bulk of this was confiscated and in 1725 the Bailiff received half the value of the confiscated opium as a reward for his efforts. Neeltje was sentenced to exile, and Helena to a leper colony. Both widows asked for a retrial and were sentenced to a fine of 8000 rix-dollars in 1725.[34]

REMARRIAGES IN GENERAL; SOME REMARKABLE ONES IN PARTICULAR

A widow or widower who wanted to remarry had to observe the same rules that applied to the first marriage. However, apart from this, he or she was subjected to an additional number of rules. Thus there were more prohibited degrees within which it was not permitted to marry than in the case of the first marriage. For instance, it was forbidden for the widower to marry the blood relatives of his deceased wife, just as it was forbidden for the widow to marry the blood relatives of her deceased husband. By the solemnization of the marriage husband and wife were considered as one unit, as a result of which the prohibition to marry was applied not only with regard to the blood relatives but also with respect to the relatives by marriage and within the same degrees.[35]

A widow was not permitted to remarry within three months after her husband's death – called the 'weeping period' – to make sure that she was not pregnant by her late husband.[36] Where her husband had disappeared without trace, the wife was allowed to remarry after a certain period of time. The Statutes of Batavia do not mention the length of this period. Regarding this, as in some parts of the Netherlands, the authorities gave a separate decision for each case. An example is the case of the wives whose husbands were assumed to have been killed at sea in 1719. Two years later the wives obtained permission to remarry. Concerning the other parts of the Netherlands there was a fixed waiting period of five years, a rule which was settled in article 467 of the Indian Civil Code.[37]

The surviving spouse with underage children was not to be permitted to remarry without having made arrangements with the Orphan Masters concerning the shares due to these children out of the estate of the deceased.[38] The remarrying widower could keep his guardianship of the children, but the remarrying widow was not allowed to continue as guardian. The responsibility passed to her husband or to a specially appointed guardian. The impossibility of continuing the guardianship resulted from the loss of her full capacity to act by the remarriage. Again, she was subject to her husband's marital power with all the consequences given.

Young and/or rich widows were extremely popular among men on the lookout for wives, men with large debts, or poor widowers with children. An example of the last category is the lawyer Johan Bitter. Leonard Blussé has described Bitter's life so excellently that we shall talk about him only briefly.[39] Johan Bitter, a lawyer, went to the Indies to begin a legal career in the service of the VOC. On 12 September 1675 he arrived with four children as a widower in Batavia; his wife and one of his children had died on the two-month-long passage between South Africa and Batavia. He entered the Council of Justice as a Councillor. Very soon he discovered that the income he received was totally insufficient to provide for himself and the upbringing of his four children. Then one of his colleagues drew his attention to a very well-to-do elderly Eurasian widow, Cornelia van Nijenroode. He set out to court her and succeeded in persuading her to marry him. The marriage was not only attractive to him but, as Blussé has already written, also to her because of Bitter's academic background and his high status as Councillor of Justice. Although Bitter was penniless, yet his high office would offer opportunities that were denied to her as a widow; furthermore it would keep open the doors to the salons of the Company élite. However, probably the most important consideration would be that Bitter's office could provide Cornelia with the legal backing necessary for her business dealings; people would think very carefully before cheating her.

Such a marriage with a poor man being a risk for a wealthy woman, Cornelia obviously did not want to marry under the common matrimonial property regime, the universal community of property already mentioned. She did not want to take a chance; she therefore called in the help of legal advisers to draw up a watertight antenuptial contract, which Cornelia and Johan signed in March 1676. The same month they married. Shortly after the marriage they started to make life hell for each other. The main problems were firstly that Johan did not allow Cornelia to carry on her business, but wanted to administer her properties himself; and secondly, that Cornelia kept him on too short a leash. Regarding the second problem she admitted it, and solved it by giving him in advance the money to which he was only really entitled after her death. Now he could at least administer that. Regarding the first problem the couple agreed that Cornelia could keep the other possessions to herself and administer, invest and redeem them as she liked.

Nevertheless a great many lawsuits followed, also because of Johan's embezzlement of Cornelia's money. In 1677 Cornelia requested a divorce from bed and board. The fact is that a full divorce was not possible; this was only allowed in the case of adultery or malicious abandonment. Cornelia's request was granted in 1679, but revised in 1684. The troubles continued and were ended only by Cornelia's death in the summer of 1692. At that time there was not much left of all her wealth for her inheritors, her grandchildren, because of Bitter's lifestyle and because of all the money the lawsuits and lawyers had cost.

An example of someone with a large debt is provided by David van Lennep, who at the end of the eighteenth century embarked for the Indies. He had a 270,000 guilder debt which he hoped to repay by earning enough money in the Indies. Here he became Councillor of Justice, not a very well-paid job, as we know from the Bitter case. After some time he met a well-to-do widow (worth 800,000 guilders) and decided to hook her. He hoped to marry her without an antenuptial contract, so that he could pay off his debt out of the joint estate. However, from later correspondence it becomes clear that Van Lennep was turned down.[40]

The category of men prowling around for wives was described by John Crawfurd, a Scotsman who lived from 1808–16 in the East Indies, in the following way in 1820: 'As soon as a woman becomes a widow, and the body of her husband is interred, which is generally done the day after his decease, if she be but rich, she has immediately a number of suitors. A certain lady, who lost her husband while I was at Batavia, had, in the fourth week of her widowhood, a fourth lover, and, at the end of three months, she married again, and would have done it sooner, if the laws had allowed of it.'[41] This last part aims at the 'weeping period' of three months already mentioned.

A very remarkable remarriage is that of Elisabeth Abbema to Governor-General Joan Maetsuyker (1653–78). As a young girl she arrived with her family – her father was a minister – on Ternate, one of the Molucca Islands, in 1656. A few months earlier the unmarried Simon Cos had arrived on Ternate. He was appointed Governor of the Moluccas. Soon after the arrival of the Abbema family, Cos's eye fell on the daughter Elisabeth: a marriage was the result.

In 1662 the couple departed to Amboina, which is one of the Moluccas as well. However, it had its own governor and Cos had been appointed as the new one. Two years later he became very ill, and died on 24 February 1664 at the age of approximately 50 years. The marriage was childless. Elisabeth was left alone, but definitely not without means. Cos was succeeded by Johan van Dam, who arrived one year later on Amboina. Valentijn describes him as tall, slim and bad-tempered. He was approximately 40 years old and had the nickname of 'Tall John' or 'John with the trousers' because he often wore trousers for protection against mosquitos. Van Dam's eye fell on Elisabeth. This was not unwelcome to her and soon the couple became engaged. Their intention was to marry in Batavia. Van Dam, having been only a short time on Amboina, could not obtain leave again immediately. This is why Elisabeth went on ahead, alone. Van Dam requested his friend, the Governor-General Joan Maetsuyker, to take care of her until he himself arrived in Batavia. Maetsuyker, a widower since 3 June 1663, took the request to take care of Elisabeth so seriously that he even allowed her to stay in his house. He took a liking to her and persuaded her to marry him, a Governor-General, and not Van Dam, only a Governor. The wedding followed soon after.

After some time Van Dam on far-away Amboina heard about this event. Immediately he left for Batavia and found his bride there, in the meantime married to Maetsuyker. In public he did not show his rage, but in private, if he thought himself alone, he ranted and raved. Maetsuyker's spies informed him of this. When they asked if they should stop this raging, Maetsuyker answered that he could imagine Van Dam's reaction very well, and he ordered them to leave the man alone. Maetsuyker himself thought that what he had done to Van Dam was quite a serious matter, and he mentioned that in future Van Dam would be wiser not to leave his bride, and such a nice widow too, in the care of a widower. Van Dam did not feel like staying any longer in the Indies and departed to the Netherlands in the same year. The marriage between Elisabeth and Maetsuyker was dissolved by Elisabeth's death on 27 November 1674. Maetsuyker himself died on 4 January 1678.[42]

THE ROLE OF THE DUTCH REFORMED CHURCH

The Dutch Reformed Church had a very prominent role in 'European' daily life and was deeply rooted in society.[43] The recording of births, marriages and deaths was its responsibility. The solution of small legal problems and the prevention of bigger ones was also part of its task, as well as the provision of education and welfare. The Church Council was increasingly often confronted with appeals for alms. Therefore in 1621 the Poor Relief Board was set up and charged with the granting of alms,[44] which were paid out of the proceeds of collections and donations, and of a percentage of the fines imposed by the government. Thus in the seventeenth century, Maria van Aelst, widow of the Governor-General Antonio van Diemen (1636–45), donated money to the poor of Batavia, and in the eighteenth century Governor-General Petrus Albertus van der Parra (1761–75), born in Ceylon, left his chief inheritance to the widows of Colombo and a smaller one to the poor of Batavia.[45]

Apparently, many people appealed to the Board, for in April 1627 the decision was made to give no more, or at least less money, to the many native women supported by the Board.[46] Also the notes of the Church Council tell us that many 'European' widows – with or without children – were supplied with alms or loans. Sometimes widows were allowed to live in the almshouse. Also there were seven houses, especially rented on behalf of sick wives or poor widows. If the latter were healthy, they had to take care of the sick wives.[47]

Concerning the remarriage of widows, difficult problems were sometimes given to the Church Council to solve. Thus it had to find a solution to Catalina Charles's problem. Catalina Charles married Jan van Bacchum tot Haerlem in the Dutch town of Haarlem in 1621. After the marriage, Jan went on ahead to the Indies, where he died, Catalina said she had been told. Thereupon she married Jan Albertsz in Haarlem in 1627. The couple departed to the Indies and found Jan van Bacchum tot Haerlem there in excellent health. The Church Council decided to involve the Council of Justice in solving this problem. Together they resolved that Catalina had to live with her first husband and that the second one had to go back to the Netherlands. Apparently, he did not leave, because one year later Jan van Bacchum complained that Catalina's second husband spent every day with her. This is why he asked for a divorce. The Church Council did not permit this, but they promised to ask the government to send the second husband to Amboina. We learn nothing more about him, whereas we are told more about Jan van Bacchum, for in 1631 Catalina complained to the Church Council of his bad behaviour. The Church Council thereupon decided to remit the case to the Fiscal, the public prosecutor in the Council of Justice, because both Jan and Catalina had behaved so badly that they had to be punished, to serve as an example to other people. I do not know what became of this couple afterwards.[48]

The Church Council was often presented with cases of widows who wanted to remarry but finally changed their minds, or widows who complained that their fiancés had renounced the marriage. In most of the cases the Church Council decided the marriage had to take place. Sometimes the Church Council received petitions for remarriage which for the time being could not be sanctioned because the widow had not been a widow long enough; as we have already said, widowhood had to last at least three months. It also happened that the Church Council refused permission because of the fact that the widow had just given birth to a child by her late husband or, in the case of a missing spouse, because it was not yet sure that her husband could be presumed to be really dead.

A rather exceptional case is that of Trijntje Floris, a widow, who wanted to marry for the third time, this time to Pieter Dircksz. She did not obtain permission for this, because even during her second marriage the rumour went that her first husband was still alive in the Netherlands. Pieter and Trijntje continued to request confirmation of their marriage, and the Church Council for its part persisted in demanding evidence of the fact that Trijntje's first husband had died. Further, Trijntje and Pieter were told not to go near each other in order to prevent further scandals. However, in 1626, Trijntje requested a divorce from Pieter, to whom she claimed to be engaged. Thereupon the Church Council answered that they did not know of any legal contract between the two of them; that this was the reason why the Council did not want to separate those who had never been united. The case continued to drag on, and in 1631 it was evident that Trijntje had been excommunicated, and that the church members were forbidden to see her.

In 1634 the Church Council again occupied itself with the question of Trijntje's remarriage, this time to Crijn Maersz. Again the answer was a negative because her first husband was still alive. Thereupon Trijntje applied to the Governor-General and his Council with the request to be allowed to marry Crijn in front of the Church or the Court. The Governor-General consulted the Church Council on this matter. This Council judged – enumerating a string of Bible texts on adultery – that Trijntje's remarriage could not and should not be allowed. The Council's president addressed her, reprimanding her for making this indecent request, and warned her to lead a better life in future. We do not know if she did so, but it is certain that the Church Council's notes do not mention any more scandalous facts about her.[49]

SUMMARY

In the initial stages of the VOC in the Dutch East Indies it was the intention to establish settlements consisting of purely European colonists. Contacts with native women were not encouraged. Because of the problems caused by the bad characters of most of the European women and wives, and the problems with producing European children, in 1634 the VOC directors from the Netherlands decided to reverse their policy by promoting marriages with Asian women. If they were Christians or converted to that faith, and if the solemnization of the marriage had been according to Dutch law, they and their offspring acquired European status. This meant that they were no longer covered by their own law, but by the law in force for the Europeans. Concentrating on our subject, the same legal consequences of the marriage and of its dissolution by death were applicable to all the 'European' wives. Where their legal position as widows was concerned, for instance, their limited capacity to act was changed into the full capacity in consequence of the husband's death, to whose marital power they had been subjected as wives.

With regard to their social position, this depended on whether arrangements had been made for them by means of an antenuptial contract or a will or, where there was universal community of property, the widow's part of the joint estate (half) was enough to subsist. If not, money had to be obtained in some way or other. Some widows found jobs, others asked for help from the Poor Relief Board of the Church or from the Governor-General. Remarriage could solve their problems. Being well-to-do, of course they had no money problems, but a widow's social life did not have the same quality as that of a wife. In general, remarriage could be advantageous for such widows, if it was to a man of a high status.

The Dutch Reformed Church had a very prominent role in 'European' daily life. Apart from the provision of alms or loans, the Church busied itself with the solution of small legal problems. Regarding our subject, this included for instance the investigation and solution of the problem of whether permission could be given for a remarriage.[50]

NOTES

1 For the previous history and the establishment of the VOC see J.K.J. de Jonge, *De opkomst van het Nederlandsch gezag in Oost-Indië*, 13 vols (The Hague and Amsterdam, 1862–88) I, 1–149.

2 De Jonge, *Opkomst*, III, 134–5; IV, i–ii.

3 *Groot placaet-boeck vervattende de placaten, ordonnantiën ende edicten van de . . . Staten-Generael der Vereenighde Nederlanden [etc.]*, 9 vols (The Hague and Amsterdam, 1658–1797) I, cols 329–46.

4 De Jonge, *Opkomst*, IV, cxxxiv–cxxxvi. The first Governor-General and his Council were appointed by the States-General by a Proclamation of 27 November 1609; see P. Mijer, *Verzameling van instructiën, ordonnanciën en reglementen voor de Regering van Nederlandsch-Indië, vastgesteld in de jaren 1609–1836* (Batavia, 1848) 3f. For the Judicial Ordinance of 1 April 1580 see *Groot placaet-boeck*, II, cols 695–704.

5 J.A. van der Chijs, *Nederlandsch-Indisch Plakaatboek, 1602–1811*, 17 vols (Batavia and The Hague, 1885–1900) I, 59f.; 62–5; 482.

6 Van der Chijs, *Plakaatboek*, I, 126–87.

7 Van der Chijs, *Plakaatboek*, I, 472–594.

8 Van der Chijs, *Plakaatboek*, IX.

9 Van der Chijs, *Plakaatboek*, I, 474f.

10 Van der Chijs, *Plakaatboek*, II, 152f.

11 De Jonge, *Opkomst*, IV, cxxxviii–cxli; H.T. Colenbrander and W.Ph. Coolhaas, *Jan Pietersz. Coen: Bescheiden omtrent zijn bedrijf in Indië*, 7 vols (The Hague, 1919–52) I, 534, 555, 574.

12 Van der Chijs, *Plakaatboek*, I, 461–4.

13 Colenbrander, *Coen*, I, 731f.

14 F. Valentijn, *Oud en Nieuw Oost-Indiën . . .*, 5 vols (Dordrecht and Amsterdam, 1724–6) IV, pt 1, 248.

15 Colenbrander, *Coen*, I, 555.

16 Colenbrander, *Coen*, IV, 529.

17 Colenbrander, *Coen*, IV, 736–8.

18 Colenbrander, *Coen*, I, 795f.; IV, 602f.; De Jonge, *Opkomst*, IV, cxli, 280f.; V, 2–3.

19 De Jonge, *Opkomst*, V, liii.

20 Colenbrander, *Coen*, IV, 530; see for the school: *Oud Batavia*, 2 vols (Batavia, 1922) I, 51.

21 J.K.J. de Jonge, 'Geschiedkundig onderzoek omtrent de vroeger genomen proeven van volkplanting in de Nederlandsche Oost-Indische bezittingen', in *Verslag aan den koning, uitgebragt door de staats-commissie . . . betreffende Europeesche kolonisatie in Nederlandsch Indië* (The Hague, 1858) 136, 152.

22 J.L. Blussé van Oud-Alblas, *Strange Company: Chinese Settlers, Mestizo Women and the Dutch in VOC Batavia* (Dordrecht, 1986) 161; *Oud Batavia*, I, 125f.

23 Blussé, *Strange Company*, 162. I agree with Blussé when he says in n. 5 that 'Indian' in this context of course meant Asian.

24 De Jonge, *Opkomst*, V, 196; J. Gelman Taylor, *The Social World of Batavia: European and Eurasian in Dutch Asia* (Madison, 1983) 14.

25 See for instance articles 40 and 354 which were changed in 1927, and art. 284 pt 3, which was added in 1896.

26 Van der Chijs, *Plakaatboek*, I, 546 (Statutes of Batavia); IX, 407 (art. 16 New Statutes of Batavia).

27 D.G. van der Keessel, *Praelectiones iuris hodierni ad Hugonis Grotii introductionem ad iurisprudentiam Hollandicam, Voorlesinge oor die hedendaagse reg na aanleiding van De Groot se 'Inleiding tot de Hollandse rechtsgeleerdheyd'*, 6 vols (Amsterdam and Cape Town, 1961–75) 2, 30, 2; see also H. de Groot, *Inleidinge tot de Hollandsche Rechts-geleerdheid* (The Hague, 1631[1]; last edition Leiden, 1965) II, 30, 2. The text is translated with brief notes and a commentary by R.W. Lee, *The Jurisprudence of Holland*, 2 vols (Oxford, 1926–36).

28 *Groot-placaet-boek*, II, cols 2633–6; Van der Chijs, *Plakaatboek*, II, 340–3. The Charter was proclaimed at Batavia in 1662.

29 For the Orphan Chamber in the Dutch East Indies see H.C. Gall, 'De weeskamer in Nederlands-Indië 1624–1848. Aspecten van haar uitsluiting bij testament', in *Tombola: Acht rechtshistorische loten* (Leiden, 1988) 25–39. For the instructions for the Orphan Chamber see Van der Chijs, *Plakaatboek*, I, 173–87 (1625); 513–25 (Statutes of Batavia); IX, 209–37 (New Statutes of Batavia).

30 Articles 132 and 133.

31 Van der Chijs, *Plakaatboek*, III, 140, 421; IV, 168; V, 642f.; X, 276; *Oud Batavia*, II, 3 n. 2.

32 Van der Chijs, *Plakaatboek*, III, 350; IV, 6; V, 598; VIII, 768f.; *Oud Batavia*, I, 318; J. Mooij, *Bouwstoffen voor de geschiedenis der protestantsche kerk in Nederlandsch-Indië*, 3 vols (Weltevreden and Batavia, 1927–31) III, 637; Gelman Taylor, *The Social World of Batavia*, 83–5.

33 Van der Chijs, *Plakaatboek*, I, 583–6 (Statutes of Batavia); IX, 154–85 (New Statutes of Batavia).

34 V.I. van de Wall, *Vrouwen uit den Compagnie's tijd* (Amersfoort, 1923) 175–87; F. de Haan, *Priangan: De Preanger-Regentschappen onder het Nederlandsch Bestuur tot 1811*, 4 vols (Batavia, 1910–12) I, pt 2, 26f.; W.Ph. Coolhaas and J. van Goor, *Generale missiven van Gouverneurs-Generaal en Raden aan Heren XVII der Verenigde Oostindische Compagnie*, 9 vols (The Hague, 1960–88) VII, 761f.; VIII, 30, where Neeltje's surname is Hoek.

35 For the prohibited degrees see Van der Chijs, *Plakaatboek*, I, 538f. (Statutes of Batavia); IX, 83–5 (articles 5–13 of New Statutes of Batavia).

36 Van der Chijs, *Plakaatboek*, I, 541 (Statutes of Batavia); IX, 87 (art. 25 of New Statutes of Batavia).

37 Permission given by the Governor-General and his Council on 1 August 1721, cf. Van der Chijs, *Plakaatboek*, IV, 152; A.S. de Blécourt and H.F.W.D. Fischer, *Kort begrip van het oud-vaderlands burgerlijk recht* (Groningen, 1967) 90.

38 See note 29 above.

39 Blussé, *Strange Company*, 172–259; Van de Wall, *Vrouwen uit den Compagnie's tijd*, 61–73.

40 Blussé, *Strange Company*, 175f.

41 J. Crawfurd, *History of the Indian Archipelago*, 3 vols (Edinburgh and London, 1820) I, 147.

42 Valentijn, *Oud en nieuw Oost-Indiën*, I, pt 2, 323f., 391; II, pt 2, 220f.; III, pt 1, 57; pt 2, 91; IV, pt 1, 302–4, 306; Van de Wall, *Vrouwen uit den Compagnie's tijd*, 91–111.

43 For the notes of the Church Council see Mooij, *Bouwstoffen*. In this section separate notes have not been made in the case of general remarks, which are found *passim* in the Church Council's notes.

44 Mooij, *Bouwstoffen*, I, 103f.

45 *Oud Batavia*, I, 315; Mooij, *Bouwstoffen*, I, 784; Gelman Taylor, *The Social World of Batavia*, 60.

46 Mooij, *Bouwstoffen*, I, 284f.

47 Mooij, *Bouwstoffen*, I, 326.

48 Mooij, *Bouwstoffen*, I, 319f., 331, 379.

49 Mooij, *Bouwstoffen*, I, 211f., 225, 248f., 257f., 260, 277f., 391, 438, 463f.

50 The author wishes to thank Enid Perlin-West for editing her English text and René Lombarts for his critical remarks. I also draw attention to the contribution by Dieneke Hempenius-van Dijk, 'Widows and the Law', [this vol., ch. 5]. In my contribution no separate references are made to it.

7

WOMEN WITHOUT MEN

Widows and spinsters in Britain and France in the eighteenth century

Olwen Hufton

The history of women continues to be a growth industry. In 1982, when this chapter was conceived, I lamented that relatively little attention had been given by historians to widows and spinsters and that one might go so far as to say that women had been largely examined through their reproductive capacities and their sexuality. The family has been the Atlas upon whose giant shoulders the world of women's history has reposed. We have echoed Richard Steele when he said that a woman is 'a Daughter, a Sister, a Wife and a Mother . . . no other than an additional part of the species'.[1] In so far as all women were daughters, a majority became wives and mothers, and many were sisters, one cannot fault Steele. All women lived in societies in which marriage and motherhood were regarded as the norm, spinster-hood and infertility as a blight, and in which the notion of the family economy, of the family as a composite working unit permitting the sustenance of the whole, was axiomatic. Outside the family was apparently some kind of twilight existence for women. *Hors de la famille*, *point de salut* was the pithy phrase recently used by Nicole Castan in the conclusion of her brilliant exposé of female criminality in eighteenth-century Languedoc.[2] The women with whom she was concerned – thieves, prostitutes and confidence tricksters – were recruited from cohorts of spinsters and widows for the most part outside the protective influence of the family.

Since 1982 the widow, if not the spinster, has received greater attention without becoming a major focus of study. The remarrying widow in particular has been looked at by demographers and social historians and for the sixteenth and seventeenth centuries in particular, new work has been done on the relationship between the widow and the guild to which her husband belonged. However, there has been no attempt as yet at either a national or a comparative international overview. The recent *History of Women in the West* [Harvard University Press, 1992] passed over widows and spinsters without comment. This absence legitimates an updating of my original article by a more extensive bibliography and an indication of where new work has been done.[3]

Richard Wall's observation still remains true. 'The extent to which women head households, live entirely alone or never marry are clearly key elements of the social structure of any society. It is somewhat surprising, therefore, to find that the phenomena have attracted very little attention in comparison with the attention given, for example, to the notion of the stem family.'[4]

My first intention was to entitle this exploration 'Women Alone', but on reflection I became convinced that such a title would be misleading. One's family of origin shaped one's potential for living and working; one's whole working life, whether one married or not, was coloured by notions of the family. For some the family was an albatross draped around their necks, and few achieved solitude in a world where the poor lived crowded together and the rich had chains of familial dependants.

To confine one's observations to France and the British Isles in the eighteenth century may be unduly to limit generalizations which apply to many European societies over a longer period. It is clear that there is a very long history of social attitudes towards spinsters and independent women which historians of witchcraft, of mysticism, and of the Spanish and Portuguese Inquisition are in process of unfolding for the sixteenth and seventeenth centuries; there is enough to suggest some continuity of attitudes.[5] However, this tentative essay in reconstruction aims at exploring possible sources and lines of development which have revealed themselves while the author was in pursuit of different themes of specialist research. The kind of material used is largely that of poor law and crime records, household listings, and memoirs. Any eighteenth-century scholar must be aware that the period sees the emergence in literature of the spinster as a stereotype – one to be despised, pitied and avoided as a sempiternal spoilsport in the orgy of life. I shall on the whole be sparing with fictional creation because the problem with literary sources is their rapidly changing nature. The novel is an eighteenth-century creation precluding comparison with earlier work and we are safer, for the moment, to eschew the lively and dangerous for what we can know in the way of solid fact.[6]

DEMOGRAPHY

Firstly, what do the demographers tell us about the numbers of permanent spinsters and widows in the eighteenth century? The short answer is not a great deal but enough to make us think hard because there is a significant difference between the French and British experience over the century.[7] Without lingering on different demographic techniques or on their relative plausibility or limitations, let us say that demographers have chosen to identify the never-married person as someone above the age of 50 who died celibate. (Though the probability of marriage for the spinster over 30 was remote, marriage was far from unknown.) The work of the demographers can only understate the incidence of spinsterhood. Dupâquier's summary for France says that evidence points to 7% of the generation born 1660–64, 6.6% of that born 1690–91, 8.5% of that born 1720–24, and 14% of that born 1785–9 as being permanently celibate. Dupâquier does not assess the widow stock in the population but says of the first half of the eighteenth century that a woman widowed in the age group 20–29 had about a 67% chance of remarriage compared with an 80% chance for a widower in the same age range. For the age range 30–39, 46% of widows (72% of widowers) would remarry; widows in the age group 40–49 had a 20% chance (widowers, 52%). Other assessments have placed the widow stock in the population at about 12–14%.[8] The message is a doubling of those who could not expect to marry over the period and some decline in the percentage of widows who could expect to remarry.[9]

British demographers, by different methods, tell a different story for England. Never-married persons (unfortunately not distinguished by sex) reached a high point among the cohorts born in the late seventeenth century. Of those born in 1671, 16–18% would not marry, after which time the figures steadily declined. The lowest proportions occur among the cohorts entering marriage in the second half of the eighteenth century (7, 10%). Wrigley and Schofield use Never-Married Persons' (NMPs) proportions as an important factor in determining population trends: 'Marriage changes explain the great bulk of the remarkable spurt in population growth rates in eighteenth-century England. Age at marriage fell and with it the proportion of men and women who never married.'[10]

Wrigley and Schofield and a formidable series of historians and political economists seek to explain these changes by reference to real-wage performance. Though there is some lag in the correlation, very crudely their important message is that *permanent celibacy recedes in times of rising real wages and the same conditions lower the age at marriage*. It grows in times of falling real wages. The difference in the British and French record can by extrapolation be explained by differences in the economic condition of the labouring sector. Falling real wages in late ancien régime France both pushed up the age of marriage and multiplied the number of never-married persons.

French regional studies point to enormous variation in the incidence of widows and permanently celibate people in the population at any one time. Merley, for example, in a study of the Haute Loire using household listings referring to six villages, shows that on the eve of the Revolution 7–16% of the heads of households were widows and 2–17% spinsters over the age of 25. We should note that the highest numbers of widows and spinsters are found in the *same villages* (Saint Berain, Saint-Pal-en-Chalençon).[11] Household listings of certain parishes in Le Puy, capital of the Haute Loire, point to spinster and widow heads of households reaching 25%. Percentages in Lyons, the only substantial textile city which has received close scrutiny, appear slightly higher.[12] On very random evidence, the Languedocian scene was quite variegated with some of the villages of the littoral producing single figure percentages, rising with the movement of the land to figures in the late teens for the hills.[13] We have a mere nine household listings for Britain stretching from the 1690s to the 1790s. From them, Wall extrapolates that 9–14% of households were headed by widows and spinsters over the age of 25, with the greatest frequency found with women between the ages of 30 and 54. Widows are more likely to head households than spinsters: 462 spinsters and 608 widows in Lichfield in 1695; 169 spinsters and 348 widows in Stoke in 1701; 132 spinsters and 263 widows at Corfe Castle in 1790.[14] These are the only three examples offering detailed information but they give Wall sufficient courage to posit that the percentage of women heading households (not counting those living in someone else's house) as widows or non-married persons changed little from pre-industrial society to twentieth-century society until the post-war period. These examples also help us to appreciate that in looking at spinsters and widows we are dealing with a *significant minority*, larger in Britain than in France at the beginning of our period, but the reverse by the end.[15]

Demographers obviously concentrate upon the behaviour of the masses as that which determines population trends. Little demographic work is yet class-specific. Definitive spinsterhood is viewed as an attribute dependent upon economic factors. When economic growth lagged behind population growth, the result was more spinsters. Society did not make available to a proportion of its young people the means to set themselves up and to constitute a viable family economy. In practical terms this meant a failure on the part of a girl or her family to put something away to constitute a dowry and of a young man to demonstrate similar financial strength. Both were left without a partner, but the celibate male could command wage levels and employment outlets which far outstripped those of the celibate female. Female wages were not generally calculated with an independent existence in mind, whereas, if one could get work, male wages were. Falling real wages produced more spinsters and the increased number of spinsters were forced to make out in progressively more difficult circumstances. Demographers have concentrated on the sacrifice under such circumstances of their reproductive capacities. Social historians must also be conscious of the deterioration in their lot as spinsters. Wages which fell from already low levels made survival more difficult; yet they had to survive.

Aristocratic spinsters

Hollingsworth, Thomas, and Patricia Otto have made important contributions to class differential demography in their studies of the marriage behaviour of the British aristocracy.[16] In Britain, aristocratic spinsterhood would appear to have been rare during the seventeenth century, but throughout the eighteenth it maintained a level in the region of 25% rising to 30% among the daughters of the Scottish aristocracy. The behaviour of aristocratic women was therefore in direct contrast to the popular trend. Why this might be so needs careful explanation. Patricia Otto points to more women exercising an option on whether to marry or not; she cites the case of Louisa Stuart who clearly had her chances but chose instead the single state. A formidable body of historians from Lawrence Stone to Ralph Trumbach insists that aristocratic marriage in the eighteenth century was based on choice with reference to affection and that expectations of a caring relationship were enhanced. If we accept this generalization (and the evidence for doing so exists at least at an impressionistic level for the aristocracy), we must not forget the older school of economic historians who pointed out that the cost of marriage portions rose in the eighteenth century and hence that greater wealth as well as affection was expected before a marriage contract was drawn up.[17] In this highly materialistic environment, parents could only bestow upon a limited number of daughters a substantial endowment. Those in receipt of a large portion would marry, those who were not probably would not. Whereas younger sons (able to build up an income in the army, church, the law, imperial service, or the East India company) would take a wife from the middle classes, aristocratic girls did not usually marry out of their class. That decision may have been one of conscious choice (a woman assumed her husband's status) or restricted opportunity. The recognition that so many of these women existed prevents us from a too-wholehearted commitment to the idea of love rather than wealth as a prerequisite for matrimony. Pounds and shillings remained primary considerations in the marriage market and the girls who may have had, according to the sentiments' school, a warmer and more nurturing childhood, could find themselves with few prospects in their twenties other than a guaranteed livelihood from the estate and a modest dwelling at a requisite distance from the newly embellished main house.

Working-class spinsters

Among the working classes, few girls were born with spinsterhood stamped on their brows. Let us start with the model of the country girl who came into town in adolescence in the hope of accumulating a small capital sum, a dowry, which would contribute towards the hiring and stocking of a farm on marriage or, if the couple remained in the town, towards setting up the pair in business. We think of married women, the alumnae of domestic service, as farmers' wives, as engaged in the distributive trades, in cookshop or bakery, tavern or restaurant, in small industrial enterprises in which the woman was both worker and organizer of resident adolescent labour (such as she herself had been), or as worker in the clothing trades. We know that, as such, there was little chance for her to improve her material lot: the success stories of women in business are restricted to a handful of women in any capacity and these success stories are usually closely associated with the performance of the husband or father. What, then, was the lot of the unmarried servant girl approaching her thirties who might have failed in the dowry stakes by interruptions in her period of labour?

Domestic service where physical strength for fetching and carrying was obviously at a premium was par excellence for the young and unmarried, but there were households, usually of the more substantial variety, in which the older female domestic could find a niche. These were specialist maids – the nurserymaid who had proved herself capable and had graduated to nurse or nanny, girls who had proved themselves able hairdressers or who had grown up as maids to young aristocratic girls and continued as their personal maids on marriage, cooks – though in the most substantial households these were men and girls of long service to whom a family felt a commitment. There were households which actually preferred the older woman. For example, the *Etats de Population* for 1796 at Bayeux show the households of lawyers and professional men to have both an older woman (between 30 and 50) and a young one (between 15 and 25) as resident domestics. It was probably important for such a family to have a reliable personage, permanently neat and orderly, who could take and deliver messages and present a more distinguished image of the household to callers than a raw young girl. The advertisements in the British newspaper press show that such women 'housekeepers' were in some demand.[18] If one turns to account books and diaries it becomes only too apparent why those who could afford such an alternative should do so and also that those deemed to have the requisite attributes (sobriety, honesty, reliability and skill) were at something of a premium. One might cite the account of Mrs Patrick Savage of County Down who, after hiring a series of young Irish girls who had never seen a staircase, who stole the port, and who ruined the family linen, took to employing older women (at a higher cost). Although some of these proved irregular (through the demon drink) or answered advertisements for better jobs or disappeared to bring up the orphaned family of a widowed brother, Mrs Savage was, on the whole, more satisfied.[19] What happened when such women were past work? Mrs Savage never had to face such a problem, but the English gentry commanded the almshouses and the French nobility could by a reasonably modest settlement contrive admission for the respectable aged servant of good moral reputation in an Hôpital Général.[20] The clergy could only employ women *beyond* child-bearing years under post-Tridentine convention (so as to avoid scandal), and so in every French parish the priest's physical well-being rested with a pious, upright spinster or widow of autumnal years.[21]

The housekeeper of a substantial establishment was frequently of much higher social origins than the rest of the servants. Some came into positions having been widowed or having cared for a distinguished elderly relative. The clergyman's unmarried daughter who cared for an ecclesiastic in his declining years might well progress into the role of housekeeper in later years.[22] To a degree, the entry of such women curtailed mobility in the servant sector.

There existed, then, within domestic service some scope, if far from sufficient, for the spinster provided she had the right references, a reasonable appearance, good health, and the ability and willingness to spend her life in someone else's service. The wages she could command were higher than those of her younger counterpart and were paid at stipulated periods of the year, but they reflected the fact that she was lodged and fed. She had a family substitute.

Outside domestic service, the great problem for single working women was the inadequacy of the female wage which provided little more than a basic personal food ration. Without wishing to simplify the complex factors which determined wage levels, an obviously important consideration was the preparedness of women with a roof above their heads (i.e. married women, daughters living at home) to work for a pittance which did not allow for lodging, heating and lighting.[23] This clearly posed a problem for the women who did not have this support. Different kinds of women could have been in such a position: spinners, lace-makers, silk workers (*dévideuses, tireuses, liseuses de desseins*), glovemakers who at the end of a residential period as young girls had not produced much in the way of a capital sum; textile workers, daughters who had no dowry, who could not find someone to take them on for their skill alone, or who on their parents' death could not, or were unwilling to, stay under the roofs of brothers and relatives. All these could be found in what I shall call 'spinster clustering'.

Spinster clustering

'Spinster clustering' is the grouping together of women (in twos, threes and fours) to rent some kind of accommodation where they could share costs of heating and lighting and the time spent at market, in food preparation, fetching wood and water, or picking up and delivering work. I first became aware of this practice in looking at the lace-makers of the Velay, but it is also evident if one turns to the *vingtième* lists (which tax income on property and sometimes detail how the property is divided and income gained), *dénombrements de feu* (which list householders or sharing householders), and more impressionistic evidence such as *déclarations de grossesse*. [24] Indeed the tendency for unmarried women and widows to group together in this way may account for their uneven distribution in the villages of the Velay and the Bessin. In addition, there were obviously more accessible villages which the lace-merchants visited more regularly and which permitted women a steadier income than those off the beaten track.

The women who were thus established were fully accomplished workers. The young novice producing simpler pillow lace was better advised to learn her craft in Le Puy, where a philanthropic establishment (Les Béates) gave free dormitory accommodation to a girl whose labours scarcely made her self-supporting. As she became more accomplished and earned something, the establishment helped her to accumulate her earnings to constitute a small dowry, but the vicissitudes of the lace business were such that this could be very small, and as a girl reached her late twenties she hardly qualified for the institutional support the lace-maker dormitories gave. However, unless she joined the service of Les Béates, and if marriage for whatever reason was not forthcoming, there was little hope of a viable existence unless she could cut her costs by sharing with other women. It is interesting that Angus MacKay in his study of Spanish society in the fifteenth century finds similar evidence of spinster clustering.[25]

We also find a similar situation in Beauvais and Lyons. A *servante chez un ouvrier en soie* had no incentive to return to her mountain village of origin *without* a dowry earned by twelve to fourteen years of hard labour. She might by her late twenties command a range of talents within the silk industry (*dévideuse, tordeuse*, even *liseuse de desseins*) which, provided the industry was reasonably buoyant, made her employable on a daily-wage basis, even if she would not command wage levels to make her fully independent. The conditions in which resident young *servantes* in the silk industry lived – sleeping in cupboards and under looms – with the employer, his family, and an apprentice or so, *all* sharing one or two rooms, may again have accelerated a girl's wishes to exchange this environment as she advanced in years. Similarly the daughter of less substantial masters who lived at home in her parents' lifetime and worked in silk but might not have anything in the way of a dowry and might not have found a marriage-partner could find herself working for her brother and sister-in-law but be reluctant to live with them. Hence the clustering of older, unmarried women in some of Lyons' *quartiers*.[26]

We also find groups of women immigrants from nearby villages over the usual marriageable age hiring a room – frequently a cellar – in Lille and Troyes and working at cotton spinning.[27] In Paris such clustering was not confined to industrial workers; older women of varying *métiers* – street pedlars of haberdashery, combs, and pins, laundresses, staymakers, and button-makers – frequently shared rooms, even in shifts, on a communal basis. A study in Carrick-on-Suir in Ireland in 1799 shows that widows accounted for a fifth of the female population above the age of 20 and that every third person living in a house was a widow living most often with another widow.[28] For some, it must have been the only alternative, a family substitute.

Mother and daughter

An alternative to clustering is the association of widowed mother and daughter. Whereas Wall did not locate spinster clustering in his nine English household listings, this association was common. A woman of restricted earning power was likely to keep her daughter at home beyond the usual age of marriage so that the pair could be mutually sustaining (though emancipating her son). This cut off from the daughter the means of ever putting anything by and multiplied the odds on her being a permanent spinster. Of Wall's widows, 60 per cent lived with one of their children, usually a daughter, and the two pooled their earnings and tried to make out.[29] When the widow died the spinster daughter was largely at the mercy of her brothers or had to join another 'spinster network'. There is some evidence to suggest that the odds on a widow's daughter ending up a spinster were multiplied.

It is virtually impossible, as yet, to know whether proto-industrialization accelerated the trend for single women above a certain age to seek each other's society rather than live in a family network. Industry was, above all, based upon the family as a working unit which had not made a total breach with the land. Alone, neither agricultural nor industrial income sufficed to sustain the family and female wage rates in particular would not permit an independent existence. Industrialization reduced the need for a dowry and brought down the marriage age, in some places.[30] It may have reduced the numbers of spinsters in the community, but it did not proffer much scope to the woman who did *not* have a husband or father or a brother able or willing to do the ploughing or heavy work

131

involved in keeping a smallholding. A group of older women unable financially to hire a cottage with a strip of land or physically to work it might, very plausibly, be driven towards a cheap room and somewhat higher wages in town.

Prostitution

Criminal records, *maréchaussée* reports on prostitution, and the *déclarations de grossesse*, particularly relative to women above the age of 25, all bear witness to the problems of the unmarried woman seeking to maintain herself outside a family setting.[31] In periods of textile slump, wages could dry up. A protracted period of sickness or a debility like arthritis or the failing eyesight which plagued the lace-maker as she approached 40, could see her hungry and resourceless. Female criminality pivots on two issues – prostitution and petty theft. The archetypal recruit to prostitution as far as qualitative evidence is concerned is the dismissed servant girl with an unwanted pregnancy on her hands or one shown the door by an employer in some financial straits himself, followed by the textile worker in slump or hard times. If we turn to the revelatory reports of le Noir, *lieutenant de police* in Paris, we find a wonderful sociological analysis of the vice trade. Prostitutes, he told his men, can be divided into three categories: the maintained mistress under the protection of, and supported by, a man who could afford the luxury; girls in bawdy houses under the direction of a Madame who was known to the police and in control of the activities of her girls; and the street walker catering for her clientèle on her own premises, who would probably operate from a tavern. The police should concentrate their efforts on driving the third category out of existence, he said; the other two need not concern them. The activities of the police therefore tended to drive the prostitute into the institutional setting of the bawdy house. Here, though she shared her profits when trade was buoyant, she had some measure of economic protection, being fed when it was slack. The more hard-headed girl who was fortunate enough to have escaped a sexually transmissible disease may even have progressed to the role of Madame. What we know about the vice traffic of Paris and London in the eighteenth century suggests that it was in the control of women, though there were obviously taverns and rooming houses where keeper and concierge were prepared to tolerate the practice for a consideration.[32]

Single women from our lowest socioeconomic grouping are also found involved in what I once described as an economy of expedients, multiple-makeshifts which together permitted some kind of existence and which may have been the means whereby the greater part of the population lived in the eighteenth century. The combinations defy enumeration within a restricted space: strawplaiters who were hoers, weeders, and harvesters at stages of the year; salters of herring who were also kelpers and stocking-knitters; silk workers who made fireworks in their spare time; Mrs Phelps's London and Leicester outworkers (silk spinners and seamstresses) who made condoms and dildoes to order. Such examples look picturesque, though there was little of the picturesque in their living conditions. One could multiply them to infinity but demonstrate little more than that older single women living together, with an aged parent, or with a widowed or debilitated brother, are to be found in every town or village, making do as best they could. Their difficulties are made manifest above all in Speenhamland lists, or in those of *bureaux de charité.*

THE WIDOW AND THE WIDER FAMILY

How did their condition compare with that of the widow in analogous circumstances? There are similarities, but there are also some subtle and important differences. When her husband died, the widow was part of a family economy of varying degrees of viability; the critical question was whether her efforts, reinforced by those of her children, her family and his family, could be extended to make good the financial or labour deficit occasioned by his death. The widow had allies at various levels which the spinster did not. She had three distinct family groups, his family, her own, and her children (who could, of course, be a liability), all of whom were of *potential* assistance. Moreover, society as a whole could identify, or be made to identify, with her plight. In England the widow could go some way towards sustaining her quest for a viable income by using the threat of throwing her children onto the parish rate. There was also, though it did not invariably count for very much, the notion that the widow inherited her husband's attributes along with his property.[33]

These generalizations have to be tempered by reference to specific jobs and personal circumstances – the recognition that we are dealing with people with few financial reserves. However, one can suggest a few principles. Best tailored to cope with the eventuality of the husband's death was the family economy that pivoted upon the small business, especially the *café-bar, cabaret,* tavern, lodgings house, victualler's shop, cake, pie and muffin production (but not a butcher's shop). The maidservant with an eye for an uncertain future, in command of a few assets as she embarked on marriage, was well advised to push her husband in this direction, even if the business was only an ancillary part of the family economy, as most licensed premises undoubtedly were. What happened on the death of the male partner was that the widow continued to look to the business for support and the children could quickly be trained to play their part. Hence the heavy number of widows' *cabarets* and *buvettes* and of widows' children selling hot pies and sweetmeats from trays in the street. A widow could take on most shops, from the haberdashery to the undertaker's business, but, and the last example is a good case in point, she had to hire some male labour to carry out those aspects of the work beyond her physical resources or those roles which society expected a man to play.[34]

On the Continent, crafts were organized into guilds and the guilds had a number of conflicting attitudes *vis-à-vis* the widow. One was that, on the whole, the widow had a right to some protection. Provided that she could guarantee standards and employed a journeyman to do those aspects of the job which were deemed beyond her physical capacities or skills, she could remain in business. To take a few examples: women, almost everywhere, were permitted to run a printing shop but not to pull the press, which was man's work. Hence from London to Vienna we find the widow's imprimatur on eighteenth-century books.[35] On the other hand, we do not find women goldsmiths, silversmiths, pewterers, clock- or watchmakers (though they might make some of the simpler clock-parts and do engraving), because the skills necessary in these occupations were regarded as something acquired over a long period after a rigorous training.[36] The artificer's guilds were prepared to accept the defunct master's son as apprentice on favourable terms, but otherwise they could not help the widow. It should, however, be pointed out that even where a guild structure did not exist, women did not undertake these crafts, probably because the status of the dead husband was a fairly affluent one and some financial provision for the artificer's widow might exist. One does not find the artificer's widow on paupers' lists. Nor, for what it is worth, is she a literary shabby genteel. Equally striking, we do not find widows in the building or shoemaking trades or running such business in their name. As far as joinery, carpentry, and cabinetmaking are concerned, one can point to physical strength and technique. Most building workers tended to marry innkeepers' daughters because hiring was done from the tavern, and the female partner remained with the drink and catering trades which became her recourse in widowhood.[37] Shoemaking perhaps explains itself by the actual poverty of the trade. Too many sought to make a living from it: shoemakers are invariably found on lists for charity and relief. It was not perceived as a viable alternative for the widow – at least as a full-time job – though there was some scope for ill-remunerated outwork embroidering ladies' slippers, adding buttons, etc., which in some urban and rural areas constituted part of an economy of expedients.

We come to the tricky question of textile production. Outside continental towns, even in some instances where guilds did exist, there was nothing except a plethora of basic economic factors to stop the widow producing in her husband's name. She had to make good his labour in order to reproduce an integral family economy and that meant paying regular wages to someone. Everything we know about the family economy of the modest manufacturer shows how difficult it could be to maintain this. The death of a modest silk manufacturer in Tours or Spitalfields or of a frame stocking-knitter *ipso facto* meant his wife and children had to abandon the family business.[38]

Much better placed was the widow whose husband had had a quasi-official job. There was a tendency for such a job to be regarded as a kind of property in which the incumbent had a stake. Gaolers, janitors, inspectors, poor house and hospital officials of one kind and another had jobs they had either initially purchased or acquired through patronage, and much of the work involved had often been performed by the wife. Indeed, many of the positions would not have been granted to a single man. Running a jail, for example, was not regarded as a full-time job for a man. He was expected to have and indeed, given the way prison services were remunerated, needed to have, some form of ancillary income. (In England this was for a long time the sale of tap to the prisoners and/or some kind of business which could use prison labour.)[39] British Quarter Sessions records teem with information about the widows of such people. Let us take an example from Abingdon in Berkshire in which the death of the keeper of the Bridewell caused his widow to write to the assembled magistrates in defense of her job:

The Humble Petition of Elizabeth Prince, Widow of John Prince late keeper of the House of Correction at Abingdon.
That your Petitioner is left in very distressful circumstances

with family of eight children, the eldest of which being a daughter of only 14 years old and 3 of them have natural infirmities which will probably render them ever incapable of gaining their livelihood.

That your Petitioner's Husband and his Father and Grandfather have been Keepers of the House of Correction at Abingdon for a great number of years and your Petitioner has a brother and a Brother-in-law very well qualified and willing to assist her in the future management of that prison and she can find sufficient security if required for her faithful discharge of the Office of Bridewell Keeper.

Your Petitioner therefore, humbly prays to be continued in the office of Keeper of the House of Correction that she may be thereby able to provide bread for her Family which must otherwise be unavoidably thrown on the parish for maintenance.[40]

This letter, if not a masterpiece of the language, was the work of a woman who had understood the system. She based her petition on the family stake in the job, the available support of her kin group, and the threat of throwing a large family on the poor rate. She did not choose to mention that she had been doing the job over the past couple of months since his death without incident; that the Poor House in Abingdon was being run by a widow, and that her husband died in suspicious circumstances (he was murdered). The widow prevailed – we find her five years later asking for an extra turnkey. Others in a similar position were given a year in which to find a husband or at least a prospective one. In fact, between 1688 and 1775, a little over a quarter of British jails had a female keeper at some point in the period, and this does not take into account cases such as that of an estranged couple in Derbyshire in which he nominally retained the office, but she actually continued to run the business: 'The Gaoler and his wife had agreed for her to have the sole management of the prison, he to have so much a week and take his pleasure.'[41]

Middlesex and Norfolk also employed women, predominantly widows, as 'matrons'. In Middlesex, they had responsibility for lying-in women; in Norfolk, for sick prisoners and those dependent on charities. Wherever a charity was involved, a widow was likely to be the liaison; where urban bridewells were concerned, the main clientele tended to be night-walkers sentenced to hard labour and a 'matron's services' were particularly useful.[42] Keeping a widow and her brood off the parish rate was obviously a consideration, and authorities took full advantage of such jobs as they could bestow. Even food-fetching when the prisoner could not find a relative to do the job tended to be a widow's monopoly. Many county jails offered bread and water to the prisoners and those who could pay had food cooked outside the prison, in some instances by relatives, but sometimes by women who contracted to perform the service and were approved by the magistrates.

In spite of society's greater preparedness to countenance the widow in a 'man's' job, we must recognize that the situation of the working-class widow could be far more difficult than that of the spinster if she had young children to support. Here again the records of the criminal courts come to our assistance. In both Britain and France in the eighteenth century we are now aware that periods of price rises (either a run of bad harvest years or the kind of longer-term economic crisis such as that which characterised the two closing decades of the ancien régime) dramatically multiplied the numbers of widows and older single women (above the age of 25) appearing before the courts, in the second case perhaps for prostitution as well. Indeed, Nicole Castan tells us that in France the widow is the only woman represented in crime statistics in the same proportion as she is represented and appears in the population as a whole, and she probably constitutes an even greater part of the 'hidden face'.[43] This was because the community's notions of *honnêteté* (fair play) restricted the number of suits. It was not deemed right for an individual to pursue a struggling woman, particularly for the theft of food. Admittedly such fine distinctions applied more to rural Languedoc than to Paris. The same is broadly true in Britain. Even if brought to court, magistrates could show a tolerance to the widow by reducing the offence or by letting the fine ride.[44] In Britain this could be done almost systematically. Hay and Beattie demonstrate a substantial increase in the 1760s and 1780s in 'widows' thefts' of food – crimes which in more normal times would have been prosecuted as grand larceny punishable by a heavy fine and penal servitude. By reducing the crime to petty larceny and tolerating a delay in the payment of the fine (done on a large scale by Staffordshire and Surrey magistrates), the community was spared increasing numbers of parish dependants whose widowed mothers were serving a sentence. At the same time, a warning had been delivered to the woman.[45] In France periodic round-ups of cattle illegally pastured in domanial woods usually revealed the widow and her goat.[46] She did not escape sentence, but the fine was allowed to ride, and costs were not usually entered in the records. In such a way consciences were salved, but one might reasonably question how far the widow's problems were resolved.

THE MIDDLE CLASSES

Let us turn now towards the spinsters and widows of more middle-class origins: women who did not live with the threat of destitution, who could for various reasons 'make out', but who faced very specific and complex problems. Ask any historian of the early modern period about the spinster in rural society and you will be directed firmly towards the testament (or the *acte d'avancement de succession*) in which provision is made, if only by recommendation to the heir, for the daughter who never married.[47] Often such women looked after aged parents, travelled to care for sick relatives, or stepped in to care for the orphaned in the family. In her own old age, she might well be tended by a niece whose lifestyle was a replica of her own. The support of parents and in due course brothers, sisters, nephews, nieces, epitomized a range of services which the welfare state has struggled in vain to make a public concern. Women without husbands were nurses, companions, housekeepers, mother's help, foster parents. Alone, few women from this sector generated new wealth. They lived on income from property which found its way back to the family on death. They were expected to live piously and modestly – does literature provide us with the example of a profligate maiden aunt? With the growth of female literacy, such women were often prolific letter-writers, keeping scattered members of the family informed about the minutiae of family affairs. In the towns, some helped with family businesses. Historians of women have emphasized the lack of female entrepreneurial activity, yet we should look carefully at the evidence of memoirs and letters and try to reconstruct lifestyles. How many spinsters were like Mary McCracken of Belfast, daughter of a linen merchant, who had her own little enterprise of delivering flax to outworker spinners, while keeping her father's books, tending him in sickness, supporting her brother in his political activities for a united Ireland, and involving herself in philanthropic work?[48]

If one takes the membership lists of the late-eighteenth-century British and Irish societies for the aid of prisoners and the relief of certain categories of poor, one finds that the middle-class spinster and the widow predominate in the practical execution and organization of relief.[49] In France they are the backbone of the *Dames de la Charité*, pious laywomen who sometimes distributed small charitable bequests, second-hand clothing, and soup to the domiciled sick. We are dealing with societies in which *public* intervention in support of the needy was restricted and private enterprise and effort was the motor of philanthropy. A great deal of that effort was spinster-generated and the historic partnership between the vicar, pastor, priest and his maiden ladies was all significant.

Outside the family, spinster sociability, particularly in the village, focused on the church. No society in the early modern period (and indeed few in the modern period) has permitted the respectable spinster a tavern-based social life, whereas the church erected celibacy into a virtue and provided a framework within which the spinster could have a social existence – as much or as little as her time allowed. Susan Watkins shows a correlation between high spinster density and high levels of religious worship in different regions of nineteenth-century France.[50] Without straying too far into these realms we can point to a growing body of literature demonstrating the particular role of village spinsters (*les demoiselles*) during the Revolution in sheltering refractory priests, organizing clandestine masses, taking risks in holding communal recitations of the rosary, courageously defying exhortations to accept a state religion, and strenuously supporting the refractory church as it emerged from exile and began to reassert itself at the parochial level.[51] Where would the Curé of Ars in his massive clean-up of south-eastern France have been without his *demoiselles* to report on the aberrant, to organize parochial pilgrimages, and to provide the effort behind charitable enterprise?[52]

While there were clearly those for whom the family and the community could provide an existence, equally clearly there were those who for a multiplicity of reasons, economic or psychological, could not or did not look to a family for practical support. Such women might be the dowryless daughters of the lower middle classes, of school teachers, impecunious clergymen, clerks, surgeons or notaries. Our paradigm could be Mary Wollstonecraft or Miss Mitford; it could be girls whose dowries were so meagre they could not aspire to very much and rejected what there was to be had; or it could be women like Hannah More who made a positive decision to stand on their own feet. Miss Mitford and Hannah More are not perfect examples because both ended up supporting their own families. They were women of exceptional talent and hence not representative. But the means whereby they made out, at least in the beginning, are of relevance to our theme. What, asked Mary Wollstonecraft with her brand of devastating logic, can the woman of modest origins expect? She might be a governess, a companion or a mantua-maker.[53]

If Mary Wollstonecraft had been French, Catholic, and part of a cohort reaching adolescence between 1789 and 1801, she could have provided another alternative, the convent. This alternative was the one adopted by thousands of women in France: in 1789 there were 56,000 nuns. Such numbers demand reflection, at a level beyond Diderot's sensationalist approach (which converted the nun into the victim of family greed and, once inside the convent, of surreptitious deviant sexuality as well) or beyond the hagiographical approach (which converts every little sister into an embryonic Thérèse of Lisieux motivated by an unquenchable spiritual flame). One cannot speculate on levels or intensity of faith. I will instead take piety as a given and offer the reminder that one could also be pious *outside* a convent. We should concentrate on a number of basic facts. Throughout the eighteenth century, the total number of recruits to the monastic life was declining – a fact usually attributed to the Enlightenment's assault on conventual life. Yet the decline is detected almost wholly in the male sector and in the contemplative section of the female orders – Benedictines, Carmelites, Visitandines, etc. In contrast, the active orders dedicated to teaching, nursing and what we might loosely call social services (*filles repenties*, orphanages, homes for the elderly) were burgeoning. The Sisters of Charity alone accounted for 15 per cent of all nuns in 1789. They continued to do so in spite of the Enlightenment, the Revolution which dissolved them, drove them into hiding, and even imprisoned them; the nuns, unlike the monks, were not intimidated. They emerged during the Napoleonic period to reassume control of the same service sector. They proliferated and diversified into areas like *crèches* for the working mother or moral vigilance services on the factory floor, until by the second half of the nineteenth century they constituted the bulk of the Catholic clergy (58 per cent of 220,000). Meanwhile, the rest of society was heading along the paths of dechristianization. How do we explain this engaging paradox? Who were the eighteenth- and even nineteenth-century nuns?[54]

They were girls of lower-middle-class origins, though we have no overall idea of how many were urban and how many rural. They had to have on entry into the convent a dowry of 150–400 *livres* which put this way of life beyond the reach of the working-class girl. They were basically literate and, depending on the order they chose, they were opting for a hard if satisfying career.[55] Some worked in isolation in the villages – the sisters who ran the *petites écoles* in the winter only experienced the corporate life for part of the year or in old age. Others sustained a communal life while serving in a hospital or teaching an industrial technique to young girls. Their order assured them subsistence and shelter, companionship, and the feeling they were socially useful. However hard their life – and the demands made were considerable – there was always someone ready to step into their shoes who saw this way of life, for whatever reason, as preferable to marriage or the 'soft' life of the nun dedicated to prayer alone.[56]

It is very difficult to find a 'straight' assessment of the nun and her work although we are getting changes for the better. Historians of literacy and education have tended to stress the limited achievement of the *petites écoles* in the eighteenth century (35 per cent female literacy), though the trend was upwards in the nineteenth century and female education remained nun-controlled.[57] Historians have also stressed the restricted content of the nun's educational package and there has been a long debate associated with the church and state conflict which has coloured the republican and socialist historiographical tradition. Similarly, the nursing sister has been condemned for her ignorance in contrast to the increasing professionalization of the surgeon whose 'progressive' views she resisted.[58] It is also remarkably easy to point to the pitiful inadequacies of church-based welfare agencies in coping with the problems of a rapidly industrializing state and the pernicious effects – because they retarded the day of state social services – of schemes privately organized by women of myopic vision.

The brilliance of debate should not, however, blind us to a number of basic points: first, the professionalization of nursing and teaching of girls and social services in France had to take place within the framework of conventual life. Progress was made within surgery (though until the advent of antisepsis, the results must have been minimal) but, as Dora Weiner's profound and sensitive studies show for the Napoleonic record, progress in nursing care and pharmacy services occurred *within* the nursing community of nuns.[59] Hospitals were run on private funds attached to the communities. They could be used for the poorer sectors of society rather than those who could pay surgeon's fees. The nuns represented in every sense the eternal: their order was institutionalized in the hospital whereas surgeons merely came and went and expected payment. This institutional strength protected them against being under the thumb of the male branches of the medical profession. In France on the eve of the Revolution 100,000 people were hospitalized compared with 3000 in England; émigré nuns were shocked at what they found in such British establishments as did exist. Florence Nightingale remarked that if Britain had had the Sisters of Charity there would have been no need for her services.

The second recognition must be that the existence of such institutions soaked up a proportion of middle-class women and would continue to do so until there were alternative opportunities for similar employment in France. It should be noted that British women from Mary Astell, who promoted such a prospect, to Lady Mary Wortley Montagu, men such as Bishop Burnett and even writers like Samuel Richardson lamented the lack of the kind of association and professional outlet for the middle-class women in Protestant England that the convent bestowed on the Continent.[60] British women, lacking this alternative, turned to similar work (teaching, serving as companions to the elderly, infirm and lonely who could afford their services), but they lacked both the companionship and the long-term security of belonging to a community as well as the strength and status which membership in an order endowed. Nightingale was at the mercy of men in a way that a sister of charity never was. The obverse side of this was of course that the hard route followed by the British middle-class spinster who had to find a job to support herself would eventually in the late-nineteenth and early twentieth centuries allow her to secure professional status without having to take on the church as well as the state. But that is another story.

THE TEACHING SPINSTER

From the eighteenth century on in Britain we become increasingly aware of the growth, both in terms of supply and demand, in the numbers of women, especially girls, employed to educate young children, as governess either in the child's home or in school.[61] The period witnesses the rise of the girls' boarding school and its extension beyond that of a dumping ground for the illegitimate offspring of the wealthy to a place catering to a broader spectrum of girls. It sees also the full flowering of the charity school. The word 'governess' changed over the period from meaning anyone employed by an institution to care for young children to meaning someone privately employed in a home, as distinct from the teacher who now became the one employed by the institution. Whatever the significance of such a change, the main realization must be that the teaching sector (it would be unwise to label it a profession at this juncture), for girls especially, was monopolized by women of various degrees of literacy and talent of lower middle-class origins, with few financial resources; they proliferated as female education, at least of a very basic kind, became accepted as essential. Given demographic growth which produced the employees, the increase in landed and commercial wealth which provided the employers, and the lack of other outlets for the women, who regarded themselves as worthy of something other than menial work with their hands, the governess/teacher group could only multiply. Indeed, given the presence of charity schools and foundations for the children of clergymen and the like of limited income, the system was virtually self-sustaining. The low pay and poor work conditions, enclosing the woman in question in a house in lowly capacity or in an institution, guaranteed an uncontested female dominance of this sector. Women, in short, captured this territory and in the long run this occupation was to prove highly significant because the professionalization of women began in the educational sector. When female education took off in the late nineteenth century it had to achieve reform within an area already dominated by women. Moreover, until the last war, it remained a spinster-dominated sector. The governess/teacher group was also a breeding ground for female militancy; *ab initio* the most vociferous critics of the status quo were the women for whom the family did not provide means for existence. We should note that this situation is firmly rooted in the eighteenth century.

There were plenty of critics (as diverse as Defoe and Diderot) of the content of women's education.[62] Enlightenment thinkers tended to concentrate on the inadequacy of women's education to make women fit intellectual companions for men. A few, and women critics in particular,[63] believed better education would improve women's position in society. The early girls' boarding schools obviously provided much material for criticism. They varied enormously. At one end of the spectrum was the aimiable kind of establishment experienced by Jane Austen at Reading or Miss Mitford in Hampstead – the former run by a jolly widow with a cork leg who invested her late husband's resources in creating a cheerful environment for a score of girls in which academic learning was not at a premium but needlework, drama, French, and a little dancing filled the days.[64] At the other end was the oppressively pious atmosphere of the charity schools and establishments run on a religious basis, the type experienced by the Brontë girls, where mortification of the spirit was the chief object, though they scored some distinguished failures. Inadequate as the educational fare might be, it outstripped the job opportunities.

Jean Hunter, in her article on the eighteenth-century Englishwoman, shows even the *Gentleman's Magazine* to be aware of the problems caused by the lack of career opportunities outside marriage. There were articles suggesting that homes be established for unmarried gentlewomen where, in return for modest food and lodging, the woman would undertake work like spinning, embroidery, lacemaking, and knitting (note the analogy with the convent). They might be expected to produce one-half as much as an ordinary working woman. Another blamed parents for women's problems and suggested that all girls be taught 'the most useful Part of Needlework, all the Art of Economy (Household), writing and Book-Keeping, with enough Dancing and French to give them a graceful and easy Freedom both of Discourse and Behaviour'.[65] (What splendid prospects for an embryonic Mary Wollstonecraft or Emily Brontë!)

We should, of course, acknowledge that in early modern British and European society there was also a dearth of outlets for the educated man without capital who needed patronage for a position in the church or civil service and money for a military commission; in no way, however, does his plight begin to approximate that of the spinster. There was no East India Company for women.

In fact, the only thing to be said in defence of the eighteenth-century status quo was that female education was labour-intensive. Literary memoirs reveal a massive turnover in female staff, a fact confirmed by the newspapers. Schools were created and closed as groups of women, single and widowed, combined to rent premises on credit or by scanty savings sought to emancipate themselves from service in a private house. Education became a minor industry. Some may at some stage have been reabsorbed into their families. Others emerged in print as critics of the system.

Increasing female literacy created new markets for plays, books and tracts, the opportunity for women to write for each other. The odds, however, on gaining a viable income from literary activity were low; though writing could be a fulfilling source of subsidiary income, it scarcely helped the single woman in her short-term search for self-sufficiency. Yet, the fact of women in print, women who had tried to make a living in a hostile world, was without doubt immensely important as a consciousness-raising exercise.

What of the widow? If such a personage inherited little from her husband then there was obviously little to distinguish her from our semi-educated spinster. On the other hand, the widow's jointure gave the aristocratic woman considerable wealth and all codes of law recognized the rights of the widow over the income from her husband's property and profits from his office or business. Her relationship within the family obviously changed. She passed into a directorial capacity of property and children: she was arbiter of her destiny, free from the tutelage of husband or family. She could enjoy her freedom or be pursued in the marriage market. She could even, like Mrs Thrale or the Duchess of Leinster, marry gloriously and defiantly beneath her, making her own personal choice. In the literature of the period – letters, diaries, and tracts – emerges a hysterical obsession among middle- and upper-class males. In the event of their death, would their widows squander their wealth on a gigolo figure who excited their sexual appetites after a lifetime of repression and boredom?[66] There were plenty of disquieting examples around (enough in fact to make one wonder why historians of love and sexual titillation have not looked more closely at the second marriage).[67] The wealthy, merry widow is there in her own right. *Mutilée de guerre*, hardened by experience or made giddy with freedom, one can write her up as one chooses. Alone perhaps among the women who have been my concern, her *monde* was *en rose*.

This cursory analysis of the never-married woman and the widow in eighteenth-century society does not lend itself to ready conclusions. Above all it has pointed to the economic problems of the woman fending for herself in this society and has suggested that if she did not have some family connection she had to find an alternative. Those suggested were spinster clustering, or continuing residential work, domestic service, governess work, teaching in boarding school, the convent, prostitution, and in due course the expectation of a poor-law institution or hôpital général. I hope I have suggested some avenues for further investigation such as Speenhamland, poor law and hospital records, criminality records, correspondence attached to the Quarter Sessions, newspaper advertisements, and the interstitial information embodied in memoirs. I think an important development to note is the prevalence of middle-class widows or spinsters in

education and welfare services because this points to future developments. We should see widows and spinsters in the forefront of
pressures for change from the eighteenth century onwards.

THE ETYMOLOGY OF 'SPINSTER'

In the light of this, we should perhaps end with an etymological
codicil. According to the *Oxford English Dictionary*, the word
'spinster' was not used to denote marital status until the second
decade of the seventeenth century. It was a professional term and
continued to be used as such until the end of the century but, in the
closing decades, it was also used to denote marital status. The first
three decades of the eighteenth century saw the analogy drawn
between 'spinsters' and 'old maid'. In parlance and literature (though
not in legal records, where it denotes the unmarried woman of all
levels of society under a viscounty) the word came to denote an
ageing woman and implied certain pejorative attributes – such as a
narrowness of spirit and a tendency to gossip over the teacups. This
development may in some way be connected with the growth in
numbers of upper-class spinsters and the development of the novel.
Be that as it may, when we consider the degree to which these women
had to construct lifestyles for themselves and were often pushed into
circumstances hardly consonant with their birth and when we note
the struggles of working-class women who had to find some means
of support in a hostile world, then we should be considering how
one changes the meaning of language. In my view at least, the
definition of the word spinster should include heroic attributes to
convey the sense of someone who struggled against odds and social
disapprobation and yet survived and in some cases made the survival
of subsequent generations easier.[68]

NOTES

A superscript number after a date indicates the edition of the work cited

Archives
Archives Départementales Hérault (ADH) C 6765 Plaintes et Placets
Archives Municipales, Bayeux (AMB) F Etats de population, an 4, an 7
Archives Nationales (AN)
Y 12830 Lenoir to Commissioners, November 1778 Berkshire Record Office
(BRO)
1785 Easter Sessions. Quarter Session Roll 205: 'The Humble Petition of
Eliza Prince'

1 R. Steele, *The Spectator* [London] 3 (1950) 70f.

2 N. Castan, *Justice et repression en Languedoc à l'Epoque des Lumières* (Paris, 1980) 235.

3 Amongst new work, J. Dupâquier *et al.* (eds), *Marriage and Remarriage in the Populations of the Past* [London, 1981]; M. Bordeaux, 'Droit et femmes seules. Les pièces de la discrimination', in *Madame ou Mademoiselle? Itinéraires de la solitude féminine, 18e–20e siècles* (Paris, 1984); B.A. Todd, 'The remarrying widow: A stereotype reconsidered', in M. Prior (ed.), *Women in English Society, 1500–1800* (London, 1985); M. Palazzi, 'Abitare da sole. Donne capofamiglia alla fine del settecento', *Memoria* 18 (1986); M. d'Amelia, 'Scatole cinesi: Vedove e donne sole in una società d'ancien regime', ibid.; L.A. Clarkson, 'Life after Death: Widows in Carrick-on-Suir, 1799', in M. MacCurtain and M. O'Dowd (eds), *Women in Early Modern Ireland* (Edinburgh, 1991).

4 R. Wall, 'Woman Alone in English Society', *Annales de Démographie Historique* (1981) 303–16.

5 Important similarities exist, for example, in the work in progress by Angus Mackay of the University of Edinburgh on Spanish *converso* women in the fourteenth and fifteenth centuries and in L. Roper, *The Holy Household: Women and Morals in Reformation Augsburg* (Oxford, 1989).

6 I. Watt, *The Rise of the Novel: Studies in Defoe, Richardson, and Fielding* (London, 1957) 144f.

7 E.A. Wrigley and R. Schofield, *The Population History of England, 1541–1871: A Reconstruction* (London, 1982) 260.

8 This would appear to have been a western European norm in the period (Castan, *Justice et repression*, 235), reaching levels of 11 per cent of the total female population in eighteenth-century Spain where the remarriage of widows was discouraged by the church, cf. R.M. Capel-Martinez, *Muher y sociedad en España (1700–1975)* (Madrid, 1982) 30. In Britain, the percentage in the eighteenth century is usually taken to be lower, in the range of 8–10 per cent: R. Malcolmson, *Life and Labour in England 1700–1780* (London, 1981) 176.

9 Cf. J. Dupâquier, *La population française au XVIIe et XVIIIe siècles* (Paris, 1979) 60f.

10 Wrigley and Schofield, *Population History of England*, 260–3; see also D. Weir, 'Rather Never than Late: Celibacy and Age at Marriage in English Cohort Fertility 1541–1671', *Journal of Family History* 9 (1984) 340–54.

11 J. Merley, 'La Haute Loire de la fin de l'ancien régime aux débuts de la Troisième République', *Cahiers de la Haute Loire* (1974), 51.

12 M. Garden, *Lyon et les Lyonnais au XVIIIe siècle* (Paris, 1970) 670.

13 J.P. Bobo, *Une communauté Languedocienne au XVIIIe siècle* (Master's thesis, Montpellier, 1965); A. Molinier, *Une paroisse du Bas Languedoc, Serignan, 1650–1792* (Master's thesis, Montpellier, 1968); J.M. Oustry, *Démographie, subsistances et aspects socio-économiques de Bédarieux, 1800–1830* (Master's thesis, Montpellier, 1972); C. Bonnafons, *Une paroisse montpelliéraine. Sainte Anne, 1680–1789* (Master's thesis, Montpellier, 1973); Merley, *La Haute Loire*, 51.

14 Wall, 'Woman Alone in English Society', 141.

15 English demographic work has focused heavily upon the village, and it might well be that a close examination of demographic aspects of the town will reveal a larger concentration of widows driven townwards in the search for work or possibilities of a livelihood. In the Le Puy region there appears to be a correlation between high spinster and widow density in the lace-making villages.

16 T.H. Hollingsworth, 'The Demography of the British Peerage', *Population Studies* 8 Supplement (1964); D. Thomas, 'The Social Origins of Marriage Partners of the British Peerage in the Eighteenth and Nineteenth Centuries', *Population Studies* 26 (1972) 99–111; P.C. Otto, *Daughters of the British Aristocracy and Their Marriages in the Eighteenth and Nineteenth Centuries with Particular Reference to the Scottish Peerage* (Dissertation, Stanford, 1974) 283.

17 L. Stone, *The Family, Sex and Marriage in England 1500–1800* (London, 1971); R. Trumbach, *The Rise of the Egalitarian Family: Aristocratic Kinship and Domestic Relations in Eighteenth-Century England* (London, 1978); G.E. Mingay, *The Gentry: The Rise and Fall of a Ruling Class* (London, 1976), is much more interested in younger sons than younger daughters; Otto, *Daughters of the British Aristocracy*, 260–6, 270.

18 For France: AMB. For England: J. Hecht, *The Domestic Servant Class in Eighteenth-Century England* (London, 1956) 26–9.

19 The Ulster antiquary Colin Johnston, 'Flashes from Domestic Life Long Ago', *Irish News*, 18 October, 1961, collected many anecdotes from account books he had in his possession.

20 Hufton, *The Poor of Eighteenth-Century France* (London, 1974) 151.

21 The 'Plaintes et Placets' addressed to the military governor by priests of the diocese of Lodève reveal several incidents of insults to elderly housekeepers about their role in the priest's household (ADH: C6765).

22 Cf. Hecht, *The Domestic Servant Class*, 19. Housekeepers in large establishments were often women of good family, even from the gentry.

23 Hufton, *The Poor of Eighteenth-Century France*, 26–41.

24 Cf. A. Lottin, 'Naissances illégitimes et filles mères à Lille au XVIIIe siècle', *Revue d'Histoire Moderne et Contemporaine* 17 (1970) 278–322. It should be noted that clustering could be a way of life for more affluent women too. For example, at Montcollier House, Belfast, two widows, Mrs Wilson and Mrs McKay, and three spinsters, the Misses Bland, all lived together and shared the housekeeping: Johnston (see note 19 above).

25 I am indebted to Angus Mackay of Edinburgh University for this information.

26 Cf. P. Goubert, *Cent Mille Provinciaux au XVIIe siècle* (Paris, 1968) 339: 'Quant aux femmes seules, filles ou veuves, à peu pres incapables de vivre avec deux ou trois sols par jour, elles se groupaient par deux ou trois dans de minuscules logements, pour diminuer les frais de loyer et de chauffage.'
    The fifth floors (immediately under the roof) in the poorest Lyonnais quarters were leased out to single girls who paid an individual rent. The

greater possibility of clustering in a town than in a country cottage and finding work may have pushed single women more and more towards the town, cf. Garden, *Lyon et les Lyonnais*, 162.

27 Lottin, 'Naissances illégitimes', 318–20.

28 Clarkson, 'Life after Death', 247.

29 Wall, 'Woman Alone in English Society', 314.

30 S. Chassagne, A. Dewerpe and Y. Galupeau, 'Les ouvriers de la manufacture de toiles imprimées d'Oberkampf à Jouy-en-Josas (1760–1815)', *Mouvement Social* 97 (1976) 82f.; S. Chassagne, 'La formation de la population d'une agglomération industrielle Corbeil-Essones (1750–1815)', *Mouvement Social* 95 (1976) 99–102.

31 Hufton, *The Poor of Eighteenth-Century France*, 306–17; Castan, *Justice et repression en Languedoc*, 238f.

32 Literary sources, not least Defoe's *Moll Flanders* (London, 1721–2) and Cleland's *Fanny Hill* (London, 1748–9), suggest a vice trade largely controlled by women.

33 See Malcolmson, *Life and Labour in England 1700–1780*, 176, n. 53, for a good bibliography on the English widow.

34 Good advice books (such as Eliza Heywood, *A Present for a Serving Maid*, London, 1743) encouraged women thus to invest their dowries.

35 Cf. C.J. Mitchell, 'Women in the Book Trades in the Eighteenth Century', Unpublished paper, University of Melbourne, Australia. This is some of the first work to draw upon the new British Library computerized catalogue of eighteenth-century publications and shows that about 50 per cent of publishing houses were run as family businesses in which the woman worked, but 10 per cent were in the hands of women alone, usually widows. I am indebted to Dr Mitchell for allowing me to consult his work.

36 L. Mottu-Weber, 'Apprentissages et économie Genevoise au debut du XVIIIe siècle', *Revue Suisse d'Histoire* 20 (1970) 321–53; N.Z. Davis, 'Women in the Crafts in Sixteenth-Century Lyon', *Feminist Studies* 8 (1982) 65f. (on the role of widows).

37 AMB, an 4. This phenomenon was particularly marked in France.

38 Hufton, 'Women, Work, and Marriage in Eighteenth-Century France', in R.B. Outhwaite (ed.), *Marriage and Society: Studies in the Social History of Marriage* (London, 1981) 196–7.

39 I am indebted to Joanna Innes of Somerville College, Oxford and to Richard Williams of the University of Reading for providing me with the information relative to the running of British jails from their work in progress.

40 Abingdon 31 March 1785 (BRO, 1785; Quarter Session Roll 205).

41 J.C. Cox, *Three Centuries of Derbyshire Annals*, vol. 2 (London, 1890) 28.

42 The notion of women as managers of women, particularly of prostitutes, was also observed in French *dépôts de mendicité*.

43 Castan, *Justice et repression en Languedoc*, 235.

44 Peter King of Clare Hall, Cambridge has found that 15 per cent of all women offenders in Essex were also widows, which bears a precise correlation with the French example. Peter King was particularly

concerned in his work with defining crime as part of the life-cycle experience of certain social sectors, and he depicts female criminality as essentially occurring before marriage and in widowhood.

45 D. Hay, 'War, Death and Theft in the Eighteenth Century', *Past & Present* no. 95 (1982) 120–55; J. Beattie, 'The Criminality of Women in Eighteenth-Century England', *Journal of Social History* 8 (1975) 101–7.
46 In contrast to the poachers and the large-scale illegal pasturers of cattle renowned for their violence, she constituted a minor problem for the seigneurs but an easy arrest for the seigneurial police.
47 Estate papers could be exploited much more effectively than they have been to date to look at the treatment of spinsters and widows. Dr Jill Edwards, who recently classified the Stonor Papers, drew my attention to the potential of this source and my own recent cursory examination of the records of the Ufton Park Estate and the Duke of Wellington's estate, both held by the Museum of English Rural Life, University of Reading, confirms this view.
48 M. McNeill, *The Life and Times of Mary Ann McCracken: 1770–1866* (Dublin, 1960). This book is a remarkable, indeed model, biography of a single woman whose activities may well have been duplicated by several of her friends.
49 McNeill, *Mary Ann McCracken*, 293–6.
50 S.C. Watkins, *Variation and Persistence in Nuptiality: Age Patterns of Marriage in Europe, 1870–1960* (Dissertation, Princeton, 1980).
51 R. Dupuy, 'Les femmes et la contre Revolution dans l'ouest', *Bulletin d'Histoire Economique et Sociale de la Révolution Française* (1980), 61–70; Hufton, 'The Reconstruction of a Church: 1796–1801', in C. Lucas and G. Lewis (eds), *Beyond the Terror* (Cambridge, 1983) 24–5, 28.
52 P. Boutry and M. Cinquin, *Deux pélérinages au XIXe siècle: Ars et Paray-le-Monial* (Paris, 1980). The first two chapters of this work draw important gender differences between the responses of men and women to the work of the Curé of Ars.
53 C. Tomalin, *The Life and Death of Mary Wollstonecraft* (New York, 1974) 41.
54 F. le Brun, *Histoire des Catholiques en France du XVe siècle à nos jours* (Paris, 1980) 216f. (number of nuns), 217 (Benedictines, etc.), 345f. (Sisters of Charity).
55 See Hufton, *The Poor of Eighteenth-Century France*, for a general idea of their work.
56 M. Laget, 'Petites écoles en Languedoc au XVIIIe siècle', *Annales* 26 (1971) 1398–1418.
57 F. Furet and M. Ozouf, *Lire et écrire: l'Alphabetisation des Français de Calvin à Jules Ferry*, vol. 1 (Paris, 1977).
58 C. Bloch, *L'Assistance et l'Etat en France à la veille de la Révolution* (Paris, 1908) 74; M. Foucault, *Naissance de la clinique* (Paris, 1963); Hufton, *Bayeux in the Late Eighteenth Century* (London, 1967) 97; R. Mandrou, 'Un problème de diététique à la veille de la Révolution', *93e Congrès national des sociétés savantes* (Paris, 1971).
59 D. Weiner, 'The French Revolution, Napoleon, and the Nursing

Profession', *Bulletin of the History of Medicine* (1972) 274–305; C. Jones, 'The Filles de la Charité in Hospitals', in *Actes du Colloque International d'Etudes Vincentiennes* (Rome, 1983) 239–82.

60 Cf. F. Smith, *Mary Astell* (New York, 1916); R. Halsband, (ed.), *Complete Letters of Lady Mary Wortley Montague*, vol. 3 (London, 1967) 97; Bishop Burnett, *History of Our Own Time*, vol. 2 (London, 1723–34) 653; S. Richardson, *Clarissa Harlowe*, Everyman edn (London, 1962) 62.

61 It seems surprising that we do not as yet have a major work devoted to the eighteenth-century governess.

62 E. Jacob (ed.), *Women and Society in Eighteenth-Century France* (London, 1979) contains a good selection of views on this theme.

63 Bathusa Makin, *An Essay to Revive the Antient Education of Gentle Women* (London, 1673).

64 W.J. Roberts, *Mary Russell Mitford: The Tragedy of a Blue Stocking* (London, 1913) 48–65; D. Cecil, *A Portrait of Jane Austen* (London, 1978) 43f.

65 J. Hunter, 'The Eighteenth-Century Englishwoman according to the Gentleman's Magazine', in P. Fritz and R. Morton (eds), *Women in the Eighteenth Century and Other Essays* (Toronto, 1976) 73–88.

66 One of the best monuments to this theme must be Richardson's 'Letter from a Gentleman, Strenuously Expostulating with an Old rich Widow, about to Marry a Very Young Gay Gentleman', in *Familiar Letters on Important Occasions* (London, 1741) 90.

67 Two instances of the reactions of intimate friends and relations to widows who married beneath their social status.

68 An earlier version of this chapter appeared in *Journal of Family History* 9 (1984) 355–76.

8

NOBLE WIDOWS BETWEEN FORTUNE AND FAMILY

Yme Kuiper

There is an urgent need for more women's history of upper-class women.

David Cannadine[1]

Estate papers could be exploited much more effectively than they have been to date to look at the treatment of spinsters and widows.

Olwen Hufton[2]

At the age of 29 I was unfortunate to lose my husband and this great calamity made me retreat from the world. I lost all interest in things, life disgusted me, and how I spent those first years I hardly know. By choice I was often alone and so thrown on my own resources, I withdrew from people and affairs and was continually absorbed in the past. Owing to my husband, who had travelled a great deal, my taste and judgement had been changed and developed and owing to the seriousness of life I sought interests and occupations above my years. One day, when I opened a chest which I had brought along from Leeuwarden [the capital of the province of Friesland] on my marriage, I found in it a number of interesting notes, books, letters, rare drawings and my mother's first housekeeping book started in 1834. In the same chest I also found a beginning of my grandfather's memoirs; this piece of writing immediately took my interest and from that moment I resolved to start something similar.

Adriana ('Jeanne') Wilhelmina, Lady van Andringa de Kempenaer, born into a noble family with many children, was 60 years old when she wrote down these words in one of her albums in 1918. Until she died in 1926 Jeanne continued to work regularly on what she herself called 'a family story with anecdotes'. A childless widow, she had already started this story in 1898. At that time she was in possession of the carefully preserved family archives and her mother, aged 85, was still alive. Eight years later, however, Jeanne's castle at Wychen near Nimwegen was burnt down. Both the family archives and her recorded memories, by now a manuscript numbering hundreds of pages, went up in flames. 'Gone in one night, indeed in a few hours, all the precious souvenirs of my whole life, my beautiful furnishings with many antiques, porcelain, silver, linen, books, accounts and letters. Nothing left of my husband other than a few bijoux, but not a single letter, nor of my mother, who died in August 1906.'

Several noble house and family archives in the Netherlands contain unpublished memoirs written by women. In this regard the family recollections of Jeanne van Andringa de Kempenaer (1858–1926) are far from unique. But her writings are remarkable for their extensiveness, the many striking observations of life in aristocratic circles and the writer's psychological acumen in portraying the people around her. Unconsciously and unintentionally, Jeanne's memoir also registers the standards and values (the cultural codes) of the select social group to which she belonged: from strongly developed feelings of social superiority to subtle expressions of gender identity, besides Jeanne's own interpretation and use of these codes. Without this kind of primary, qualitative source, we cannot form an adequate picture of the social and mental world of married noblewomen, spinsters or widows from a distant or recent past.

NOBLE WIDOWS

In this chapter my main focus will be on the life histories of two noblewomen: Sara Adel van Huls (1718–92), from a patrician family in The Hague and widow of the Frisian nobleman, statesman and poet Onno Zwier van Haren (1713–79); and Jeanne van Andringa de Kempenaer, widow of her second cousin Quirinus van Andringa de Kempenaer (1850–88), a rather introverted and wealthy gentleman, fond of travelling. The availability of detailed sources on the life of these two dowagers increases our knowledge of the activities of aristocratic widows and their class's assumptions and expectations concerning widowhood. As for the former, a great deal naturally depended on the age at which a woman was widowed. Did she have (grown-up) children and to what extent was she able or willing to act on a financially or otherwise independent basis? As for the latter, every society and certainly a traditional élite like the nobility has its own cultural code. How was a noble widow supposed to behave and present herself? Were there certain taboos? What was the attitude of her peers to a second marriage? As anthropology has shown, many societies distinguish the following phases in a woman's life: 'virgin', 'mother' and 'widow'.[3] What social and cultural meanings were attached to this threefold division by the Dutch nobility of the eighteenth and nineteenth centuries? Apparently the ancient Romans had a high regard for the *univira*, the woman who remained faithful to her husband by not re-marrying.[4] Was this view shared by the Dutch nobles in the eighteenth and nineteenth centuries? And how frequent was the practice of remarriage among men and women in the Dutch élite? According to Carroll Smith-Rosenberg, in her well-known article on love and rituals among women in nineteenth-century America, there was a separate women's world in this society with behavioural and cultural codes that deviated from the men's world.[5] What do the life histories of the two heroines in this chapter tell us about the possible existence of a typical noblewoman's world, based on networks of relatives, women friends, widows and spinsters?[6]

As early as the sixteenth century, following the example of the larger dynasties, the Dutch nobility adopted the custom of calling a widow from their own circles a 'douairière', i.e. dowager. Thus Sara called herself 'the dowager Van Haren' throughout her widowhood, while Jeanne, at the early age of 30, was addressed as the 'dowager Q.J.C. van Andringa de Kempenaer'. From a legal point of view in the history of Dutch nobility the term properly refers to the special widow's inheritance or portion (in French *douaire*), consisting, for instance, of an annuity or the usufruct of certain properties.[7] From a cultural point of view the term suggests a lasting bond between a widow and her deceased husband. In practice, as earlier research into the position of aristocratic women in early modern Europe shows, widows often took over the role of the husband in the private family sphere and in the administration of his property.[8] In what ways were legal, cultural and economic practices interrelated in the widow-hoods of Sara and Jeanne and how did these practices affect their personal actions?

As Natalie Davis advises for historical inquiry into women in the early modern age, I have tried in this preliminary investigation to give full consideration to the effect of the factors of power, social structure, property, symbolism and time.[9] By mentioning these factors Davis rightly calls attention to both the material and the ideological circumstances under which women and widows lived. In this connection social historians have pointed out that the 'family' factor also exercised a profound and lasting influence on the behaviour and attitudes of women.[10] Thus the wealth of a family determined the marital and social prospects of spinsters and widows in particular. Obviously this list would not be complete without the notion of gender – briefly: the cultural classification of male and female.[11] Least of all here, because precisely in the case of upper-class women the 'gender' factor may have been more important in defining their social freedom than in the case of women from an economically poor stratum, whose position was strongly determined by 'class'.[12]

Guided by these kinds of questions and considerations, I therefore propose to tell the life stories of two Dutch noble widows from the eighteenth and nineteenth centuries. A question which immediately arises here is whether their positions and experiences as widows were representative of aristocratic culture in the Netherlands of the eighteenth and nineteenth centuries.[13] I believe they were. Although for a large part of their lives Sara and Jeanne belonged, one by marriage and the other by birth, to a regional élite of leading families, namely the nobility of the province of Friesland (in the north of the Netherlands), the political careers of their fathers and husbands gave them direct access to the highest circles in the country. Born into a distinguished bourgeois ('patrician') family, Sara's marriage to a talented and influential nobleman made her a welcome visitor at the court of stadtholder Prince William IV and his wife Anna of Hannover, daughter of the English king George II, in Leeuwarden and later in The Hague. Thus Sara suckled Anna's only son for a period of time. And nine of her ten children were married to Dutch and German nobles or persons from Holland's wealthy patriciate. Virtually the same applies to Jeanne. She too had noble and patrician ancestors; her father came from a large family ennobled by King William I in the early nineteenth century, while her mother was the only daughter of a very affluent patrician father and noble mother. Almost all her five sisters and two brothers married partners from the nobility or patriciate. Already in Jeanne's youth the regional aristocracies had been more or less integrated by marriage into a national élite.[14]

DEMOGRAPHIC BACKGROUNDS

To give an adequate idea of the widowhoods of Sara and Jeanne, I shall first briefly sketch the demographic situation of the specific social group, the nobility in the province of Friesland, to which they and their families belonged. My data derive from a demographic enquiry relating to a population of more than 1000 persons from 50 noble families who were born between 1700 and 1875.[15]

Marriages in the Frisian nobility rarely ended in divorce in the period I covered and so they almost always ended by the death of a partner. Generally in both the eighteenth and nineteenth centuries the number of widows far exceeded the number of widowers. It was only during the first years of marriage, owing particularly to the effect of death in childbirth, that the life expectancy for married men was higher than that of their wives.

The average duration of a marriage did not increase much between 1700 and 1880, from twenty-three to twenty-seven years. But we should be well aware that this is an average. Some marriages were very short, for instance when a woman died after the birth of her first child; other marriages lasted relatively long, although a union of fifty years was highly exceptional. In the entire population of both the Netherlands and the province of Friesland there was a striking discrepancy between the number of widows and widowers in the nineteenth century. In 1830 the ratio was 44:100, and in 1899 50:100 in the Netherlands and 53:100 in Friesland.[16]

So, given the much higher death rate than in our time, this regional group of nobility between 1700 and 1900 always contained a great many widows and widowers of various ages. A second question which presents itself is: how many of them remarried? Suppose that there was a kind of taboo among this nobility on the remarrying of widows in particular. If this kind of norm did in fact affect the number of remarriages by widows – as Olwen Hufton assumes for eighteenth-century England and France: widowhood as the rule and the re-marrying widow as the exception – this would also have to emerge from the figures.[17] What do our figures show? We find that during both the eighteenth and the nineteenth centuries widowers married much more often than widows. Around the middle of the eighteenth century, for instance, more than 15% of widowers remarried, and a century later this figure had not changed. Of the widows around 1750 some 10% remarried, but around 1850 this figure had dropped to a bare 5%. Remarkably, around 1850 widowers remarried three times as often as widows. To check whether this was an exceptional situation, one can compare the English landed nobility, the nobility in the German state of Westphalia and the patriciate of Geneva in the same period of 1700–1875.[18] The comparison shows that the Frisian élite hardly deviated from the foreign élites in this regard.

The trend of a decrease in the number of remarrying widows among the Frisian nobility had already started in the seventeenth century. Consulting the large Genealogical Register of the Frisian nobility, one sees that in the fifteenth and sixteenth centuries men and women regularly married three times, sometimes even four.[19] In her research into remarrying widows of the village of Abingdon in England between 1540 and 1720, Barbara Todd also shows a declining trend.[20] Her explanation is striking. In the case of more wealthy widows she not only points to purely demographic factors but also to the wife's increasingly strong emotional bond with her husband, even after his death; this emotional bond then varies from feelings of love to a sense of duty. Moreover, Todd points out that in the course of time more and more widows themselves preferred to remain unmarried. However, in his study on the long-term development of marriage and love in England Alan Macfarlane states that from the fourteenth till the twentieth century English society encouraged or at least tolerated remarriage.[21] It is not clear whether his claim holds good for all social strata in pre-modern England. Investigators of English aristocratic élites, including Lawrence Stone and Trumbach, have shown for the gentry that the richest part of this self-confident élite used various strategies in the eighteenth and nineteenth centuries to keep the ranks closed. Thus fathers, brothers, brothers-in-law and sons quite often prevented their daughters, sisters, sisters-in-law and mothers from marrying or remarrying.[22]

My enquiry bears out that between 1700 and 1900 many more women remained unmarried than men, as was the case for the British nobility, the patriciate of Geneva and the nobility of Westphalia. A further striking statistic is that women from the Frisian nobility were much less prone to marry beneath their station, an event referred to with horror as a *mésalliance*. An even lower rate of 'bad matches' is found among the nobility in the German states of Hessen and Westphalia.[23] Roughly half of the married men between 1700 and 1875 chose a noble partner, whereas four out of five women in the eighteenth century and still two out of three in the nineteenth married a nobleman. Precisely this strong social endogamy can be seen as the externalization of an existing mentality within this group.

So women, and possibly widows too, were expected to marry or remarry 'ebenbürtig', equal to their station. Presumably these women will have internalized this strong class-consciousness during their upbringing. For, as far as we can tell from the sources, the young Frisian ladies too seem to have largely determined their own choice of partner.[24]

When during a naval review in Rotterdam in the autumn of 1737 Onno Zwier van Haren espied a lovely young girl between all the eminent statesman and soldiers, and she turned out to be equally charmed, Onno and Sara soon made up their minds. A few months later they married. Indeed, less than six months after the wedding Sara gave birth to her first child, which was highly unusual for this kind of aristocratic marriage. In her memoirs Jeanne says that it took her some time to get used to her cousin Quip van Andringa de Kempenaer. But she soon had to admit that he was the man of her heart. Like Sara and Jeanne, their sisters and friends had little to do with so-called arranged marriages. Marriages in the Frisian aristocracy of the eighteenth and nineteenth centuries conformed rather closely to the ideal of the 'companionate marriage' as described by Lawrence Stone.[25] According to him, this type of marriage was mainly popular among the landed nobility and the gentry. In contrast to marital life in the highest stratum of the nobility, where love and the choice of a marriage partner did not usually coincide, the companionate marriage was characterized by friendship and intelligent comradeship between wife and husband. It was the wife who was allowed supervision of the housekeeping and the servants. She was also closely involved in the upbringing of the children. The marriages of both Sara and Jeanne were undoubtedly of this type. The big practical difference between their widowhoods was the fact that Jeanne became a childless widow at a very young age. As for the remarrying Frisian noblewomen, they too were more or less free in their choice of partners. Strikingly, they almost always married another aristocratic partner.

Finally, looking at the marriage pattern among the close relatives of Sara and Jeanne, we recognize for the most part the same demographic situation. Of Sara's six daughters and four daughters-in-law, only her eldest daughter and youngest daughter-in-law remarried – the first a senior Swiss officer, the second a Dutch baron. Two of Jeanne's sisters were widows. Like Jeanne, both had been widowed at an early age, namely 49 and 31; they did not remarry, in contrast to two of Jeanne's three brothers-in-law. To Jeanne's grief and chagrin her favourite brother Marius remarried as well, at the ripe old age of 65 with a noble lady fifteen years his junior.

SARA 'DOUAIRIÈRE DE HAREN' AND THE REPUTATION OF THE VAN HAREN FAMILY[26]

On 12 January 1759 the dowager princess of Orange, Anna Hannover, widow of stadtholder William IV, Prince of Orange and Count of Nassau, died in The Hague. At that time Onno and Sara van Haren could not foresee what serious consequences their patroness's death would soon have for Onno's political career and the reputation of their family. The following winter Onno, Sara and their children became involved in a moral scandal that was initially kept in the family. Onno allegedly committed what his signed confession calls 'the *crimen tentati incestus* with two of my children'. In the same document he solemnly promises his brother-in-law, the husband of Sara's sister, and two sons-in-law, the husband and fiancé of his eldest daughter Amelia and his third daughter Carolina, to leave The Hague and the province of Holland immediately and never to return. At his country estate in faraway Friesland Van Haren no longer posed a threat to these daughters and had no more influence in the political centre of the Republic, the States-General and the stadtholder's court in The Hague. In March 1760 the Van Haren family took up residence at their country seat. In April 1761, however, they returned to their house in The Hague. At receptions virtually everybody ignored the once-so-popular couple. Evidently the Hague *beau monde* knew all about the family scandal.

In the States-General too Van Haren was *persona non grata*. A committee soon decided that Van Haren would not be allowed to appear as representative of Friesland in the States-General until he had proved his innocence. Onno returned to Friesland for good and sought rehabilitation by asking the highest court of law in Friesland for an acquittal. In May 1761 he himself published an elaborate defence which attracted a great deal of interest throughout the Republic. Van Haren naturally declared that he had been forced to sign the confession by a group of intriguers. But in October 1762 the Court of Friesland passed a verdict of *non liquet*. The court discharged Van Haren but did not pronounce him innocent. According to the version of the story most favourable to Van Haren, he had regularly inspected the fracture of his daughter Marianne. According to another version, he had made her older sisters dance naked for him when they returned from a ball at night. In a third version Van Haren had entered the dressing-room of his daughters and had suddenly embraced one of them and kissed her bosom. This was seen by a servant, who related the event to a chambermaid of a person hostile to Van Haren. The most damaging version, finally, reported that Onno had fathered children on his two eldest daughters. Though the real facts of the incest case are obscure to this day, it was clearly part of political infighting and court intrigue.[27]

Although her family sided against Van Haren, Sara always believed in the innocence of her husband, as did the other daughters and sons of Onno and Sara. The family withdrew to their estate in a small village in South Friesland; in the winter they moved to a house in Leeuwarden, the capital of the province. In this period Onno wrote to a friend with whom he kept up a literary correspondence in which he was fond of quoting the Roman classics or the great writers and poets of contemporary European literature: 'Je passe tranquillement mon temps dans mon cabinet à m'entretenir avec Pope qui me dit "all that is, is well".' The broken statesman devoted himself to writing poetry and tutored his children in geography and English among other subjects. In his main poem 'De Geuzen' ('The Beggars') he extolled the loyalty of his Sara, though another satirical poem reveals that she was not his first love.[28]

In May 1777, less than six months after a great fire had almost completely destroyed the family estate, Onno and Sara drew up a so-called 'reciproque testament' in their temporary residence.[29] This is a joint testament in which the testates benefit each other mutually. In the eighteenth century it was a very common form of testation among the Frisian nobility; it was prohibited by the nineteenth-century legislators.[30] As the heirs to all their goods Onno and Sara designated eight of their ten children, explicitly disinheriting the two daughters in The Hague. Furthermore, they gave to each other, to the partner who lived longest, the usufruct of the entire inheritance. The remaining partner was not required to produce an inventory of the goods and so could do with them as he or she saw fit. This usufruct would eventually function as Sara's *douaire*, her widow's portion.

Onno died in 1779 and was taken by ship, in the presence of his sons, to the family grave at St Annaparochie, a village in the north of Friesland. Sara would survive him by fourteen years. News of the complete disinheritance soon reached the aristocratic circles in The Hague. The letter of mourning sent by Sara mentions only eight children. The many reactions to this show how unusual her course of action was, all the more when one realizes that the principle of equal inheritance among sons and daughters was firmly established in Friesland, also among the noble families, who in those days nearly always arranged their inheritance by testament. Attempts by the two disinherited daughters and their parties to get at least their legitimate share of the inheritance – which would only devolve to them on their mother's death – were completely unsuccessful.

The prevailing law in Friesland in Sara's time placed a married woman under so-called marital guardianship, entailing that her husband administered her estate (and her part of their common estate).[31] A widow, by contrast, was considered by the law to be of full legal capacity. She could administer her estate and could also be a guardian to her children, unlike a married woman.[32] And indeed, the dowager van Haren emerges from the sources as an independently operating woman.

Sara was just over 60 when Onno died. In the first years after his death three of her four sons and two of her daughters remained unmarried. Initially they stayed close to their mother. They had no independent incomes, and the family lived mainly on the rents from the tenant farmers. In the same period the restoration of Lindenoord, the country estate, was completed and, as in the years with Onno, the dowager continued to keep a staff of about fifteen servants, all the sons and daughters having their own valet or maid. It is striking that, despite their father's dubious reputation, all but one of the children managed to contract financially rewarding and *ebenbürtige* marriages. For a large part this was no doubt due to the influence of the widow Van Haren and the respect she enjoyed among her adult children. The letters to her children, often written in French, also reflect the authority which she still exercised over them. Her approach here was tactful and cordial in a refined way. In October 1782 she wrote a letter from Lindenoord with local news about the hunting season to her third son, who was 27, still unmarried, and who had recently taken his doctor's degree in law in Utrecht. She signed the letter with the telling words; 'Votre bonne amie et tendre mère la Douairière de Haren'.

In 1785, eight years before her death, Sara, many times a grandmother, lost her eyesight. Only shortly before she had helped one of her daughters-in-law in confinement. Because of her handicap she now completely relied on the aid of her only unmarried daughter Marianne, who was 41 years old and had always lived with her mother. In the same year Sara's youngest daughter Wilhelmina

Carolina died. After consulting with Wilhelmina's widower, the nobleman and military officer Jasper Gerrit van Ittersum, Sara took their only child Margarethe Isabella, into her home to be brought up by her and Marianne. The matrifocal family now often stayed for long periods in the Burmania house in Leeuwarden. From the childhood recollections of this granddaughter Margarethe , which she started to write down in French at the age of 15, we learn a lot about Sara's last years. We constantly find evidence of the great respect that the dowager Van Haren enjoyed in her family and aristocratic environment. She was still capable of exerting a powerful influence on the actions of her children. She advised her unmarried second son Willem, who was well over 40, to get to work on a certain Lady Cecilia, the wealthy daughter and sole heiress of a prominent Frisian noble family. Later Willem in fact married Cecilia, despite the legal proceedings which Cecilia's fiancé took against her for breach of promise. The lovers fled to Germany to get married there.

Proud Sara refused to be reconciled with her two daughters in The Hague, even when she had gone blind and her powers were failing. Nor could she be swayed by the fact that the two sons-in-law who had played such an infamous role in the scandal had died years ago. The feud of the Van Haren family with the distinguished Dutch families Van Hogendorp and Van Sandick was carried on into the generation of her grandchildren. In the winter of 1792 Sara organized a few parties during the Provincial Council assembly in Leeuwarden; in the following winter she died in her town residence after an illness of several weeks, continually surrounded by her solicitous children. An old lady friend of the dowager helped watch over her at night. Ten days after her death Sara was buried in the family grave at St Annaparochie. At her own request the ceremony was a sober one and only her sons and a son-in-law followed her on her last journey. A long period of official mourning ensued. Family members and staff wore mourning attire, engagements for large parties were cancelled, and the shutters of the house in Leeuwarden remained closed for months. The property that Sara left her children was estimated at Dfl. 217,000, but the estate had also run up many debts. Now that the mother no longer acted as the pivot of the family – the eldest son Duco was not really equal to his role as *chef de famille* – the complicated estate became the object of a long tug-of-war between the Van Haren brothers and sisters. It was not until a quarter of a century later, in 1818, that the final partition took place.

Though the history of the Van Haren family was eccentric, many aspects of Sara's life as a widow corresponded to the social position of other noble widows in Friesland at the end of the eighteenth century. Reasonable access to large estates usually allowed widows to continue their accustomed lifestyle. Often estates were not immediately distributed and so a large group of widows with children, depending of course on their age, carried on living as families. In effect this meant that the daily lives of these widows between the ages of 40 and 60 did not differ all that much from their previous existence as wives. Childless and very old widows often lived together with unmarried sisters or daughters but were by no means isolated from wider family circles. One is immediately struck by the strong emotional ties between mothers and daughters or between sisters, whether or not married or widowed. Many a widow's testament mentioned legacies for staff members who had faithfully served her for decades. Another facet of the average widow's existence which requires a separate discussion but which can only be touched upon here is the involvement of noble widows in church and religion. Highly regular church attendance, intensive contacts with ministers or offices of charity via the church for instance – all these are the rule rather than the exception until deep into the nineteenth century.

Sara died at the end of the eighteenth century, Jeanne was born in the middle of the nineteenth. In the meantime wide-ranging cultural developments had taken place.[33] Sometimes we find traces of these when we compare the memoirs passed down to us by Sara and Jeanne. Jeanne's age, as her memoirs clearly show, was much more prudish than Sara's. Also the family life of aristocratic families in the nineteenth century seems increasingly to adopt features from that of the upper middle classes. And in Jeanne's lifetime there is growing criticism of and opposition to the élite to which she belonged by birth.

A VICTORIAN WIDOW: JEANNE, LADY VAN ANDRINGA DE KEMPENAER[34]

Jeanne was the ninth and last child of a large family. When she was born in 1858 her father was 52 and her mother 45. She remembered her father as an amiable but very conservative man; for many years he was burgomaster of a Frisian rural district and also member of the Dutch Upper House. His favourite pastimes, as Jeanne writes, were dining out, receiving and hunting. He died in 1870 in the family's town house in Leeuwarden when Jeanne was 12 years old. For the next thirty-six years, until her death, Jeanne's mother was the dowager Van Andringa de Kempenaer. In many ways Jeanne's mother was a talented and well-educated woman. She placed a much higher value on domesticity and devoutness than her husband had. For the next three generations the Van Andringa de Kempenaers were staunch Orangeists and royalists. Both King William II and his son King William III had honoured the family with a visit to Oostenburg at St Annaparochie when the father was still the head of local government there.

In writing the family memoirs Jeanne, who was childless, obtained a great deal of information about the family from her mother, who died at the ripe old age of 93. In the first years of her widowhood Jeanne often stayed with the family of a sister in The Hague who was also a widow. In the 1890s she always spent the summer with her mother at the family's country estate Harstastate at Hogebeintum in Friesland. After Jeanne's mother had been widowed, she wore mourning as tradition prescribed. 'Not to mourn', Jeanne remarks, 'was regarded as the height of vandalism by our class in 1870.' Not only the children but also the servants were given mourning attire. The widow herself did not appear in public for weeks and Jeanne was kept from school during the same period. At the funeral of Jeanne's father there were no women present, though grandsons aged 8 and 10 did attend. For the rest of her life Jeanne's mother would effectively continue to wear mourning. In this way she not only made her status as widow clear to the outside world but also her feelings. Likewise Jeanne's mother no longer took part in the so-called 'society' of Leeuwarden or The Hague and she never again organized a dinner or reception. Yet she did not entirely cut herself off from the world. She followed with great interest contemporary developments in church and theology. She felt an affinity with the rising modernism in the Dutch Reformed Church.

It is all the more striking that three of Jeanne's sisters chose a different religious direction from their mother. Their 'conversion' took place after they had been educated at a boarding school in Wageningen in the province of Gelderland, led by two piously orthodox ladies (as Jeanne writes with some aversion). This simple fact underlines how important boarding schools in the nineteenth century were for a Dutch élite that was becoming increasingly integrated at a national level. It was there that lifelong friendships were formed with boys and girls from other provincial élites and that certain views and attitudes were fostered. Jeanne's descriptions of her sisters clearly show how they fit into our general picture of the orthodox Revival in the Netherlands: the devotional exercises at home, the involvement in sewing, knitting, Sunday and nursery schools and the visits to the poor.[35] During her widowhood Jeanne herself, as her memoirs reveal, reacted fiercely against the orthodoxy of her sisters and brothers-in-law. In Catholic Wychen near Nimwegen, where she had bought a castle in 1903 for Dfl. 30,000, she never really felt at home in the village community. The reason why she bought the castle, as she later held, was that she would be living close to her favourite brother and some close lady friends. But anybody who reads Jeanne's memoirs right through will suggest another reason, namely an intense preoccupation with her noble ancestry. A typical detail of her predilection for a certain aristocratic grandeur is her demand that the key of the gate be brought to her on a silver tray every night.

Strikingly, it is above all men who represent the family tradition, both in the past and in the present, according to Jeanne's memoirs. She speaks highly of her great-grandfather and her father and strongly identifies with her husband and youngest brother. A fine example of the gender mechanism in Jeanne's upbringing is the following story. As a girl of 16, the very age at which she is tutored at home by a governess, she eavesdrops on a conversation about the family's financial affairs. To her astonishment she infers from her brother-in-law's remarks that the great fortune on which the family depended came not from her father but from her mother. It was also characteristic of the young Jeanne that at the time of her marriage with her cousin Quip, as she frankly admits in her memoirs, she knew nothing about her (future) financial position. She understood nothing of the marriage settlement deed and the testaments of Quip and herself which the notary had duly read out to them. This would change drastically once she became a widow and chatelaine. Yet Jeanne had already been an enterprising person in her teens. A telling recollection here is about the search for a lost umbrella. On a family trip to Paris Jeanne left her umbrella in a hackney cab after seeing the horseracing at Longchamp. Without permission and so without a chaperone Jeanne had spent hours the next day trying to get back her lost possession, which in the end she did.

Jeanne strongly identified with her family's past. In 1918 she bought for Dfl. 136,000 what was once part of her mother's enormous estate, the Harstastate at Hogebeintum and the surrounding land. Every Sunday in summer she faithfully went to the church on the terp of Hogebeintum, where she would sit in the family pew. Also she had her husband, who had died in The Hague, reburied next to the church, intending to be buried there herself, as in fact she was in 1926. At the end of her life she wrote with resignation in her memoirs; 'Smaller and smaller, too, grows the circle of acquaintances, empty places everywhere and everything is changing. More and more I live in the past and then all the dead become living speaking beings with whom I relive all those times, I hear their voices, listen to their stories and then I feel once again the desire to rescue some things from oblivion, hoping in this way to please somebody in the family.'

Jeanne survived all her brothers and sisters. She herself was childless and quarrelled with her brother and his children until her death. This may help to explain why her testament nominated the rest home Sonnenburgh of the Dutch Reformed Church in Leeuwarden as her sole and universal beneficiary. Her testament also contained many, sometimes substantial legacies, for beloved family members, for her best friend Lady Quarles van Ufford, for her servants, for an orphanage in Alphen aan de Rijn, for the poor relief in Ferwerd and the church at Hogebeintum. According to her great-nephew A.W. den Beer Poortugael, 'aunt Jeanne' was 'small, firm, highly educated and aristocratic in her demeanour'. 'Proud of her ancestry', he added with disapproval, and 'highly conservative in her social views'. But it is precisely Jeanne's memoir which shows how this view might be qualified. Her memoirs confirm that Jeanne held highly conservative views, but they also show that she was very sensitive to the needs and interests of the women around her. I shall give just one example. When describing the early death of one of her sisters, she bitterly reproaches her brothers-in-law for the many pregnancies which they made their wives go through. And these passages also show that Jeanne's fury did not confine itself to words on paper. At times in her recollections one also hears a voice from the women's movement of the period. Thus Jeanne was quite aware that the changes after the Great War offered women greater social opportunities, and she applauded those changes. On the other hand, certain forms of increased informality and democracy went much too far in her view. 'Our class is no longer treated in a friendly way', she tellingly writes. When writing her memoirs, Jeanne had ambivalent feelings about her own time. As a rich, independent and intelligent widow Jeanne was free to do many things, but as 'the dowager Van Andringa de Kempenaer' she was also a prisoner of her own view of the past.

CONCLUSIONS

What conclusions can be drawn from the life stories of two noble widows living in what we could call 'the long nineteenth century' (1780–1914)? They have shown that research into the position of noble widows should take five factors into account. First, the economic and legal position of such a widow. Although Sara died at the end of the eighteenth and Jeanne at the beginning of this century, there were hardly any structural differences between the situations of the two widows in this regard. As widows they enjoyed more freedom of action than as married women, and both lived on family capital. This money allowed them to keep country estates, town houses and the necessary staff, so that they could effectively continue the lifestyle of married women from the leisured classes.

A second factor is their noble ancestry and the nature of their widowhoods. Both Sara and Jeanne, as the sources show, were accustomed by upbringing and marriage to the fact that women played a leading role in the home.[36] Like other widows from the Frisian landed nobility of the eighteenth and nineteenth centuries, they also felt perfectly capable of administering the family estate. Both widows, for instance, made contracts with their tenants and, if necessary, engaged the services of a notary or lawyer to do so. A third element is the age at which a woman was widowed and whether she had children. The situations of Sara and Jeanne were very different in this regard. Sara's main concern was to serve the interests of her children and grandchildren. As the dowager Van Haren she was the pivot of Onno's 'patriline'.[37] In this respect Jeanne, being childless, was necessarily more concerned with the past; the interests which Jeanne wanted to serve were basically those of the reputation of her family. Though in her memoirs she likes to talk about very young, very rich widows constantly receiving new marriage proposals – despite their lack of beauty – Jeanne more or less took her own widowhood for granted. Her mother was a widow, her sisters were widows, and none of them remarried. An interesting idea for future research into aristocratic widows would be to focus more specifically on the possibly different ways in which they identified with the history of their ancestors and their living relatives. An important key to an understanding of Jeanne's memoirs is, for instance, the strong, often ambivalent relationships she had with her brothers and sisters. In the fourth place, Sara's widowhood and especially that of childless Jeanne show that the contacts with older women – unmarried sisters and cousins, close relatives who were also widows, friends and companions – produced to some extent a specific form of sociability without this directly presupposing the existence of a separate women's culture.

The fifth factor, finally, is what I would like to call the personal factor or, if you like, the personality of an individual widow. The famous Dutch feminist, anarchist and jurist Clara Wichmann made the following provocative statement in 1913: 'In the life of every woman it is the personal, not the social relationships which are really decisive.'[38] Now that 'narrativism' and 'thick description' in cultural history have become such important trends in the nineties, many are likely to regard this statement as highly topical and apt.[39] To some degree this chapter is also an narrative experiment in writing the history of the concrete lives of women, in this case aristocratic widows. More importantly, it shows the need to see these lives as the products of biographical facts, social circumstances and cultural constructions.

NOTES

1 D. Cannadine, *The Decline and Fall of the British Aristocracy* (New Haven and London, 1990) 7.
2 O. Hufton, 'Women without Men: Widows and Spinsters in Britain and France in the Eighteenth Century', *Journal of Family History* 9 (1984) 367 [this vol., ch.7, 150 note 47].
3 K. Hastrup, 'The Semantics of Biology: Virginity', in S. Ardener (ed.), *Defining Females* (London 1978) 49–65.
4 J. Bremmer, this vol., ch.3, 38.
5 C. Smith-Rosenberg, *Disorderly Conduct: Visions of Gender in Victorian America* (New York and Oxford, 1985) 53–76, 305–13.
6 See also I.Q. Brown, 'Domesticity, Feminism, and Friendship: Female Aristocratic Culture and Marriage in England, 1660–1760', *Journal of Family History* 7 (1982) 406–24.
7 Cf. S. Marshall Wyntjes, 'Survivors and Status: Widowhood and Family in the Early Modern Netherlands', *Journal of Family History* 7 (1982) 396–405; Sherrin Marshall, *The Dutch Gentry, 1500–1650: Family, Faith, and Fortune* (New York, 1987) 53–68.
8 I. Blom, 'The History of Widowhood: A Bibliographic Overview', *Journal of Family History* 16 (1991) 191–210; M. Palazzi, 'Female Solitude and Patrilineage: Unmarried Women and Widows during the Eighteenth and Nineteenth Centuries', *Journal of Family History* 15 (1990) 443–59; R. Kalas, 'The Noble's Widow's Place in the Patriarchal Household: The Life and Career of Jeanne de Gontault', *The Sixteenth Century Journal* 24 (1993) 519–39; M.E. Wiesner, *Women and Gender in Early Modern Europe* (Cambridge, 1993) 74.

9 N.Z. Davis, '"Women's history" in Transition: The European Case', *Feminist Studies* 3 (1976) 83–103.

10 P. Stearns, 'Old Women: Some Historical Observations', *Journal of Family History* 5 (1980) 201–16; L. Stone, *The Family, Sex and Marriage in England 1500–1800*, 1977[1] (abridged and revised edn, Harmondsworth, 1979) 81–9; M. Slater, *Family Life in the Seventeenth Century: The Verneys of Claydon House* (London, 1984) 25–59; D. Kertzer, 'Anthropology and Family History', *Journal of Family History* 9 (1984) 201–16; Hufton, 'Women without Men', this vol., ch. 7; M. Abbott, *Family Ties: English Families 1540–1920* (London, 1993) 39–70.

11 J. Scott, 'Gender: A Useful Category of Historical Analysis', *American Historical Review* 91 (1986) 1053–75; 'Women's History', in P. Burke (ed.), *New Perspectives on Historical Writing* (Cambridge, 1992) 42–66.

12 Wiesner, *Women and Gender in Early Modern Europe*, 240–1, 252–5.

13 J. Hokke, '"Mijn alderliefste Jantielief". Vrouw en gezin in de Republiek: regenten vrouwen en hun relaties', *Jaarboek voor vrouwengeschiedenis* 8 (1987) 45–73.

14 Y. Kuiper, *Adel in Friesland 1780–1880* (Groningen, 1993) 563–6.

15 Kuiper, *Adel in Friesland*, 85–136.

16 My colleague and friend Meindert Schroor has kindly traced these data.

17 Hufton, 'Women without Men', this vol., ch.7.

18 L. Stone, *An Open Elite? England 1540–1880* (Oxford, 1984) 87–93; H. Reif, *Westfälischer Adel 1770–1860: Vom Herrschaftsstand zur regionalen Elite* (Göttingen, 1979) 252f.; L. Henry, *Anciennes familles genevoises: Étude démographique: 16e–20e siècle* (Paris, 1956).

19 M. de Haan Hettema and A. van Halmael Jr (eds), *Stamboek van den Frieschen vroegeren en lateren Adel* (Leeuwarden, 1846).

20 B. J. Todd, 'The Remarrying Widow: A Stereotype Reconsidered', in M. Prior (ed.), *Women in English Society 1500–1800* (London and New York, 1985) 54–92.

21 A. Macfarlane, *Marriage and Love in England: Modes of Reproduction 1300–1840* (Oxford, 1986) 231–9.

22 Stone, *An Open Elite?*; R. Trumbach, *The Rise of the Egalitarian Family: Aristocratic Kinship and Domestic Relations in Eighteenth-Century England* (New York, 1978); see also J. Powis, *Aristocracy* (Oxford and New York, 1984).

23 Reif, *Westfälischer Adel*, 241; G. W. Pedlow, 'Marriage, Family Size, and Inheritance among Hessian Nobles, 1650–1900', *Journal of Family History* 7 (1982, 333–52) 338.

24 J. J. Hermsen *et al.* (eds), *'Nu eens dwaas dan weer wijs': Belle van Zuylen tussen Verlichting en Romantiek* (Amsterdam, 1990), especially the contributions of J.-D. Candaux, H.S. Haasse and R. van der Plas.

25 Stone, *Family, Sex and Marriage*, 217–53.

26 This section is based on various family archives. In the State Archives, Leeuwarden, Friesland: the family archives of Van Canter, Van Haren, and Van Sloterdijck; Collection Nepveu. In the Provincial Library, Leeuwarden: Collection Hareniana.

27 A.J.C.M. Gabriëls, *De heren als dienaren en de dienaar als heer. Het stadhouderlijk stelsel in de tweede helft van de achttiende eeuw* (The Hague, 1990) 159–62, 273–6 and 409–14.

28 A.J. Stakenburg, *Onno Zwier van Haren: De Geuzen* (Santpoort, 1943) 19, 27f.

29 U. Huber, *Beginzelen der Regtkunde in Friesland en elders gebruikelijk* (Leeuwarden, 1774) 64.

30 Y.M.I. Greuter-Vreeburg, *De codificatie van het erfrecht* (Zutphen, 1987) 64–9.

31 A. H. Huussen Jr, 'Rechtspolitische Aspekte der Ehe- und Familien-Gesetzgebung in den Niederlanden vom 16.–19. Jahrhundert', in H. Mohnhaupt (ed.), *Zur Geschichte des Familien- und Erbrechts* (Frankfurt am Main, 1987) 93–119.

32 Hempenius-van Dijk, this vol., ch. 5.

33 I. Weber-Kellermann, *Frauenleben im 19. Jahrhundert: Empire und Romantik, Biedermeier, Gründerzeit* (Munich, 1983).

34 This section is based on the following archives. In the State Archives, Leeuwarden: the family archive Van Andringa de Kempenaer; notarial archives. In the State Archives, Middelburg, Zeeland: the family archive Den Beer Poortugael.

35 See also T. de Bie and W. Fritschy, 'De "wereld" van reveilvrouwen, hun liefdadige activiteiten en het ontstaan van het feminisme in Nederland', *Jaarboek voor vrouwengeschiedenis* 6 (1985) 30–59.

36 T. Lummis and J. Marsh, *The Woman's Domain: Women and the English Country House* (London, 1993).

37 For a useful and elegant interpretation of this concept see K.W. Wachter and P. Laslett, 'Measuring Patriline Extinction for Modeling Social Mobility in the Past', in K.W. Wachter *et al.* (eds), *Statistical Studies of Historical Social Structure* (New York, 1978) 113–35.

38 J. van den Bergh van Eysinga-Elias and Clara Wichmann, *De vrouw in Nederland voor honderd jaar en thans* (Amsterdam, 1913).

39 Cf. L. Hunt, 'Introduction: History, Culture, and Text', and A. Biersack, 'Local Knowledge, Local History: Geertz and Beyond', in L. Hunt (ed.), *The New Cultural History* (Berkeley and Los Angeles, 1989) 1–22 and 72–96, respectively.

9

THE ULTIMATE JOURNEY
Satī and widowhood in India

Lourens P. van den Bosch

> There is humanity in all inhuman barbarism,
> if only we try to discover it.[1]

It is a human phenomenon that, when confronted with other cultures, the attention is caught usually not by the plain and the ordinary, but by the extraordinary, the fanciful or the bizarre. The striking contrast with one's own culture creates surprise and evokes numerous questions. It is therefore understandable that the practice of so-called 'widow-burning', *sutti'ism*,[2] has from the beginning attracted the attention of travellers who visited India. The sad fate of many a widow was related by them in their itineraries in vivid and contrasting colours.[3] This one-sided attention to the tragic and the grotesque has often led to a distorted picture of Indian culture, creating the impression that *sutti'ism* was once practised by broad strata of the population. This was never the case.[4] It was only occasionally performed, and in most cases restricted to members of specific castes. So, during the heyday of *sutti'ism* at the end of the eighteenth and the beginning of the nineteenth century H.Th. Colebrooke, a famous indologist and judge in the High Court of Calcutta, could remark: 'happily martyrs of this superstition have never been numerous'.[5] None the less, it is significant that this controversial practice was incorporated in religious tradition and even praised in brahminical texts. It reveals a number of ideas about women and widowhood and their relations to men, which have been clearly expressed in the course of brahminical tradition.

In this chapter I shall concentrate on two contrasting series of funeral rites which are performed when a woman loses her husband. Firstly, if she expresses her wish to follow her deceased husband on the funeral pile to the hereafter she is named a *satī*, 'a virtuous or faithful wife', and extolled in many texts as a divine being, worthy of worship. In the course of tradition detailed ritual procedures have been developed for the voluntary immolation of a *satī*. Secondly, I shall describe the brahminical rites in case a woman accepts the heavy burden of widowhood. Both rites reveal certain features of women and widowhood and are expressive of the traditional brahminical ideology with respect to women which for so long has moulded Indian civilization. They reveal certain dominant ideas about women, or widows, which may be summarized as the denial of their own religious identity in this world. In traditional brahminical ideology women have been always defined in terms of their fathers, husbands or sons. These ideas have been transmitted, elaborated and adapted over many centuries and have been closely intertwined with the practice of *suttee*. This will be seen from the following short historical outline of what is often, but wrongly, called 'widow-burning', in which I shall also describe the absorption of the practice into the western imagination.

The descriptions of *sutti'ism* from the second century BC up to the present day display a great continuity in symbolism and seem to justify more general statements based on an ideal-typical reconstruction. The information on 'widow-burning' became more detailed when the East India Company became responsible for the administration of Bengal and related areas. Much research was done by civil servants and missionaries in order to gain a better understanding of the extent and spread of the practice. The traditional themes related in the itineraries were again under discussion, but now within the context of the administration of law. The western fixation on its humanitarian aspects, especially on its various abuses with respect to widows, which were grist to the mill of the British missionaries, led to a lack of understanding of the symbolic dimension of the ritual. For this reason I have chosen to deal in this article with the position of the *satī* and the widow within the context of the funeral ritual and to elucidate its symbolic idiom.

THE HISTORY OF 'WIDOW-BURNING'

One might expect the first information on *sutti'ism* to be in ancient Indian texts, but these are conspicuously silent on it. Diodorus of Sicily is the first Greek author to incorporate a graphic description of it in his history.[6] The account centres on an Indian general, Ceteus, who entered the service of the Macedonian ruler Eumenes and commanded an Indian contingent.[7] Ceteus fell in a battle against Eumenes' arch-rival Antigonos near Paraetacani in Asia Minor in 316 BC and was cremated with military honour together with one of his two wives.[8] The geographer Strabo (c. 64 BC–AD 25) also mentions the practice of *suttee* among some tribes in the Punjab, e.g. among the Kathaioi. He refers to earlier authors such as Aristobulos and Onesicritus, contemporaries of Alexander the Great.[9] The reports of Diodorus and Strabo seem to indicate that 'widow-burning' was sometimes practised among tribes, especially in the north-west of India. The graphic account of 'widow-burning' by Diodorus struck the imagination to such an extent that it was often copied by classical authors. As such, it has deeply influenced the western imagination.[10]

We may assume that the practice of *sutti'ism* was a highly emotional and controversial affair from early days on. Diodorus and many later authors described the shock which the practice produced among the observers. Though the wife immolated herself voluntarily on the funeral pile with the corpse of her husband, they could not understand it and looked for other explanations. Both Diodorus and Strabo suggested a fantastic theory, which is still mentioned in some itineraries of the seventeenth century.[11] This runs as follows: in former times lascivious young wives sometimes poisoned their husbands by secret means in order to get rid of them and to enjoy themselves with their new lovers. To deter these wicked wives from murdering their husbands they were compelled to be burned with them.[12] It will be clear that this theory is not very satisfactory. In the first place the voluntariness of the act on behalf of the woman concerned is totally disregarded, and, secondly, no valid explanation is given for its occasional occurrence.

The Greek descriptions of 'widow-burning' are important, because the most ancient Indian texts do not mention the custom at all. The Vedic texts, specially authoritative in brahminical tradition, offer scarcely any starting-points, nor do they justify the practice.[13] Moreover, the most ancient brahminical legal codes, the *dharmaśāstras*, which purport to be based on Vedic tradition, do not contain any injunction in this respect. This seems to indicate that *sutti'ism* did not originate in Vedic tradition, but was only later incorporated in it. According to the historian V. Smith it began in the fifth century AD in the north-west of India in a culture blending Scythian, Iranian and Vedic traditions.[14] *Sutti'ism* would have been practised only by some families belonging to the warrior class (*kshatriyas*), but it was not widely spread.[15]

During the first five centuries of our era 'widow-burning' is only occasionally mentioned in preserved Indian texts.[16] The legal code of Vishnu relates that the widow after the death of her husband has the choice of preserving her chastity for the rest of her life, or ascending the pile with his corpse.[17] The author of this legal code thus introduces the practice as a valid alternative to widowhood; in this conception he is later followed by others.[18]

From the second half of the first millennium the custom seems to have spread over great parts of the Indian subcontinent, especially among certain families of the warrior class.[19] Moreover, from this period onwards, *sati*-stones were erected, memorial stones for those heroic women who voluntarily followed their deceased husband. In that capacity these *sati*-stones formed, as it were, the counterpart of the memorial stones erected for heroes (*vira*) slain in the battle.[20] The custom was very controversial in brahmin circles and led to heated discussions. Some regarded it as a form of suicide and, for that reason, as a most reprehensible act,[21] but others praised it as a supreme sacrifice. By this immolation the wife achieved well-being in the hereafter for her deceased consort.[22] In the course of time the restriction was added that the wife of a deceased brahmin was allowed to be burnt with his corpse only on the same funeral pile.[23] In other words: the practice of *sutti'ism* became accepted in certain circles of brahmins and warriors in the first half of the second millennium, but the protests against it did not die away and even continued during the following period.[24]

With the advent of the second millennium 'widow-burning' became slightly more common, as may be inferred from the increase of the number of *sati*-stones in this period. Moreover, the increase in contacts between the Middle East and Europe on the one hand and the Indian subcontinent on the other led to many descriptions by travellers and scholars with a different cultural background.[25] The famous North African traveller Ibn Battūta, who lived in the first half of the fourteenth century, reported, for instance, a shocking 'widow-burning' in his itinerary. He was so moved by the scene that he nearly fainted and would have fallen from his horse if his friends had not been near.[26] The Muslim Mughals, who ruled over great parts of the Indian subcontinent from the beginning of the sixteenth century onwards, allowed *sutti'ism* if the wife concerned made this choice voluntarily.[27] They ordered that the local governors should carefully check this voluntariness before ritual cremation could take place. The Portuguese authorities in Goa, however, forbade the practice absolutely by an edict of their first governor Alfonso d'Albaquerque.[28]

Western descriptions of 'widow-burning' increased with the expansion of the European trade in the Orient. The question of the religious character of *sutti'ism* gradually became more important. This especially concerned the period after 1765, when the East India Company took control of Bengal and its adjacent territories and was charged with the collection of revenues and the administration of justice. With this development a new colonial chapter started in the history of the Indian subcontinent. The harmonization of the administration of justice with the culture of its inhabitants and respect for their religious freedom was a foremost concern of the British.[29] In this context the question arose whether the practice of *suttee* should be regarded as essentially rooted in religion.[30] For this reason the Court of *Nizamat Adalat* (Supreme Court) made a careful study of those Hindu scriptures which were supposed to be authoritative in matters of religion. On the basis of this report the Court formulated more detailed rules by means of which *sutti'ism* should be tested.[31] The Court took as a general premise that the British administration should allow the practice in those cases in which it was sanctioned by the religion of the Hindus, but it should be prohibited in those cases in which it was forbidden by the same authority.[32] The rules formulated by the Court had regard, firstly, to the voluntariness on behalf of the wife; secondly, her age, because she should have reached the years of discretion; thirdly, the prohibition of the use of intoxicating drugs, because this obstructs a deliberate choice; fourthly, the prohibition of pregnant and menstruating women from this practice; and lastly, the obligation of the mother to take care of a young child, as well as the obligation of the family of the deceased man to take care of the older children.[33] With these regulations the British administration hoped to maintain the practice according to the religious tradition of the Hindus without interfering in it.[34] The presence of civil servants, who were to supervise on behalf of the British administration, led in some Hindu circles to the view that the East India Company implicitly approved of the practice of 'widow-burning'.[35] In this context the missionary J. Peggs voiced the opinion of some natives: 'Now she must burn; for the *Boro Sahab* (the Great Gentleman) has sent her permission to burn.'[36]

With the expansion and consolidation of the colonial administration over great parts of the Indian subcontinent the question arose whether the British did not have a universal task in the field of civilization and whether they should not forbid such barbaric practices as 'widow-burning' and the like.[37] The missionaries of the Baptist Missionary Society in Bengal (Serampore) were especially active in the mobilization of public opinion in England in the first three decades of the nineteenth century. They collected many facts to show how repugnant some religious customs were.[38] In Bengal a discussion about 'widow-burning' and its foundation in the Vedic literature was started by prominent Hindus.[39] Rammohun Roy, one of the great religious reformers of Hinduism in Bengal at the beginning of the nineteenth century, was a serious advocate of its abolition, but he was against an official prohibition.[40] The House of Commons ordered an investigation into the practice of 'widow-burning', which took place between 1821 and 1827. A mass of materials was collected,[41] but this did not lead to a satisfactory answer to the question of the nature and meaning of the custom. The governor-general of the East India Company, William Bentick, forbade the practice in 1829 after having investigated whether the prohibition would have deep emotional repercussions among the Hindus and the native soldiers which might be dangerous for the British administration.[42] He concluded that the custom was not deeply rooted in the religion of the Hindus. For this reason he did not regard it as a religious custom.[43] In 1861 the prohibition of 'widow-burning' came into force in the independent Indian principalities.[44] In this respect the British colonial authorities had been successful.

So, much material was collected by both the British colonial administration and the missionaries about the practice of 'widow-burning', but it was mainly legal and practical in nature.[45] It concerned, for instance, the frequency of the custom in the various parts of the country and its occurrence among various groups, or castes. They particularly questioned why *sutti'ism* was more frequently practised in some circles and in some areas than in others. Lastly, they investigated how 'widow-burning' was legitimated from a religious point of view by the various groups concerned.[46]

The direct responsibility of the British administration for the maintenance of law and order in India and its implicit involvement in the practice of 'widow-burning' led to heated reactions. Many 'orthodox' Hindus regarded the practice as an act of great holiness, to which only a few ladies were elected by divine grace.[47] The missionaries, on the other hand, spoke about a 'shocking murder' and sought attention for the poor victims of this 'shocking super-stition'.[48] They put forward many arguments, which they cunningly derived from the religious tradition of the Hindus and added to them objections more humanitarian in nature.[49] They stressed the fact that the practice of *sutti'ism* was not mentioned at all as an obligation in the authoritative religious scriptures. On the contrary, a pure and sober life in continence was enjoined upon Hindu widows by the great majority of religious texts. The frequent cruelties by relations of the victim during the performance of the practice were in flat contradiction to the official religious rules and justified a total prohibition.

When one studies Bentick's views on the Sati Regulation Act, as formulated in his Minute on Sati, it becomes clear that he was influenced by some of the missionaries' arguments,[50] and he maintained as a universal imperative: 'no innocent blood shall be spilt'.[51]

In the discussion of the practice of 'widow-burning' attention was paid not only to demographic and judicial problems, but also to the origin and function of the custom. Often the custom was supposed to have its origin in Indo-European tradition, and parallels were drawn with similar customs from other Indo-European peoples.[52] Or it was thought that the immolation of the wife was occasioned by the idea that the deceased husband continued his married life in the hereafter.[53] The existence of the custom in only certain circles of Hindus was explained on functional grounds. In this context, an important role was also attributed to financial interests and considerations of prestige.

When we review the preceding it becomes clear that the religious and symbolic dimension of *sutti'ism* has frequently been disregarded, although the various descriptions often allude to it.[54] It is a striking feature that many of its symbolic forms and some of its precepts have not changed over a very long period. Even in recent cases of *satī*, reference is made to this traditional cultural-symbolic idiom. This continuity seems to indicate that certain ancient ideological notions at the basis of this ritual have been handed down unchanged in Indian tradition.[55] In the following paragraph we shall deal with these notions.

THE IMMOLATION OF A *SATĪ*

The reports on *sutti'ism* by missionaries often suggest that, under the cloak of religion, a bizarre murder of the widow is committed by the family of her husband because of material interests.[56] For all that, the early itineraries also present a rather different image, which is more in agreement with the traditional Indian view: a *satī* should be regarded as a virtuous woman who, by immolating herself on the funeral pile of her deceased husband, achieves well-being for him in the hereafter.[57] Diodorus of Sicily, for instance, relates that the two wives of General Ceteus, who was killed in battle, fought for the honour of being cremated with him.[58] His colleagues judged that one wife was sufficient and no compulsion was used. The elder wife was disqualified on account of her pregnancy,[59] while the younger one gained the honour. According to Diodorus, the elder lady behaved as if a great disaster had been announced to her, and she ripped off the wreath with flowers on her head and tore her hair out. The other one rejoiced in her victory and went to the pyre crowned with fillets which her maidservants had bound in her hair, and magnificently dressed as if for a wedding ceremony. She was escorted by her kinsfolk, who sang in praise of her virtue. On the road to the funeral pyre she stripped off all her ornaments and jewels and gave them to her servants and friends. At the place of cremation she took leave of her household and was assisted by her brother, when she mounted the pyre, where she reclined beside the corpse of her husband. The entire army walked three times around the funeral pyre before it was lit. No ignoble cry escaped from her mouth, while a numerous crowd was watching the cremation ceremony. Reading Diodorus one gets the impression that the younger wife was not regarded as a victim, but as a victor.[60]

Some of the elements of Diodorus' description often recur in reports by later travellers on 'widow-burning':[61] as in, for instance, the confirmation that the virtuous wife (*satī*) is dressed like a bride, she is abundantly adorned with jewellery and her head is decked with flowers. Moreover, music, songs of praise and dance are often fixed parts of these festivities. For this reason it is not a sad event, but a happy one: the wife joins her husband in order to follow him as a bride to the hereafter. She presents herself to him in her bridal dress and with her bridal jewels, just as during the marriage ceremonies. The sacrament of marriage is, as it were, demonstrated again at the cremation fire in this critical stage.[62] From this point of view it is inaccurate to speak about widow-burning, because the wife concerned is not regarded as a widow, but as a bride who stays with her husband. The many attributes with which she adorns herself and the many actions which she performs do not refer to her status as a widow, but to her status as a bride. Of course, new notions are introduced at the same time to express her imminent death, as may be seen in the following example from Rajasthan. When Maharana Jawan Singh of Udaipur (Mewar) died in 1838, his wives dropped their veil and took their hair down as a public proclamation of their intention to follow their master as *satīs* to the hereafter.[63]

Specific references to wedding ceremonies are often incorporated in *sutti'ism* and used to express the reconfirmation of marriage. Diodorus already points to these notions, but they are also found in more recent cases. When the wife of Sardar Sham Singh of Attari received the message that her husband had been killed in the battle against the British during the pacification of the Punjab in 1845, she burnt herself with her bridal dress.[64] The 18-year-old Roop Kanwar, who became a *satī* in 1987, also dressed herself as a bride and was abundantly adorned with jewellery, according to the descriptions in the newspapers.[65] In devotional pictures she is represented in her bridal dress and sits on the pyre, while she holds the corpse of her beloved husband in her lap. The cremation fire functions in all these contexts as the fire where the sacrament of marriage is renewed.

In the itineraries there are many regional variants of the cremation ceremony of a *satī* (*satīdahana*).[66] Moreover, castes and families have their own specific traditions. From the earliest times two different forms of *sutti'ism* are distinguished. The first is known as *sahamarana* or *sahagamana*, and the second as *anumarana* or *anugamana*.[67] In the first case the wife is cremated together with the corpse of her husband on the same pyre. In the second case the wife immolates herself on a different funeral pile and at a different time. In the latter case the wife cremates herself with a symbolic object which refers to the deceased man such as, for instance, his slippers, his turban or his wedding dress.[68]

The bipartition mentioned above recurs in many descriptions, *inter alia*, in a book on Hindu customs by the Dutch clergyman A. Rogerius, who stayed in a trading-post of the Dutch East India Company near Paliacatta on the Coromandel Coast in the first half of the seventeenth century.[69] He related that the brahmins and *vaiśyas* (the 'class' of peasants and traders) usually cremated a wife together with her deceased husband in the same fire, but the wife of a *kshatriya* (the warrior 'class') or a *śūdra* (the serving 'class') might be burnt at a later time on a different pile. Moreover, he mentioned that the brahmins erected a pile, on which the wife should be burnt lying alongside the corpse of her husband. In other cases, the corpse of the husband was thrown in a pit where a pyre was erected and lit. This pit was masked by a cloth, so that one could not see the burning fire. After the corpse was thrown in the pit, the widow jumped in holding a jar with oil on her head.[70] Rogerius stressed the fact that the wife concerned could only immolate herself voluntarily, but he also related that the *kshatriyas* and *śūdras* sometimes gave intoxicating drugs to the victim in order that she might not reconsider her promise to the deceased husband. According to his brahminical informant it was under no circumstances permitted to burn the female victims against their will.[71]

The custom of digging a fire-pit is often mentioned for the south of India, but the Bengalis preferred to fasten the victim to the funeral pile. In the west of India a pyre was usually erected and a small hut built on top of it with a roof of grass, the so-called 'grass-hut', in which the wife was placed together with her husband. In this case the wife should light the roof herself.[72] Some British civil servants insisted that the pile should be so constructed that the wife could even jump down from it at the very last minute,[73] if the heat of the fire caused her to go back on her decision, since the canonical books (*śāstras*) acknowledged the right of the widow to reconsider her decision at any time. For this reason the tying of the victim, locking her up in the grass-hut or similar activities were regarded as being in defiance of law. In common practice, though, the decision of a wife to become a *satī* was regarded as irrevocable. A *satī* who revoked her promise was a disgrace to her family and, for this reason, she was cast out, in spite of religious texts which prescribed specific penances to nullify her defilement.[74]

The voluntary decision of the wife was regarded in later canonical tradition as essential for the validity of the ritual and its beneficial effects. This decision should be taken immediately after the death of the husband and without deliberation with others. Subsequently, the wife should publicly proclaim her resolution (*samkalpa*).[75] After this proclamation her position was fundamentally changed, because she was regarded no longer as an ordinary mortal person, but as a divine being who was endowed with supernatural powers.[76] By her voluntary immolation she undid all transgressions of her husband without regard to their gravity; moreover, she sanctified her own ancestors and those of her husband to the third or seventh generation.[77] In short, the voluntary immolation of the wife was regarded as the supreme form of devotion. Some traditional religious texts even proclaimed this ideal as an integral part of the religion of the Hindus.[78]

From olden days *sutti'ism* was not regarded as a private, but as a public affair. It was attended by communal meals, festivities and processions, in which the *satī* had a central role. The Italian traveller Pietro della Valle, for instance, relates that he met a procession with a *satī* in the city of Ikkeri in south India on 12 November 1623.[79] The wife was unveiled and sat on the back of a horse. In one hand she held a mirror, in which she beheld herself with a sorrowful look, and in the other, she was holding a lemon. Above her head a great umbrella was held as a sign of supreme honour. During her procession of farewell she was accompanied by musicians with drums and many men and women followed her through the city and wished her the best. Della Valle was so impressed by this that he decided to visit the *satī* before her cremation. He met her in the courtyard of her house and related that she was dressed in a white garment, which he describes as her nuptial dress. She was abundantly adorned with necklaces, bracelets and other jewels of gold. Her head was decked with garlands of bright flowers and in her hand she held a lemon, which, he claims, was the usual ceremony. Della Valle mentions that she seemed to be happy enough, talking and laughing in conversation, as a bride in our countries would. Our author was introduced to her and relates that her name was Giaccama and that she belonged to the race of the Terlingas (Telingas). Her deceased husband was a drummer and had also married two other wives who were older than she, but neither of them was willing to die. Giaccama was about 30 years old and mother of a son and a daughter, whom she had entrusted to the care of an uncle and the two other wives of her late husband.[80] She had taken her decision after due thought and without compulsion. Della Valle asked her about the ornaments and the flowers she wore and she told him that such was the custom for a *māstī* (i.e. *mahāsatī*, a great *satī*), because she would meet her husband and therefore had reason to rejoice.

The description by Della Valle is confirmed, in its main lines, by other itineraries.[81] During the procession a *satī* is eulogized as a divine being and led round on a white horse as a symbol of royal triumph, or on an elephant or in a palanquin. If she has a low status, she may walk, but always with an umbrella as a symbol of her importance and flanked by musicians. It is conspicuous that she often holds the same attributes in her hand, according to the authors. In her left hand she has a looking glass, and in her right hand a lemon or coconut, but sometimes also an arrow.[82] Zachariae has pointed to the symbolic meaning of these attributes.[83] The lemon is an auspicious fruit, which would keep off evil.[84] Since the *satī* is in a vulnerable transitional stage, she may be attacked by evil spirits and the lemon would protect her against them.[85] The coconut would have the same effect, since it is also an auspicious fruit which wards off evil. In this context Zachariae draws parallels with rituals of possession, in which the lemon and coconut are used to expel evil spirits. Moreover, he mentions the use of the coconut in another important rite of passage, viz. marriage ceremonies,[86] although the arrow is only held by widows from certain prominent groups.[87] He also points to parallel traditions in the marriage ceremonies in which the bride also holds an arrow. The arrow not only expresses status, but may also refer to magical power.

The mirror is another important attribute which functions in ancient Indian tradition as an auspicious object and is often mentioned in lists with auspicious items.[88] According to a widespread belief, the mirror could expel all kinds of evil, especially evil spirits, but it is also supposed to be effective against the evil eye. The mirror belongs to those presents in ancient Indian tradition which should be given by the groom to the bride, and she should hold it in her left hand.[89] In this connection the parallel with the procession of the *satī* seems to the point. Zachariae is of the opinion that when, during the procession, the *satī* looks in the mirror it is an action to keep off evil, but his explanation is not fully satisfactory and seems to illuminate only one aspect of the matter. In Indian tradition the reflection of a person is often regarded as a part of the soul.[90] When a person sees his reflection in the mirror, he may infer from it that he is still in possession of his soul, while its absence points to a loss of the soul. In the contexts mentioned by Zachariae this is not unimportant, since one may easily lose one's soul in transitional ritual stages, when evil spirits threaten to abduct it. So, when a *satī* beholds her reflection in the mirror during her last procession through the city, this may indicate that she is still in possession of her soul. Because she should make her decision at the funeral pile voluntarily and should be in full possession of her mental faculties, this is of vital importance for its validity.

According to tradition a *satī* should bathe near the place of cremation and then dress herself in two white garments. Then she should renew her official decision (*samkalpa*) with a proclamation in front of the officiating brahmins. In her hand she should hold *kuśa*-grass and sesame seeds to scare off the spirits.[91] Subsequently, she should walk around the pyre three or seven times, ascend it and join the corpse of her husband.[92] When a *satī* goes to meet her husband in the hereafter, she should be in possession of all her mental faculties.[93] The fear that a *satī* might lose her mind and revoke her decision through possession by evil spirits is a striking feature and it is counteracted in many ways.

It is related that a *satī* sometimes pronounces her decision with the same formulas as she had done during her marriage ceremonies.[94] Thus, the symbolic dimension of the sacrament of marriage is also incorporated in the funeral ceremonies.[95] In this context we can observe some other parallels with the marriage ceremonies. During these ceremonies the groom offers an auspicious mirror to his bride, thus implicitly offering her image to her: in his mirror she will behold herself in future. The subsequent ritual actions, viz. the threefold circumambulation of the nuptial fire by the couple and the common taking of seven steps, confirm the sacrament of marriage and irrevocably unite the couple.[96] With this sacrament the wife moves from the sphere of her father and his family to that of her husband. She is bound to him as her lord and protector.

So we can see that features of the marriage ceremonies are embodied in the ritual cremation of a *satī*. The bridal dress, the ornaments, the flowers, the vermilion (*sindhūra*) in the parting of her hair, the attributes in her hands, the henna (*mehndī*) with which her hands and feet are painted, all this and many other ritual activities point to the sacrament of marriage. For this reason a *satī* should be regarded essentially as a bride who follows her deceased groom to the realm of heaven. In terms of the cultural-symbolic idiom her last journey should be regarded as a bridal procession to the burning pile where the sacrament of marriage is once more performed. The three-or sevenfold clockwise circumambulation of the pyre by the *satī* points not so much to funeral ceremonies[97] but to marriage ceremonies.[98] The old invitation of the groom to the bride at the so-called seventh step of the marriage ceremonies, ending with the words: 'Friend! be with seven steps united to me. So be thou devoted to me',[99] is answered at the cremation ceremony by the *satī* with a devotion unto death. She becomes one with her husband, who is the essential soul of herself.[100]

A *satī* is supposed to be endowed with many supernatural powers, as for instance, the gift of prophecy and clairvoyance. Dubois relates that women at the side of the road asked a passing *satī* to prophesy the future.[101] A *satī* was regarded as a saint and a mediatrix; for this reason her grace and intercession were often requested.[102] She was endowed with the gift of bestowing sons upon women without sons; after her death she was sometimes worshipped as a territorial tutelary deity.[103] In some itineraries it is related that people tried to touch her garments during the procession in the hope of benefiting from her power.[104] Sometimes she was asked to give best wishes to beloved persons in the hereafter.[105] Moreover, the gifts of a *satī* were venerated as valuable relics. To sum up, a *satī* was especially dear to the public on account of her mediating, beneficial and evil-averting supernatural powers. For all that, she was also feared on account of her dangerous curses and her destructive powers, as we can see from the following example. On 21 September 1845 soldiers of the Sikh army murdered Jawahar Singh, vizier of the Sikh realm in the Punjab, on suspicion of collaboration with the British. When his widows were forced by soldiers to mount the burning pile as *satīs*, they vehemently cursed the army of the Khalsa and prophesied that the country would lose its independence, that the Khalsa would be destroyed and that the women of the soldiers would be widowed. Their prophetic words were fulfilled within a year and confirmed the popular idea that a *satī* is a powerful saint, whose last words always come true.[106]

WIDOWHOOD

In his passage on 'widow-burning' Diodorus also relates how the elder wife of Ceteus behaved when she was refused admittance to the pile of her husband on account of her pregnancy. She wept, cast the wreath with flowers from her head and tore her hair.[107] This behaviour is often explained in connection with the sad and stern fate of widows, who are considered to be impure and are often despised. The low status of a widow contrasts sharply with that of a *satī*.[108] Rogerius relates that a widow who refuses to immolate herself on the pile of her husband is a shame and a disgrace before everyone. Her hair is shaven off, she is not allowed to wear jewellery or to chew betel nuts and it is out of the question for her to remarry: 'all the sorrow and the pain that one can imagine is given to her'.[109]

The prohibition on remarriage was observed among the higher castes of orthodox Hindus especially. In this respect, they distinguished themselves from many lower castes, who often practised the custom of levirate (remarriage with the deceased husband's brother), especially when the widow was in the blossom of her youth.[110] When a widow belonging to an orthodox family wanted to remarry she was generally viewed as an immoral woman.[111] Remarriage by the widow was regarded as adultery or infidelity to the deceased husband, and also as a shame for his family. According to orthodox Hindus, a wife is fortunate if she dies before her husband, because she will not be subjected to the humiliations, mortifications and insults inherent in widowhood.[112]

The transitional stage from married status to widowhood is also given ritual expression.[113] The abbé Dubois, who lived for many years in the south of India, relates that immediately after the death of her husband a widow dressed herself in her best clothes and adorned herself with all her jewels. Then she threw herself desperately upon his lifeless body, embraced it passionately and uttered loud cries. She held the corpse tightly clasped in her arms, until her parents-in-law were satisfied with this demonstration of grief and tried to restrain her from further sad embraces. When she found that all her attempts to revive her husband were useless, she rolled frenzied on the ground, tore her hair out and manifested many other signs of deep despair. She uttered a whole series of lamentations, in which she blamed her husband for her grim fate:

Why hast thou forsaken me? What wrong have I done thee, that thou shouldst thus leave me in the time of my life? Had I not for thee all the fondness of a faithful wife? Have I not always been virtuous and pure? Have I not borne thee handsome children? . . . Was I not diligent in all the duties of the household? Did I not sweep the household every day, and did I not make the floor smooth and clean? . . . Did I not cook good food for thee? Did thou find grit in the rice that I prepared for thee? . . . Who will take care of me hereafter?[114]

These charges alternated with loud lamentations by the other women who stood around her and participated in her deep sorrow. According to Dubois, accusations with blasphemies against the gods by the desperate widow were a fixed part of the ritual. They were openly charged with cruel injustice in thus depriving her of her beloved husband. The whole scene lasted till her eloquence was exhausted or till she was no longer capable of giving utterance to her sorrow.

Dubois observes that these expressions of grief follow a traditional pattern.[115] He relates, for instance, that an unhappy wife who was really afflicted by the loss of her husband did not behave according to the expectations of the family and other bystanders. She was totally stupefied and could not even utter a cry. For this reason she was despised by her own parents with the words: 'So foolish is she that, on the death of her husband, she did not utter a single word; she did nothing but cry, without saying anything.' According to Dubois, vehement and great expressions of grief in eloquent and demonstrative speech were appreciated by the family and were regarded as a sign of intelligence and education, which would contribute to the estimation of the widow.

Unlike the heroic *satī*, a widow has no special function in the cremation ceremony, but she remains in mourning until her death. She does not return to her former position in the society, like the other mourners, but is left in a liminal situation, which will characterize the rest of her life.[116] The continuation of this liminal stage is often confirmed in a special ritual, which is performed some time after the cremation, often on the tenth or the twelfth day. The soul of the departed is then supposed to be endowed with a new spiritual body, which is especially prepared by means of certain rituals. The deceased husband takes leave of his abode and starts his journey to the hereafter with his new vehicle.[117] Subsequently, the nearest relations, with the exception of the widow, abandon their impure transitional state and start participating again in normal daily activities after being purified by a special bath. The widow, on the other hand, is permanently settled in her isolated impure state during a special ritual, which is performed by her female relatives and friends. Dubois describes two variations of the final funeral rites, depending upon whether the wife of the deceased was of brahminical origin or not.

According to the traditional brahminical ritual the widow painted her eyelids with antimony, her forehead with vermilion, her neck with sandelwood paste and her arms and legs with saffron. She then dressed herself in her richest garments, adorned herself abundantly with all her jewels, twined red flowers in her hair and hung garlands of sweet-smelling flowers round her neck. Then she was brought down by the man who had performed the role of 'chief mourner' in the cremation ceremony and had lit the pyre, usually a brother or a son of the deceased man. She went in procession to the place of cremation and was accompanied by her female married relations and friends. All the women mourned with her; they beat their heads and breasts, wept and sobbed as loudly as they could. After these gestures of sorrow the 'chief mourner' performed the oblation, which confirmed the final farewell of the deceased. His soul was finally connected with a spiritual body and fully equipped for the heavenly journey. The male relations had their heads shaven again, just as they did at the beginning of the funeral ceremonies. The beginning and end of the mourning were symbolized by the shaving, while in the intermediate period the head was not shaved. After this shaving they took a ritual bath in a tank (artificial basin) and were then reincorporated in society.

In principle the situation for the widow was different from that of the other mourners. She was brought to the edge of the tank by her female relations and friends. There a heap of earth was piled, on which a little ball of mud was placed which received the name of the deceased husband. Surrounded by her female relatives and friends, the widow divested herself of all her jewels and beautiful garments. She wiped off all the pigments with which she had adorned the various parts of her body. Finally she took her *tali*, the golden marriage gift, once tied around her neck by her husband as a symbol that he had accepted her as his wife. She placed this precious ornament near the ball of earth representing her husband and pronounced the words: 'I abandon all these to prove to thee my love and my devotion.'[118] With this formula she acknowledged that her marital state in this world had come to an end, but she would bear her widowhood in devotion to her deceased lord. Subsequently, her female relations and friends were purified by the domestic priest (*purohita*) with holy water from the defilement which they had contracted by taking part in the funeral ceremonies. Finally white cotton clothes, symbolic of widowhood, were given to the widow, which she had to put on immediately.[119]

Initiation into widowhood took place in a somewhat different form in non-brahminical circles.[120] The female relatives and friends of the widow entered her house some days after the death of her husband and were given a meal. All surrounded the widow, wept with her and exhorted her to bear her miserable lot with fortitude. One after the other took her in her arms and shed tears with her, but at the end all pushed her violently to the ground. After many lamentations they finally made her sit on a small stool. Subsequently, one of her nearest female relatives cut the thread of her *tali* after having murmured some religious formulas. Then her head was shorn by the barber as a symbol of widowhood. With the performance of this ritual the unhappy wife was confirmed in widowhood for the rest of her life. Dubois remarked in this context that the term *moonda*, i.e. 'shorn-head' or 'bald-head', was one of the worst abusive words that quarrelling women could call each other. The same applied to the curse: 'may you have your *tali* cut', meaning: 'may you become a widow'.[121]

From early times many authors have related that the path of a widow was not strewn with roses. She had to remain in mourning until her death and various symbols were employed to express this state. Until the beginning of this century an orthodox Hindu widow of a higher caste was shaven once a month.[122] She was usually dressed in a simple white cotton cloth, since coloured garments were prohibited. She was not allowed to look in a mirror or to adorn herself with jewellery.[123] The application of make-up such as, for instance, collyrium, vermilion and saffron, was fundamentally wrong. The chewing of betel nut was forbidden. Furthermore, the widow was excluded from any form of amusement or family festivities such as initiation (*upanayana*), marriage ceremonies and the like. Except for her children, her very presence was regarded as an evil omen in orthodox Hindu circles.[124] She was generally regarded as impure, or in the words of a maxim: 'just as the body, bereft of life, in that moment becomes impure, so the woman bereft of her husband is always impure, even if she has bathed properly'.[125] She was often humiliated and the subject of hate and contempt. She had to sleep on the ground and restrict herself to one meal a day. She was always controlled by the family of her deceased husband in order to ensure that she might not harm or disgrace him, because his spiritual well-being was supposed to be closely connected with her behaviour.[126] Only by a life of ascetic discipline combined with prayer and other forms of worship in pious memory of her lord, might she hope to become connected with him again in the next life.[127]

HER LAST JOURNEY

In the tradition of orthodox Hinduism a wife has only two options when her husband dies. She may 'choose' to become a *sati* and is then regarded as extremely holy.[128] Indian religious literature contains many eulogies on the *sati*. The *sati* embodies, as it were, the ideal wife, who is totally devoted to her husband. By her voluntary immolation she demonstrates that she goes through the fire for him in order to achieve his well-being for him. Her death clears all his faults and brings them together again as a couple in the heavenly regions.[129] According to some conceptions, a wife cannot choose this option, because she is elected for it on account of her good *karman*. Popular tradition proclaims that the heavenly power of *sat* descends on a *satī* at the time of her decision and renders her insensible to pain.[130]

When a widow 'chooses' widowhood she is considered impure and a bad omen.[131] It is sometimes regarded as her fault that her husband died, because she is responsible for his well-being and his term of life. In this context the lamentations mentioned above are relevant. 'What wrong have I done to thee, that thou shouldst thus leave me in the time of my life. Had I not for thee the fondness of a faithful wife?'[132] These lamentations not only have a psychological meaning, but also refer to metaphysical conceptions, which are deeply rooted in traditional Hindu culture. In the *Rāmāyana*, for instance, Rāma's wife Sītā complains that the wife is held responsible for the death of her husband, even if she leads a religious life and has been totally devoted to him.[133] According to popular tradition, a wife may cause the death of her husband by her bad *karman*, even if she has no idea of it. Widowhood is thus connected with evil in a former life, for which she has now to suffer,[134] and this idea still exists in certain circles of orthodox Hindus.[135] In this context, the ascetic way of life for a widow becomes meaningful. By her acts of penance a widow can wipe out her guilt and acquire merit, which fosters the well-being of her husband in the hereafter. Many religious books of rules on right conduct, *dharmaśāstras*, recommend renunciation and asceticism for a widow as the obvious way to heaven.[136] In some brahmanic circles, asceticism is even more valued than the immolation of the *satī*, because this is considered as a form of suicide and, for this reason, condemned.[137]

Marriage symbols play an important role in the rituals I have discussed. They give expression to the idea that husband and wife form a unity and that the line between life and death in this respect is only relative. The wife is often regarded as the better half of her man. A *satī* is dressed as a bride and joins her husband on the pile to be connected with him in the hereafter as his spouse. She presents herself not as a widow, but as a spouse and a married woman. She is not regarded as a being which causes evil; on the contrary, through the ordeal by fire she promotes the well-being of her husband and his family and clears her negative *karman*.[138] In popular tradition she has sometimes been transformed into a tutelary deity of the village.[139]

A 'widow' also presents herself as a bride in front of the corpse of her husband. She too refers to the sacrament of marriage and defines herself as the spouse of the deceased man. Her marital status in this world comes to an end by his cremation and by his journey to the hereafter. After his soul has been endowed with a spiritual body he leaves this world and the wife enters widowhood. All attributes characteristic of her marital status are taken away from her. She does not, however, regain her freedom, because she remains defined in terms of her deceased husband in spite of the separation. This is expressed in the formula with which she surrenders her *tali*: 'I abandon all these to prove thee my love and my devotion.' Widowhood is characterized by love and devotion to the deceased husband. The renunciation refers to the outer features of the marital status. In orthodox Hinduism a married woman is regarded as the other half of the husband and this does not change when she becomes a widow, or in the words of an ancient medieval author: 'The wife is declared to be half of man's body, she participates equally in the husband's merit and sin; a virtuous wife, whether she burns herself on her husband's funeral pile or lives after him, tends to the spiritual benefit of her husband.'[140] For this reason she may auspiciously or inauspiciously influence the well-being of her husband by her behaviour. These religious notions have led to many rules in which asceticism, chastity and devotion to the deceased husband take a central position.[141] After the death of her husband the widow remains bound to his memory and well-being by a series of painstaking prescriptions.[142]

Many itineraries have mentioned the bad treatment of the widow. This is confirmed in Indian tradition where the widow is qualified as an inauspicious omen and treated accordingly. This treatment is not explained satisfactorily on the grounds that she is implicitly held responsible for the death of her husband. She is also regarded as permanently impure. In fact, she is a living corpse, the living half of her deceased husband. For this reason she is an 'outcast', no longer part of the regular society and restricted in her freedom of movement. She is under the control of her sons, if she is lucky enough to have sons; otherwise, she is dependent for her subsistence upon the family of her husband.[143] She lives separated from her friends and has to do the most menial and impure tasks in the household. Thus she is punished for the death of her husband and the grief she has given to his family.

In this connection a few words may be devoted to the problems of the child-widow.[144] The custom of marrying off young children and consummating marriage after the first menstruation of the girl led to a situation in which some girls became widows at an early age and were thus marked for the rest of their life.[145] Many orthodox Hindus were of the opinion that child-widows should not remarry, even if marriage had not been consummated, in spite of the fact that the ancient codes of law acknowledged such a possibility.[146] If they were without protection, these child-widows became a prey of people of the worst sort.

The way of living of the orthodox Hindu widow has been compared by some authors with that of the ascetic (*samnyāsin*), who searched after salvation.[147] The focus of comparison is then the central feature that both are marginal to traditional society. The way of life of both is characterized by great soberness and austerities, such as one meal a day and regular fastings on specific days; not the bed, but the hard floor is the place where they ought to sleep. The widow is set apart by her white cotton dress and her tonsure and may therefore be compared with the ascetic, who is also stigmatized by his clothing and shaven head. Both are not supposed to participate in social inter-course. The ascetic has to cut the ties with his family and the widow is supposed to reduce them to a minimum. His point of orientation is final release, her point of orientation the deceased husband. By all these forms of renunciation the widow is essentially considered an ascetic, who practises austerities in order to gain religious merit which extinguishes her bad *karman* and promotes salvation. Only then may she hope to join her husband in the world to come.[148] For all that, the comparison with the ascetic fails to do justice to one essential point, viz. the voluntariness of his decision. His break with traditional society and choice of a wandering life as an ascetic is determined by his ideal of release. He no longer defines his religious identity in terms of traditional society. The widow, on the contrary, has no choice and is usually bound to the family of her departed husband. There she is supervised by her male relatives according to the general rule that women should never act independently, irrespective of age.[149] For this reason women should always be kept under the control of their fathers, husbands, sons or other relatives.[150] The idea that a woman can break with her family, just like the ascetic, is totally rejected in orthodox Hinduism. The widow remains connected with her deceased husband on account of the sacrament of marriage; only her duties have become different. She remains defined in terms of her deceased husband and an independent religious identity is denied to her.[151]

From this point of view, no path of salvation exists for the widow apart from that which leads to her husband. The break with the family for the sake of world-renunciation is not suitable for women. A widow may cause damage to her deceased husband and his family on account of her 'wild' sexual energy which is then no longer controlled.[152] The ascetic way of life to which a widow is condemned is therefore not based on the ideal of world renunciation for the sake of higher knowledge and release. Her austerities should be seen in the context of guilt and penance with respect to the dead husband who is essentially the true self of his spouse.[153]

The application of symbols of marriage in funeral ceremonies of orthodox Hinduism may seem bizarre and extraordinary at first sight. On closer inspection, however, these symbols are highly expressive of the ways in which the relations between husband and spouse are conceptualised. This implies, *inter alia*, that women in this tradition are not supposed to be endowed with a religious identity of their own, but are seen as complementary to men from whom they derive their identity. At the same time women are held responsible for the results of their bad *karman* on account of former births. Up to the present day these two seemingly inconsistent ideological notions have influenced the sad fate of widows in certain orthodox circles.

NOTES

1 F. Max Müller, *Auld Lang Syne* II (London, 1899) 46.

2 For the expression *sutti'ism* and *suttee* see R.E. Yule and A.C. Burnell, *Hobson-Jobson, A Glossary of Anglo-Indian Words and Phrases*, rev. edn W. Crooke 1903 (repr. New Delhi, 1968) 878 s.v. *suttee*; E. Thompson, *Suttee, a Historical and Philosophical Inquiry into the Hindu Rite of Widow-Burning* (London, 1928) 15f.; A. Sharma, *Sati, Historical and Phenomenological Essays* (Delhi, 1988) 85 n. 5 and 86 n. 6. For the difference between *suttee* and *satī* see J. Leslie, 'Suttee or *Satī*: Victim or Victor?', *Bulletin of the Center for the Study of World Religions* 14 (1987–8) 2, 5–23; C. Weinberger-Thomas, 'Cendres d'immortalité: La crémation des veuves en Inde', *Archives de Sciences Sociales des Religions* 67 (1989) 9–37. See further the various articles in J.S. Hawley (ed.), *Sati, The Blessing and The Curse: The Burning of Wives in India* (New York and Oxford, 1994).

3 For a short description of some itineraries see e.g. R. Garbe, *Beiträge zur indischen Kulturgeschichte* (Berlin, 1903) ch. 4. For the practice of *suttee* on the Indonesian islands Bali and Lombok see C. Fryke and C. Schweitzer, *Voyages to the East Indies* (1700[1]), with introduction and notes by C. Ernest Fayle (London, 1929) 109f.

4 For an analysis of the statistical data in Bengal see B.B. Roy, *Socioeconomic Impact of Sati in Bengal and the Role of Raja Rammohun Roy* (Calcutta, 1987) 37–80 and appendices 146ff.; cf. J. Fisch, 'Jenseitsglaube, Ungleichheit und Tod: Zu einigen Aspekten der Totenfolge', *Saeculum* 44 (1993, 265–99) especially 268–9.

5 H.T. Colebrooke quoted by P.V. Kane, *History of Dharmaśāstra* II (Poona, 1974²) 636.

6 Diodorus lived in the second half of the first century BC. His work is conveniently available in *Diodorus of Sicily*, with an English translation by C.H. Oldfather and others (12 vols, London, 1933–67). The fragments on India are found in vol. 9 (containing Bks 18 and 19) with a transl. by R. M. Geer (London, 1947¹). See also R.C. Majumdar, *The Classical Accounts of India* (Calcutta, 1960) 162, 240f.

7 For the sources of this information see R.M. Geer in his introduction to vol. 9 of Diodorus Siculus, vii–xii.

8 Diodorus Siculus, ch. 19.33.1–34.8. See also E.R. Bevan, *Cambridge History of India*, I (1922: repr. New Delhi, 1968) 415.

9 See Strabo, ch. 15.1.30: 'The groom and the bride choose one another themselves, and the wives are burned up with their deceased husbands for a reason of this kind – that they sometimes fell in love with young men and deserted their husbands or poisoned them; and therefore the Cathaeans established this as a law, thinking that they would put a stop to the poisoning. However, the law is not stated in a plausible manner, nor the cause of it either' (tr. H.L. Jones, Loeb Classical Library); see also ch. 15.1.62.

10 See M. Winternitz, *Die Frau in den indischen Religionen* I (Leipzig, 1920) 71ff.; W. Heckel and J.C. Yardley, 'Roman Writers and the Indian Practice of Suttee', *Philologus* 125 (1981) 305–11; R. C. Vofchuk, 'The Women of India as pictured by Greek and Latin Authors', *Annals of the Bhandarkar Oriental Research Institute* 69 (1988) 141–54.

11 Diodorus Siculus, ch. 19.33.2; Strabo, ch. 15.1.30. The same theory is suggested in the example given by François Bernier (1620–88), *Bernier's Voyage to the East Indies containing the Late Revolution of the Empire of the Great Mogol* (English edn, London 1658¹), tr. and annotated by A. Constable (London, 1891), revised by V.A. Smith (London, 1934) 308ff., especially 310f.; L.A. Dubois, *Hindu Manners, Customs and Ceremonies*, 1806 (Oxford, 1968, repr. of the edn of 1906³) 35; A.K. Ray, *Widows are not for Burning, Actions and Attitudes of Christian Missionaries, the Native Hindus and Lord William Bentick* (New Delhi, 1985) 10f.

12 Diodorus Siculus, ch. 19.33.2. See also V.N. Datta, *Sati, Widow Burning in India* (New Delhi, 1988) 5.

13 H.H. Wilson, 'On the Supposed Vaidik Authority for the Burning of Hindu Widows and on the Funeral Ceremonies of the Hindus', *J. Roy. As. Soc.* 16 (1854) 201–14, republished in his *Essays and Lectures Chiefly on the Religion of the Hindus* II (London, 1862); Winternitz, *Frau in den indischen Religionen* (see note 10 above), 61f.; A.S.Altekar, *The Position of Women in Hindu Civilization*, 1938¹ (Delhi, 1987) 122ff.; Kane, *History of Dharmaśāstra* II (see note 5 above), 627; See also H.T.

Colebrooke, 'On the Duties of a Faithful Hindu Widow', originally published in *Asiatic Researches* 4 (1795) 209–19, republished in *Miscellaneous Essays* (Madras, 1872²) 133–40 with references to the older literature in note 1 above. See also Raja Radhakanta Deb, 'Remarks on the Burning of Widows', *J. Roy. As. Soc.* 17 (1859) 209–20, republished in Wilson, *Essays and Lectures* II, 293ff., especially for the opinion that Vedic tradition contains starting points for the practice of *suttee*. See also Müller, *Auld Lang Syne* (see note 1 above) II, 43ff.

14　V.A. Smith, *The Oxford History of India* (Oxford, 1919) 62. The data mentioned by Diodorus Siculus and Strabo seem to point to the northwest of India; the data found in the *Mahābhārata* (see note 16 below) and the Jain tradition corroborate this suggestion. Cf. also Thompson, *Suttee* (see note 2 above), 20ff.; N.M. Penzer (ed.), *The Ocean of Story*, IV (London, 1924) 255ff. (appendix I); J.C. Jain, *Life in Ancient India as Depicted in the Jain Canons* (Delhi, 1962) 163.

15　For the supposition that widow-burning would have its origin in the 'non-Aryan' culture of India see Thompson, *Suttee*, 20f.; Ray, *Widows are not for Burning* (see note 11 above), 2f.; Datta, *Sati* (see note 12 above), 3.

16　See *Mahābhārata* ll. 116–18, where the story of the death of Pāndu is related. His two wives, Kuntī and Mādrī, both claim the honour of following their beloved husband on the funeral pile. Mādrī, a Bactrian princess, walks off with the prize. She is dressed in her richest garments, abundantly adorned with golden ornaments, and escorted by musicians to the pyre, where she is cremated with her husband; cf. also Altekar, *Position of Women*, 120.

17　See Vishnu Smirti 25.14 (in the section on women); cf. J. Jolly, *The Institutes of Vishnu*, 1880¹ (repr. Delhi, 1977: *Sacred Books of the East*, vol. 7) 111 for the translation.

18　Kane, *History of Dharmaśāstra* II, 624ff. (with n. 1477). He refers, among others, to the codes of law of Angiras and Sankha. Cf. also W. Ward, *The Hindoos, History, Literature and Religion*, 1815² (New Delhi, 1981) 235ff.; J. Peggs, *India's Cries to British Humanity* (London, 1830²) 29ff., later repr. under the title: *Cries of Agony, a Historical Account of Suttee, Infanticide, Ghat Murders and Slavery in India* (Delhi, 1984); Winternitz, *Die Frau in den indischen Religionen* (see note 10 above), 59ff.; Sharma, *Sati*, 31f.

19　For a short survey see Winternitz, *Frau in den indischen Religionen*, 62ff.; Kane, *History of Dharmaśāstra*, II, 624ff.; Altekar, *Position of Women*, 115ff.

20　Winternitz, *Frau in den indischen Religionen*, 68–70; Thompson, *Suttee*, 28ff.; S. Settar and G.D. Sontheimer (eds), *Memorial Stones* (Heidelberg and Dharwad, 1982); Weinberger-Thomas, 'Cendres d'immortalité' (see note 2 above), 24 and nn.

21　See, e.g., Weinberger-Thomas, 'Cendres d'immortalité', 11 and n. 4 (references to other literature).

22　See e.g. Winternitz, *Frau in den indischen Religionen*, 62; Altekar, *Position of Women*, 124ff.; Kane, *History of Dharmaśāstra* II, 631ff.; Sharma, *Sati*, 15ff.

23　See, e.g., Kane, *History of Dharmaśāstra* II, 633; J. Leslie, 'A Problem of Choice, The Heroic *Satī* or the Widow-Ascetic', in J. Bronkhorst (ed.), *Panels of the VIIth World Sanskrit Conference*, vol. IX, J. Leslie (ed.), *Rules and Remedies in Classical Indian Law* (Leiden, 1991) 49.

24 See, e.g., Sharma, *Sati*, 15ff. and nn.; Roy, *Socioeconomic Impact*, 54.

25 See, e.g., R. Garbe, *Beiträge zur indischen Kulturgeschichte* (Berlin, 1903) 143ff.; Th. Zachariae, 'Zur indischen Witwenverbrennung', *Zeitschrift des Vereins für Volkskunde* 14 (1904) 198–211; 302–13; 395–407; 15 (1905) 74–90; Winternitz, *Frau in den indischen Religionen*, 7ff.; K. Gupta, *The Social Status of Hindu Women in Northern India (1207–1707 A.D.)* (New Delhi, 1987) 243ff.

26 Ibn Battūta, *The Travels of Ibn Battūta (A.D. 1325–1354)*, tr. with revision and nn. by H.A.R. Gibb, III (Cambridge, 1971) 614f.

27 S. Chaudhuri, 'Satī as a Social Institution and the Mughals', *Indian History Congress Proceedings* (New Delhi, 1976) 218–23; S. Chaudhuri, 'Medieval Indian Society, State and Social Custom. Satī as a Case of Study', *The Calcutta Historical Journal* 8 (1983–84) 38–60.

28 See Peggs, *India's Cries* (see note 18 above), 64.

29 See, e.g., Thompson, *Suttee*, 57ff.; Datta, *Sati*, 19ff.; P. Spear, 'The Mughals and the British', in A.L. Basham (ed.), *A Cultural History of India* (Oxford, 1975) 348ff. See also J.T.F. Jordens, 'Hindu Religious and Social Reform in British India', in A.L. Basham (ed.), *A Cultural History of India*, 365ff.

30 In 1805 the governor-general of the East India Company, Lord Wellesley, asked the advice of the Court of *Nizamat Adalat* (Supreme Court) with respect to this subject: see Datta, *Sati*, 22.

31 See Datta, *Sati*, ch. 2.

32 Parliamentary Papers (see note 41 below), *Papers relating to East India Affairs, viz. Hindoo Widows and Voluntary Immolations by Order of the House of Commons*, vol. 18 (1821) 32 containing The Extract Judicial Consultations, 5 December 1812. See also Kane, *History of Dharmaśāstra* II, 633.

33 For these directions see the 'Draft of Directions to be issued by Magistrates to the Public Darogahs', Calcutta 9 October 1813, published in: Peggs, *India's Cries*, 51f. In the following years these regulations were further refined.

34 The freedom of the Hindu religion was guaranteed in Statute 36 Geo III Cap. CXII sec. 12. See also Datta, *Sati*, 143; Roy, *Socioeconomic Impact*, 108. Spear, 'Mughals and the British', in Basham, *Cultural History* (see note 29 above), 259f. See also A.A. Yang, 'Whose Sati? Widow Burning in Early nineteenth Century India', *Journal of Women's History* 1 (1989) 2, 8–33.

35 See, e.g., Bentick's Minute on Sati, dated 8 November 1829, in C.H. Philips, *The Correspondence of Lord William Cavendish Bentick* I (Oxford, 1977) 335–45, especially 337. For a survey of opinions see Datta, *Sati*, 19ff.

36 Peggs, *India's Cries*, 14f.

37 See Spear, 'The Mughals and the British' and Jordens, 'Hindu Social and Religious Reform', in Basham, *Cultural History* (see note 29 above), chs XXV and XXVI.

38 Ward, *The Hindoos* (see note 18 above), 235ff.; J. Peggs, *The Suttees' Crie to Britain* (London, 1827); and *India's Cries* (see note 18 above), 1ff.; Ray, *Widows are not for Burning*, 21ff.; Sharma, *Sati*, 57ff. and nn.; Datta, *Sati*, 71ff.

39 See, e.g., Ray, *Widows are not for Burning*, 36ff.; Roy, *Socioeconomic Impact*, 81ff.

40 See Roy's advice, quoted in Bentick's Minute on Sati (11 November 1829): 'The practice might be suppressed, quietly and unobservedly, by increasing the difficulties and by indirect agency of the police', in Philips, *Correspondence of Bentick* (see note 35 above) I, 335ff. Cf. also Rammohun Roy, *Translation of a Conference between an Advocate for and an Opponent of the Practice of Burning Widows Alive from the Original Bungla* (Calcutta, 1818); *A Second Conference between an Advocate for and an Opponent of the Practice of Burning Widows Alive* (Calcutta, 1820); *Brief Remarks Regarding Modern Encroachment on the Ancient Rights of Females according to the Hindoo Laws of Inheritance* (Calcutta, 1822); and the pamphlet *The Abstract of the Arguments Regarding the Burning of Widows Considered as a Religious Rite* (Calcutta, 1830). See further Ashis Nandi, 'Sati, a Nineteenth Century Tale of Women, Violence and Protest', in V.C. Joshi (ed.), *Rammohun Roy and the Process of Modernisation in India* (Delhi, 1975), 170ff.

41 Great Britain Parliamentary Papers, House of Commons, *Papers Relating to East India Affairs, viz. Hindoo Widows and Voluntary Immolations by order of the House of Commons*, vol. 18 (1821); vol. 23 (1824); vol. 24 (1825); vol. 26 (1826–7); vol. 28 (1830).

42 For the Sati Regulation Act XVII, AD 1829 of the Bengal Code, 4 December 1929, see Philips, *Correspondence of Bentick* I, 360–2; see also Datta, *Sati*, 88ff.

43 Sati Regulation Act XVII: 'The practice of *suttee* ... is nowhere enjoined by the religion of the Hindus'. Cf. also Bentick's Minute on Sati (see note 35 above).

44 See Thompson, *Suttee*, 117ff.; R.K. Saxena, *Social Reforms, Infanticide and Sati* (New Delhi, 1974) 77–143; Datta, *Sati*, 151ff.

45 See the British Parliamentary Papers (see note 41 above); cf. also Ward, *Hindoos*, 235ff.; Peggs, *India's Cries*, 1–112; R. Hartley Kennedy, *The Sutti, as witnessed at Baroda, November 29th, 1825* (London, 1855).

46 See H.T. Colebrooke, 'Duties of a Faithful Widow', *Asiatic Researches* 4 (1795) 209–19; Wilson, *Essays and Lectures* II, 270ff.; Raja Radhakanta Deb, 'Remarks', in Wilson, *Essays and Lectures* II, 293ff.

47 See, e.g., Kane, *History of Dharmaśāstra* II, 624ff.; Sharma, *Sati*, 57ff.

48 Ray, *Widows are not for Burning*, 26 referring to W. Carey. See also Ward, *Hindoos*, 235ff., and Peggs, *India's Cries*, 8f.

49 Ward, *Hindoos*, 246 and Peggs, *India's Cries*, 29f. and 34f. Peggs enumerates the arguments which are given in various missionary periodicals, e.g., *The Friend of India*.

50 See Philips, *Correspondence of Bentick* I (letter 157: Bentick in his Minute on Sati, 8 November 1829) 344: 'The first and primary object of my heart is the benefit of the Hindus. I know nothing so important to the

improvement of their future conditions, as the establishment of a purer morality, whatever their belief, and a more just conception of the will of God. The first step to this better understanding will be dissociation of religious belief and practice from blood and murder. They will then, when no longer under this brutalizing element, view with more calmness, acknowledged truths.'

51 Ibid., 344.

52 See, e.g., R. Garbe, *Beiträge zur indischen Kulturgeschichte* (Berlin, 1903) 143ff.; Penzer, *Ocean of Story*, IV, 255ff.

53 This explanation is not very satisfactory because no explanation is given for why married men did not similarly follow their deceased wives and why the custom occurred only occasionally and then only in specific circles.

54 An exception to this is A.K. Coomaraswami, 'Satī: A Defense of the Indian Woman', *Sociological Review* (April 1913). See also A.K. Coomaraswami, *The Dance of Shiva* (New York, 1957 revised edn) 109ff. Recently attention has been drawn to the symbolic aspects of the ritual by Weinberger-Thomas, 'Cendres d'immortalité' (note 2 above), 16ff.

55 For a discussion of recent cases of *satī* see K. Sangari and S. Vaid, 'Sati in Modern India: A Report', *Economic and Political Weekly*, 1 August 1981, 1285–8; *Seminar*, February 1988 with articles by K. Sangari, 'Perpetuating the Myth', 24–30; S. Vaid, 'Politics of Widow-Immolation', 19–24; V. Dhagamwar, 'Saint, Victim or Criminal', 34–9; and others. See, further, D.K. Stein, 'Women to Burn: Suttee as a Normative Institution', *Signs* 4 (1978) 2, 253–68; ibid., 'Burning Widows, Burning Brides: The Perils of Daughterhood in India', *Pacific Affairs*, 61 (1988) 3, 464–85. Weinberger-Thomas, 'Cendres d'immortalité', 16ff.; L.P. van den Bosch, 'A Burning Question, Satī and Satī Temples as the Focus of Political Interest', *Numen* 37 (1990) 174–94 and 'Pilgrimage, Prestige and Protest: On the Origin of Recent *Satī* Temples in India', in H.T. Bakker (ed.), *The Sacred Centre as the Focus of Political Interest* (Groningen, 1992) 143–60; M. Tully, *No Full Stops in India* (London, 1991) 210–36 (The Deorala Sati); S. Narasimhan, *Sati, Widow Burning in India* (New York, London and Toronto, 1992). See, further, L. Harley, *Religion and Rajput Women: The Ethic of Protection in Contemporary Narratives* (Berkeley, Los Angeles and Oxford, 1992) 112–53 (*Satimata* tradition: The Transformative Process) and 154–181 (*Satimata* tradition: The Role of Volition); Hawley, *Sati, The Blessing and The Curse*; J. Fisch, 'Jenseitsglaube, Ungleichheit und Tod: Zu einigen Aspekten der Totenfolge', *Saeculum* 44 (1993, 265–99) especially 266–7.

56 For the descriptions see, e.g., Ward, *Hindoos*, 235ff.; Peggs, *India's Cries*, 3ff. Cf. also Sharma, *Sati*, 57ff.; Ray, *Widows are not for Burning*, 21ff.

57 See Leslie, 'Suttee or *Satī*: Victim or Victor' (note 2 above), 5ff. See also A. Hejib and K. Young, 'Satī, Widowhood and Yoga', in Sharma, *Sati* (note 2 above), 73–84.

58 Diodorus Siculus, ch. 19.34.1–3.

59 This is in accordance with canonical prescriptions; see, e.g., Kane, *History of Dharmaśāstra* II, 633.

60 According to Diodorus Siculus, ch. 19.34.6 the event was eulogized, although some of the Greeks were horrified and qualified the cremation as a barbarous custom.

61 For a general description of the ritual of *suttee* according to Indian textual tradition see Colebrooke, *Miscellaneous Essays* (note 13 above), 133ff.

62 See, e.g., Weinberger-Thomas, 'Cendres d'immortalité', 24. For the sacrament of marriage see also R.B. Pandey, *Hindu Samskāras, Socio-Religious Study of the Hindu Sacraments* (Delhi, 1969²) ch. 7, especially 225ff.; S. Stevenson, *The Rites of the Twice-Born* (London, 1920); W. Harman, 'The Hindu Marriage as a Soteriological Event', in *International Journal of Sociology of the Family* 17 (1987) issue 2, 169–82.

63 See H. Bushby, *Widow-Burning, a Narrative*, (London, 1855) 7; Saxena, *Social Reforms*, 87f. For details on the dressing of the hair see, e.g., Weinberger-Thomas, 'Cendres d'immortalité', 21.

64 See L. Griffin, *Ranjit Singh* (New Delhi, 1957) 66.

65 See, e.g., *The Illustrated Weekly of India*, 4–10 October, 20ff. See also Van den Bosch, 'Burning Question' (note 55 above), 174ff.

66 See, e.g., Weinberger-Thomas, 'Cendres d'immortalité', 29ff.

67 For these expressions see, e.g., Thompson, *Suttee*, 15; Kane, *History of Dharmaśāstra* II, 627f.; Sharma, *Sati*, 86 n. 10; Leslie, 'Suttee or *Satī*: Victim or Victor', 5ff.

68 The custom of using the slippers is mentioned in several Sanskrit texts, e.g. the Brāhma Purāna; cf. Colebrooke, 'Duties of a Faithful woman', 138; Ward, *Hindoos*, 236. Mundy mentions the turban; P. Mundy, *The Travels of Peter Mundy in Europe and Asia, 1608–1667* II, R.C. Temple (ed.) (London, 1914). See also Weinberger-Thomas, 'Cendres d'immortalité', 40 and n. 35.

69 A. Rogerius, *De Open-deure tot het verborgen heydendom* (1651¹), W. Caland (ed.) (The Hague, 1915).

70 Rogerius, 78ff. For a traditional copper-plate see J. H. van Linschoten, *Itinerario ofte Schipvaert van Jan Huygen van Linschoten naar Oost ofte Portugaels Indien* (1596¹), H. Kern (ed.) in 3 vols and revised by H. Terpstra (Amsterdam, 1956) II, plate 58/59 facing p. 24. For the English edition see A. C. Burnell and P.A. Tiele, *The Voyages of Linschoten to the East Indies*, 2 vols (London, 1875–85).

71 For the use of intoxicating drugs see also Zachariae, 'Witwenverbrennung' (see note 25 above), 1904, 305 and n. 1.

72 See W. Crooke, *The Popular Religion and Folklore of Northern India*, 1896¹ (Delhi, 1968) 188; Zachariae, 'Witwenverbrennung', 307 and n. 3; for a drawing in an ancient itinerary see Mundy, *Travels* II, 35.

73 Datta, *Sati*, 55ff. with notes referring to the Parliamentary Papers of 1825, vol. XXIV; Gupta, *Social Status of Women*, 262ff.

74 See, e.g., Colebrooke, 'Duties of a Faithful Woman', 137: 'If the woman regretting life, recedes from the pile, she is defiled, but she may be purified by observing the fast called *prājāpatya*'. Cf. also Weinberger-Thomas, 'Cendres d'immortalité', 18.

75 See, e.g., Colebrooke, 'Duties', 134ff.; Kane, *History of Dharmaśāstra*, II, 634. Cf. also Hejib and Young, 'Satī, Widowhood and Yoga' (see note 57 above), 76 n. 349.

76 For a discussion of recent cases see Van den Bosch, 'Pilgrimage, Prestige and Protest' (note 55 above) 143ff. with references to other literature.

77 See, e.g., Altekar, *Position of Women*, 126; E. Abegg, *Das Pretakalpa des Garuda-Purāna, eine Darstellung des hinduistischen Totenkultes und Jenseitsglaube* (Berlin, 1956²) 140ff. (tr. of Garuda Purāna X.35–35); Leslie, 'Suttee or *Satī*', 5ff. Cf. also Rogerius, *Open-deure*, 80.

78 See S.A. Dange, *Encyclopaedia of Puranic Beliefs and Practices*, IV (New Delhi, 1989) 1258 s.v. *satī*, with references to various Purānas. Cf. also Kane, *History of Dharmaśāstra* II, 625ff.

79 See P. della Valle, *The Travels of Pietro della Valle in India*, 1664¹, E. Grey (ed.), 2 vols (London, 1892) II, 273ff. For a critical evaluation of Della Valle see Zachariae, 'Witwenverbrennung' 1904, 302ff. See also D. Barbosa, *The Book of Duarte Barbosa, an Account of the Countries Bordering on the Indian Ocean and their Inhabitants, Written by Duarte Barbosa and Completed in the Year 1518 A.D.* (originally published in Ramusio, Vienna, 1550), tr. from the Portuguese by M.L. Dame, 2 vols (London, 1918–21) I, 214ff.

80 Della Valle, *Travels*, II, 266f.; 274f.

81 Zachariae, 'Witwenverbrennung', 1904 and 1905; Weinberger-Thomas, 'Cendres d'immortalité', 24 with references to other literature in n. 36. See also Gupta, *Status of Women*, 245ff.

82 Rogerius, *Open-deure*, 78 is of the opinion that these attributes depend upon caste and estate. See also Zachariae, 'Witwenverbrennung', 1904, 206ff.

83 Zachariae points to a note in Grey's edition of the Itinerary of Pietro della Valle (see note 79 above), 266: 'The mirror and the lemon may, or may not, have a symbolical meaning.'

84 Zachariae, 'Witwenverbrennung', refers in this context, among others, to Crooke, *The Popular Religion and Folklore of Northern India* II, 36. Cf. also Weinberger-Thomas, 'Cendres d'immortalité', 24f.

85 According to Zachariae, 'Witwenverbrennung', 398 the yellow colour, just like red and black', might scare the spirits. A lemon is also sometimes put in the mouth and the nostrils of a dying person to protect him against evil spirits; Weinberger-Thomas, 'Cendres d'immortalité', 19.

86 Zachariae, 'Witwenverbrennung', 1904, 404f.

87 In this context he refers to the *kshatriyas* of Travancore and the Nambudiri brahmins of the Malabar coast; Zachariae, 'Witwenverbrennung' 1905, 78.

88 Zachariae, 'Witwenverbrennung' 1905, 78.

89 Śankhāyana Grihya Sūtra 1.12.6–7.

90 See J.J. von Negelein, 'Bild und Schatten im Volksglauben', *Archiv für Religionswissenschaft* 5 (1902, 1–37) 21ff.

91 See, e.g., Kane, *History of Dharmaśāstra* II, 633f.

92 See Colebrooke, *Essays*, 134f.: 'Reflecting that this life is nought: my lord and master to me was all, she walks around the burning pile.'

93 See, e.g., Garuda-Purāna, Pretakalpa X, 48ff., (tr.) Abegg, *Pretakalpa* (see note 77 above), 142f.

94 See Weinberger-Thomas, 'Cendres d'immortalité', 19.

95 See Colebrooke, *Essays*, 135. He refers to the *samkalpa* formulated by

Angiras in which it is stated that wife and husband shall enjoy the delights of heaven together.

96 For a description of the marriage ceremonies see Stevenson, *Rites of the Twice-born* (see note 62 above), chapter on marriage; Pandey, *Samskārās* (see note 62 above), especially 215–19.

97 Cf. also W. Caland, 'Een Indogermaansch lustratie-gebruik', *Verhandelingen en Meededelingen Koninklijke Akademie van Wetenschappen*, afd. Lett., 4e reeks, deel 2 (Amsterdam, 1898) 275ff. In funeral ceremonies an anti-clockwise direction is often mentioned.

98 See Zachariae, 'Witwenverbrennung' 1904, 306 and n. 3. The Leipziger manuscript of the Sahāgamanavidhi mentions seven *pradakshinas*. See also Stein, 'Burning Widows' (see note 55 above), 467.

99 See Parāskara Grihya Sūtra 1.8.1. H. Oldenberg (tr.), *The Grihya Sūtras, Rules of Vedic Domestic Ceremonies* I (Oxford, 1886) 283.

100 See Garuda Purāna, Pretakalpa 10.45. E. Abegg (tr.), *Pretakalpa* (see note // above), 141: 'Sie wird mit dem toten Gemahl, der ihres innersten Selbtes Seele ist, eins.'

101 Dubois, *Hindu Manners* (see note 11 above), 362. See also W.H. Sleeman, *Rambles and Recollections of an Indian Official* I (London, 1893) 27f., 160.

102 Dubois, *Hindu Manners*, 358; Leslie, 'A Problem of Choice' (see note 23 above), 46.

103 Weinberger-Thomas, 'Cendres d'immortalité', 25.

104 See Zachariae, 'Witwenverbrennung' (see note 25 above) 1905, 86 n. 1, in which he refers to authors such as Stavorinus, Tavernier and Careri.

105 Ibn Battūta, *Travels of Ibn Battūta*, III, 615. See also Gupta, *Social Position of Women*, 260 n. 59.

106 See Datta, *Sati*, 160f.; Narasimhan, *Sati* (see note 55 above), 90. Cf. also Doddwell, *The Cambridge History of India* V, 547f.

107 Diodorus Siculus 19.34.3 (Loeb edn, vol. VII, 323).

108 Many ancient itineraries make mention of this difference. See, e.g., Albiruni, *India* II, 155 (Sachau edn): 'If a wife loses her husband by death she cannot marry another man. She only has to choose between two things – either to remain a widow as long as she lives or to burn herself; and the latter eventually is considered to be preferable, because as a widow she is ill-treated as long as she lives.' A similar description is given by Ibn Battūta, *Travels* III, 615. For the position of widows see also Altekar, *Position of Women*, 115–65; Gupta, *Social Status of Women*, 243ff.; S. Vatuk, 'Old Age in India', in P. Stearns (ed.), *Old Age in Preindustrial Society* (New York, 1982) 46–103; I. Badhwar (in cooperation with others), 'Widows: Wrecks of Humanity', *India Today* (15 November 1987), 69–75; S. Manna and P. Chakraborty, 'The Position of Hindu Widows in Ancient India: A Glance over Indian Social History', in *Folklore* (English Monthly devoted to the Cause of Indian Folklore Society) 14 (Calcutta, 1990) 217–23; Narasimhan, *Sati* (see note 55 above), especially 36ff.

109 Rogerius, *Open-deure*, 80: 'alle verdriet ende onlust wort haer aenged-haen die men soude konnen bedencken'. See, further, Winternitz, *Frau*

in den indischen Religionen, 86ff. with references to many descriptions in Indian authors of the nineteenth century.

110 See, e.g., Winternitz, *Frau in den indischen Religionen*, 93ff.; Kane, *History of Dharmaśāstra* II, 583ff.

111 See, e.g., Della Valle, *Travels*, I, 83. Similar statements are found in L. di Varthema, *The Travels of Ludovico de Varthema (1502–1508)*, tr. from the original Italian edition of 1510 by J.W. Jones and ed. with nn. and introdn by G.P. Badger (London, 1863) 207. See further Winternitz, *Frau im indischen Religionen*, 92ff. for other references.

112 Gupta, *Social Status of Women*, 245ff.

113 Dubois, *Hindu Manners*, 350ff., 482ff., 491ff.

114 Ibid., 351.

115 Ibid., 350–2.

116 For the liminal stage see also V. Turner, *The Forest of Symbols, Aspects of Ndembu Ritual* (London, 1967) ch. 4.

117 See Dubois, *Hindu Manners*, 490ff.; L.P. van den Bosch, 'Dood en Religie, over funeraire riten in het oude India', *Nederlands Theologisch Tijdschrift*, 40 (1986) 209–26 and 'On the Anthropology of the Mortuary Ritual', *Journal of the Asiatic Society of Bombay*, 62–3 (1987–8 [1992]) 8–27.

118 Dubois, *Hindu Manners*, 492.

119 Dubois, *Hindu Manners*, 492f.; Weinberger-Thomas, 'Cendres d'immortalité', 24ff.

120 Dubois, *Hindu Manners*, 353ff.

121 Dubois, *Hindu Manners*, 352f. For a collection with proverbs relating to the widow see, e.g., O. von Boehtlingk, *Indische Sprüche* (Abh. für die Kunde des Morgenlandes: Leipzig, 1873²; repr. Nendeln 1966), 724, 2814, 2085, 3673, 4118. For recent cases of shaving see Badhwar, 'Widows' (see note 108 above), 74f.

122 For the history of tonsure see Kane, *History of Dharmaśāstra* II, 587ff. and Altekar, *Position of Women*, 159ff. Cf. also V.N. Narasimmiyengar, 'Tonsure of Hindu Widows', *Indian Antiquary* 3 (1874), 135ff.

123 See Zachariae, 'Witwenverbrennung', 1905, 81 n. 1.

124 See Winternitz, *Frau in den indischen Religionen*, 86–102 with many references to the older literature. Gupta, *Social Status of Women*, 247ff.; Leslie, 'A Problem of Choice', 54; Badhwar, 'Widows', 69, 74.

125 So Tryambaka, Strīdharmapaddhati 4.9.5, J. Leslie (tr.), *The Perfect Wife: The Orthodox Hindu Woman according to the Strīdharma-paddhati of Tryambakayājvan* (Delhi, 1989).

126 See, e.g., Dubois, *Hindu Manners*, 353f.; Gupta, *Social Status of Women*, 247ff.

127 See Kane, *History of Dharmaśāstra* II, 583ff.; Badhwar, 'Widows', 69–75, especially 71. Cf. also B. Saraswati, 'The Kashivasi Widows', in *Man in India* 65 (1985) issue 2, 107–20.

128 See, e.g., Weinberger-Thomas, 'Cendres d'immortalité', 25; Leslie, 'A Problem of Choice', 46; Van den Bosch, 'Pilgrimage, Prestige and Protest' (see note 55 above).

129 See Abegg, *Pretakalpa*, 142; Kane, *History of Dharmaśāstra*, II, 631; Dange, *Encyclopaedia*, IV, 1258.

130 Weinberger-Thomas, 'Cendres d'immortalité', 28f. and 41 and n. 47; R.S. Rajan, 'The Subject of Satī: Pain and Death in the Contemporary Discourse on Satī', *Yale Journal of Criticism* 3 (1990, no. 2, 1–27) 7.

131 See also Winternitz, *Frau in den indischen Religionen*, 97ff.; Kane, *History of Dharmaśāstra* II, 585 quoting the Skandha Purāna: 'The widow is more inauspicious than all other things; at the sight of a widow no success can be had in any undertaking.' It is not only the sight of a widow that is inauspicious; even dreaming of her is regarded as an announcement of death; cf. J. von Negelein, *Der Traumschlüssel des Jagaddevas* (Giessen, 1912) 132f.; 171f.

132 See note 113 above.

133 *Rāmāyana* 6.32.7. Cf. Winternitz, *Frau in den indischen Religionen*, 89, 97f.; J.J. Meyer, *Sexual Life in Ancient India, a Study in Comparative History of Indian Culture* (New York, 1953; original German edn 1928) 406ff. (The Widow).

134 Kane, *History of Dharmaśāstra* II, 583ff.; Hejib and Young, 'Sati, Widowhood and Yoga', in A. Sharma, *Sati* (see note 2 above), 73ff.; Leslie, 'A Problem of Choice', 49ff.

135 See, e.g., Winternitz, *Frau in den indischen Religionen*, 98.

136 See, e.g., Meyer, *Sexual Life*, 406ff.

137 Leslie, 'A Problem of Choice', 50. See also Altekar, *Position of Women*, 128f.

138 Ideas of being elected on account of good *karman* sometimes go side by side with ideas of extinguishing bad *karman*; cf. Weinberger-Thomas, 'Cendres d'immortalité', 26.

139 Van den Bosch, 'Pilgrimage, Prestige and Protest', 143ff. with references to other recent literature.

140 Brihaspati, quoted by Kane, *History of Dharmaśāstra*, II, 584f. Cf. also L.P. van den Bosch, 'The Marriage of the Dead in Ancient India: On the Interpretation of Vaikhānasasūtra V.9', in Leslie, *Rules and Remedies*, 71 (see note 23 above).

141 See, e.g., Manu 5.157–166; 9.29–30. For the translation see G. Bühler, *The Laws of Manu* (Oxford, 1886) 196f., 332.

142 See also Winternitz, *Frau in den indischen Religionen*, 104. The distinction made by him between civil widowhood and religious widowhood does not seem relevant to me.

143 Winternitz, *Frau in den indischen Religionen*, 97f.; Kane, *History of Dharmaśāstra* II, 586ff.

144 Behramji Malabāri and Rāmabāi were two important social reformers in the last century who tried to ameliorate the position of child-widows and protested against child-marriage; see Müller, *Auld Lang Syne* II, 113ff. Müller refers in this context to the Census Report of 1881, in which 669,100 widows below the age of 19 are mentioned, of which there are nearly 80,000 below the age of 9. The Remarriage Act of 1856 did not function, in spite of the good intentions of the British administration and its reformist advisers; L. Caroll, 'Law, Custom, and Statutory Social Reform: The Hindu Widow's Remarriage Act of 1856', *Indian Economic and Social History Review* 20 (1983) 363–80; R. Singh

Vatsa, 'The Remarriage and Rehabilitation of the Hindu Widows in India 1856–1914', *Journal of Indian History* 54 (1976) 713–30.

145 Winternitz, *Frau in den indischen Religionen*, 87ff.; Kane, *History of Dharmaśāstra* II, 437ff.; Weinberger-Thomas, 'Cendres d'immortalité', 27. See further P. Athavale, *Hindu Widow: An Autobiography* (New Delhi: tr. from the edn of 1928); F. Max Müller, 'An Indian Child-Widow', in his *Chips from a German Workshop* I (London, 1894²) 464ff.

146 See, e.g., Kane, *History of Dharmaśāstra* II, 599ff.; and 608ff. Alterkar, *Position of Hindu Women*, 143ff.

147 So, e.g., Hejib and Young, 'Sati, Widowhood and Yoga', 73ff.

148 Kane, *History of Dharmaśāstra* II, 587ff. For the ascetic path of the widow see Leslie, 'A Problem of Choice', 46ff.

149 See, e.g., Manu 5.147, tr. Bühler, *Laws of Manu*, 195.

150 See, e.g., Manu 9.3. For parallels see Bühler, *Laws of Manu*, 327 and nn. to 9.2–3.

151 See also L.P. van den Bosch, 'Some Reflections on the Concept of Person in Ancient Indian Texts', in H.G. Kippenberg *et al.* (eds), *Concepts of Persons in Religion and Thought* (Berlin and New York, 1990) 229–77, especially 258ff.

152 For the notion of uncontrolled female energy see D. Kinsley, *Hindu Goddesses, Visions of the Divine Feminine in the Hindu Religious Tradition* (Berkeley and London, 1986) 116–31 (Kālī). See also W.D. O'Flaherty, *Women, Androgynes, and other Mythical Beasts* (London and Chicago, 1980); Weinberger-Thomas, 'Cendres d'immortalité', 33ff.

153 Cf. Hejib and Young, 'Sati, Widowhood and Yoga', 79ff.

10

WIDOWS IN ISLAM

Willy Jansen

It is difficult to generalize about the position of widows in Islam. Not only may actual positions vary greatly depending on the nationality, class, ethnic group, or the age and number of children of the widow, but Islamic notions about widows have also changed over time. Interpretations of Quranic norms concerning widows in Islamic jurisprudence and common beliefs have changed with time and context. Widows on the Arabian peninsula in the early days of Islam might have little in common with present-day widows in North Africa. Yet in this chapter we will make an effort of comparison, firstly to show the contextuality and thus the diversity of widowhood as well as the divergence of the interests of widows from those of other women. Secondly, to show the similarities between widows in different times and places, which are not so much due to historically persistent religious rules, but more to the ambiguities inherent in widowhood. The socially ambiguous status of widows potentially enables them to gain a considerable influence over their private and public life, but can also cause them to be reduced to poverty; it potentially allows them to command respect, but may just as easily lead to disrespect. I will illustrate this with two cases: the widows surrounding Muhammed the Prophet in early Islam, notably Khadîja, the widow he married, and 'Aisha, the young wife he left as a widow; and the widows in present-day Algeria, notably Amina, the widow of a fighter for Algeria's independence. The material for the first case is derived from written sources, that for the second from fieldwork in a west Algerian town in the early eighties.[1]

Widows in Islam are usually studied from the perspective of religion and jurisprudence, guided by questions as to how Islamic rules make special reservations for widows and what Islam has done for widows. Here a reverse perspective is taken, that of the widows.

Our question will be what widows have done for Islam. How could widows, from their specific position, influence belief and practices in Islam? What were the consequences for themselves and other women? Such a reversal of the usual question is interesting, because it perceives women as active religious agents instead of passive victims of Islam. Moreover, it may lead us to more interesting findings about widows in Islam.

WIDOWS IN EARLY ISLAM

Khadîja

Of the widows who have played an important role in the early days of Islam, the first to be mentioned is Khadîja, who was born about AD 555 as the daughter of Khuwailid of the kuraish family from Abd al-'Uzza. Khadîja was the widow of a rich trader, whose company she ran after his death. She had also lost another husband, although the sources contradict each other on whether she lost him through death or divorce; with both men she had children. Khadîja owned several trade caravans which used to travel during winter as well as summer.[2] It was in this capacity as caravan owner that she hired Muhammed to work for her and sent him as her agent on a trading mission to Syria. She was 40 years old when she asked the 25 year old Muhammed to marry her. According to one version of the story, her father was against the marriage and she had to get him drunk before he gave his permission.[3]

As a wealthy widow and independent businesswoman Khadîja commanded several resources which she used to the benefit of Muhammed and the new religion. Her main contribution was financial. With her wealth she enabled the poor orphan Muhammed to finance his ventures. Her support of him meant that she risked considerable losses due to the hostility of the great merchants. Yet it was not this economic support but the moral support Khadîja offered the Prophet during the excitement and agitation of the first revelations that was most admired by later Muslims.[4] Muhammed turned to her when he doubted his commission as a Prophet, and she encouraged him to believe in his calling.[5] Khadîja was the first to believe that the revelations to Muhammed came from Allah and so she became the very first Muslim. It is thus well known and agreed who the first Muslim and the first female Muslim was, while the sources disagree on who the first male Muslim was.[6] Khadîja also let Muhammed profit from her family network: a cousin of her second husband later became Muhammed's trading partner, and her own cousin Waraqah, a Christian, supported the Prophet in his belief that he could have visions like Christians and Jews. Moreover, she gave Muhammed, as far as we know, two sons and four daughters, of whom only his daughter Fâtima survived him. The marriage of Khadîja and Muhammed was a monogamous one; it was only after her death that he became polygamous. Apparently, her personality, economic dominance and high social status sufficed to keep it that way.

Khadîja thus used the advantages of widowhood, especially decision-making powers in economic and personal matters, to start and maintain a relation with the Prophet and to support his endeavours. She was not the only widow to influence the new religion; nor were all widows so well-off in her time. To understand widowhood at the time of the rise of Islam let us first look at the context in which Quranic texts about widows must be placed.

Women and the Quran

At the time of the revelations the Arabian peninsula was experiencing a number of social and economic changes. The period was marked by tribal strife and warfare. The rise of a trading economy in towns like Medina and Mecca led to a disintegration of tribal cohesion in favour of new trading alliances. These developments had serious consequences for women, who were at that time economically and socially totally dependent upon the tribe. According to the picture painted by many Muslim historians, women in the pre-Islamic period could be divorced at will, had no rights to their children or alimony and were treated like a commodity. They had no right to their father's or husband's inheritance, but instead were themselves objects of inheritance.[7] The wars left a large number of widows and fatherless children, and these weaker members of the tribe suffered most severely from the diminishing tribal cohesion.[8]

The revelations of God to Muhammed can be seen as a reaction to these circumstances. Many Quranic verses on women intend to improve the position of orphans and widows by granting women in general more economic rights, thus extending the increasing individualization of property to women also. Women are given rights to property through inheritance, bridewealth (*mahr*), and personal control over property, but also rights to maintenance and alimony, and rights to custody (*hadâna*) over the children. Moreover, several Quranic verses urge the protection of widows and orphans. Their impact on the actual life of widows and orphans, however, should not be over-estimated. The Quran is not primarily a legislative document, but rather the declaration of the fundamental Islamic ethic. Its ethical provisions are not always transformed into legally enforceable rules, and there is also a wide divergence between rules and practice. In other words, widows and orphans seldom fully enjoy the protection and support they should receive according to the Quran. But Quranic norms remain important because they are recognized as binding on the individual conscience, and they can tell us something about the Islamic ethic concerning widows. Moreover, widows in the past and at present have referred to the Quranic norms when they struggle for a better position.

Within the historical context of seventh-century Arabia, Islam can be seen as an emancipatory force. An analysis of Islam as improving women's position compared to that in the pre-Islamic period is given both by modern western scholars and Muslim apologists. This approach, though, poses two problems. Firstly, how should we deal with the inconsistency between the powerful widow Khadîja, who inherited considerable wealth, ran her own business, hired her own employees and selected her own marriage partner, and the image of women and widows during the pre-Islamic period as propertyless, powerless and destitute? Secondly, if the new religion protected orphans and widows especially, did that automatically mean that this protection was beneficial to all women?

The story of Khadîja clearly fits in better with another picture of pre-Islamic women. Early sources describe cases of noblewomen,[9] who are shown to be independent characters claiming freedom of speech, of divorce, of action, of choice of locality and absence of co-wives. This has even led some older scholars to speak of a primitive matriarchate in pre-Islamic Arabia.[10] Others pointed out that the Arab woman was not absolutely free, but that control was vested in her own male relatives, notably her mother's brother, not in her husband. Yet a woman would have far more rights than in the Islamic type of marriage system, since, in case of dispute, she would be supported by her relatives against her husband.[11] Such a system would now be called a matrilineal and not a matriarchal system. However, theories of matriarchate in general, and of matriarchate on the pre-Islamic Arabian peninsula in particular, have rightly been criticized.[12] Also, the postulate of a transition of a matrilineal to a patrilineal system cannot be accepted, as it would be too simple a description of a complex situation.[13] Nevertheless, suggestions of matriarchal or matrilineal tendencies in pre-Islamic times led to a view contrary to the idea of emancipation, that is, that the coming of Islam had a negative effect on the condition of women. In this view of Islam as reactionary, Khadîja was but one example of how women in the pre-Islamic period had rights which their later Muslim sisters no longer had. From this perspective women did not gain rights but lost rights, such as the right to choose their own marriage partner(s), to manage their own property or to obtain divorce.

Eleanor Doumato, an American historian of the Middle East, analyses this still current debate, which is couched in language of mutually exclusive extremes. According to her, it revolves around the question: 'Did Islam at its inception bring about an improvement in women's condition, or was Islam responsible for bringing about inequalities between men and women in Muslim societies?' Both positions are based on the same sources and she suggests using other sources, such as relevant Christian materials, to gain a greater insight into the period. She also criticizes the methodology employed by both sides, among other things for subsuming all women into one normative category and for considering Islam as a static entity.[14] Can the two different positions described above be reconciled if we take Doumato's critique to heart? If we see Khadîja and the noblewomen described as positive exceptions, and matrilineal tendencies extant among some groups but not among others, we are able to see how Islam was both an emancipatory force for some women on some specific points, but at the same time an anti-emancipatory force for other women on other points. Accounting for differences between women and understanding these in particular historical religious contexts dissolves the dichotomous opposition. I will try to show that Islamic legislation which was beneficial to widows in the early years of Islam was already at the same time degrading to other women.

Let us take the widows' perspective and suggest an additional explanation for the numerous and precise references in the Quran to widows and orphans: the influence of the people around Muhammed, notably widows. Information about the social group around Muhammed and his interaction with its members can be gleaned especially well from the traditions. A tradition or *hadîth* is a record of an action or saying of the Prophet. The respected collections of traditions form the Sunna, which is, along with the Quran, an important source of Islamic jurisprudence. Moreover, they are increasingly used by feminist Muslim theologians to discover the role played by women in the early days of Islam.

It has frequently been noted that Muhammed had difficulty in gaining converts in the early period. The first recruits were often slaves or came from outside the clan system.[15] That he also attracted many female followers is usually neglected; even Khadîja disappears into the background in discussions on who were the first converts. Yet the traditions tell otherwise. First there were the Prophet's wives. After Khadîja, it was Sawda Bint Zam'a, Muhammed's second wife, who was one of the first women to embrace Islam. Of his wife Hafsa it is known that she was once repudiated, for unknown reasons, but was 'restored to favour by divine command in consideration of her Muslim virtues, i.e. her devotion to prayer and fasting'.[16] According to the historian Margaret Smith, in her classic study of a famous female Sufi, women exercised a freedom in worship in the earliest days of Islam which in later days was withdrawn from them. She bases this idea on the traditions collected by Al-Suyûtî, who gives an account of the wife of 'Umar, who used to be present at the morning and evening prayers among the men in the mosque. They said to her, 'Why do you go outside [of the house] when you know that 'Umar hates it and is jealous?' She said, 'What hinders him from forbidding me to do it?' They replied, 'He is hindered by the saying of the Prophet, "Do not prevent the handmaids of God from access to the places where He is worshipped"'. According to another tradition 'Umm Safiyya Khawla bint Qays used to say, 'In the time of the Prophet and Abû Bakr, and at the beginning of the Caliphate of 'Umar, we used to be in the mosque, and the women used to mix with the men ... and 'Umar said, "I send you away, O freeborn women", and he sent us away, but we used to be present at the time of prayers.'[17] One tradition recounts how Umm Salma had asked the Prophet why women were not mentioned in the Quran like men, after which the verse was revealed which specifically mentions women as believers on equal terms with men.[18] The significant presence of women among early converts and their later diminishing of importance is a phenomenon we may also find in the first stages of other new religions.

We may expect that there were quite a few widows among the earliest female believers, although few records of them exist. Islam created a new community based on religion rather than tribal alliances. Women often converted together with their husband, but when he died for the Muslim cause it could be difficult for them if they had to return to a non-converted family. It is more likely that, instead, widows sought support and protection from their new group. From the perspective of the new community it was also important to keep these widows involved. A Muslim woman who returned to a heathen tribe was lost as a believer. Moreover, it was imperative that inheritable property of the martyrs for the faith be kept for the believers rather than revert to non-believers. Widows and the young Islamic community needed each other.

Women not only worshipped but also came to the Prophet with their problems and their questions about the new faith. These were answered in subsequent revelations.[19] Female followers, then, had an important influence on the formulation of certain Islamic rules.

Quranic references to widows: inheritance

Of particular importance were the interventions of widows which led to the formulation of new rules on important matters such as inheritance. According to the traditions the widow Umm Khadja came to the Prophet with the complaint that her deceased husband's kin had appropriated all his wealth and left her and her five young daughters destitute. Her husband's brother had defended himself by saying that he clung to the tradition and did not want to know of the new laws because women did not ride horses and fight.[20] On that occasion the words in Sûra 4:8 were revealed to the Prophet, who took pity on the woman and her children:

> Men shall have a share in what their parents and kinsmen leave; and women shall have a share in what their parents and kinsmen leave: whether it be little or much, they shall be legally entitled to their share. If relatives, orphans, or needy men are present at the division of an inheritance, give them, too, a share of it, and speak to them kind words. Let those who are solicitous about the welfare of their young children after their own death take care not to wrong orphans. Let them fear God and speak for justice.[21]

According to the tradition, the Prophet asked to leave undivided the inheritance of Umm Khadja's husband Aus ibn Thâbit, who died in AD 625 in the battle of Uhud, until Allah had taken a further decision concerning the rules of inheritance. Only when more detailed instructions were given to him in the so-called inheritance verses (Quran Sûra 4:12–15) was the estate concerned divided.[22] The favourable reaction to the widow's request might have been influenced by the fact that the Prophet himself had been wounded in the same battle of Uhud in which Umm Khadja's husband died.[23] The image of death was near and he might not have wanted to leave the descendants of those who fought for him unprovided for.

The Indian Muslim scholar Engineer, who propagates a rereading of the religious sources in a way more favourable to women, refers to the great commentator al-Razi for the context in which verse 4:11 was revealed, and in which again the complaints of a widow played a role. When S'ad bin Rabi' was martyred he left behind his wife, two daughters and brother. The brother took the complete inheritance of his deceased brother, leaving the wife and daughters without resources. The widow went to the Prophet and complained about the behaviour of her husband's brother, but the Prophet sent her away saying Allah would decide the matter. She persisted, however, and returned later to complain again. It was then that verse 4:11 was revealed, according to which a male shall inherit twice as much as a female, and on the basis of this the widow's brother-in-law was ordered to pay two-thirds of the property to the daughters. The widow was to receive one-eighth and he himself could keep the rest.[24]

These examples show that not only the inheritance rights of widows, but also those of orphan girls were protected in the new religion. Muhammed himself was an orphan, his father 'Abdullâh died before his birth and his mother Amina when he was about 6 years old. He was brought up by his paternal grandfather and later by his paternal uncle. That the sufferings he endured in his youth could be related to his stand for the protection of orphans is illustrated in Sûra 93:6–10, which also makes clear his debt to Khadîja: 'Did He not find you an orphan and give you shelter? Did He not find you in error and guide you? Did He not find you poor and enrich you? Therefore do not wrong the orphan, nor chide away the beggar.'[25] It might explain the threatening words in verse 4:10: 'Those that devour the property of orphans unjustly, swallow fire into their bellies; they shall burn in a mighty conflagration.'

Special reservations were also made for slave concubines who obtained freedom in widowhood. Masters had rights to the sexuality of female slaves. Once made pregnant by their master they could not marry other slaves. Their children were free and on an equal par with children from legal wives. They themselves became free upon the death of their master and their waiting period before remarrying was only half that of other widows.[26]

The traditions mention more occasions on which women came to the Prophet to ask clarification or enforcement of the new laws. One such action led to the prohibition on considering women as inheritable property. It came from Kubaisha Bint Maan, who complained to him that she had not inherited from her husband nor been given the freedom to marry whom she wanted. Her son-in-law Abu Qais Bin Al-Aslat had laid claim to both her property and her person. Here too the woman won, and gained the abolition of the levirate for all widows. Sûra 4:19 denounces the enforcement of the levirate: 'Believers, it is unlawful for you to inherit the women of your deceased kinsmen against their will, or to bar them from re-marrying, in order that you may force them to give up a part of what you have given them, unless they be guilty of a proven sinful act. Treat them with kindness; for even if you dislike them, it may well be that you dislike a thing which God has meant for your own abundant good.' The male population of Medina was scandalized about this new rule, which took away their customary rights over widows, both over their sexuality and their property. It had been the custom that male heritors decided themselves whether to marry the widow or not. If the inheritor was too young to marry her, she had to wait till he came of age to make a decision about her. According to an account of pre-Islamic customs preserved by the Muslim historiographer Tabari (AD 838–923), when a man's father or brother or son died and left a widow, the dead man's heir, if he came at once and threw his garment over her, had the right to marry her under the dower of her deceased husband, or to give her in marriage and take her dower. This meant that, since the dower gives a husband access to the sexuality of his wife, the inheritor could either inherit this sexual right and marry her without having to pay a new dower, or give it up but take back the dower. But if the widow anticipated him and went off to her own people, then the disposal of her hand belonged to herself.[27] Male heirs often preferred to marry the widow themselves or to marry her off to someone else, because if she went back to her family they would lose both her and the dower.

In view of male opposition to the new rules in favour of women, these were explicitly and precisely specified. But the men did not give up their prerogatives so easily and sought another way out. They took recourse to the Quranic verse which read: 'Do not give the feeble-minded the property with which God has entrusted you for their support; but maintain and clothe them with its proceeds, and give them good advice' (S. 4:5). They were convinced that the most feeble-minded among the feeble-minded were women (*an-nissâ' asfaha as-sufahâ'*). This male reaction gave rise to a debate about what was to be understood by the term feeble-minded (*safîh*). The scholar Tabari collected no less than twenty-nine interpretations of the word, without, however, pronouncing that women were fools. But he did say that 'when women are excluded from inheritance, one makes a distinction according to sex which is not present in the Quranic text'.[28]

Various Quranic verses thus allow widows access to property through inheritance, although on less favourable terms than widowers. This was a considerable improvement in the financial position of most widows, as the previously exceptional practice of some noble and some matrilineal lineages, of letting widows inherit, was now generalized for all women. This did not mean, however, that female inheritance from now on would always be practised; on the contrary, recent studies in various Muslim societies on women's inheritance show that this is seldom the case, although women can legally claim what is theirs.[29] Moreover, while it was an amelioration of women's position in the seventh century, it is a hindrance to emancipation today, because with the inheritance rules a fundamental inequality between women and men was laid down in the most important Islamic source of norms: the Quran. As for the ban on considering widows as inheritable commodities, this also was an improvement. The custom of levirate did not cease with it – in the modern Muslim world many widows marry their husband's brother – but it can help widows ensure that their decisions are respected. It gave widows more say in whom to marry than virgins.

Quranic references to widows: maintenance, 'idda, and polygyny

Part of the widow's quest for protection and support from Muhammed and the new religion resulted in statements on maintenance. Men were admonished to provide for their widows in Sûra 2:240: 'You shall bequeath your widows a year's maintenance without causing them to leave their homes; but if they leave of their own accord, no blame shall be attached to you for any course they may deem fit to pursue.' After this period the duty of maintenance of a widow who cannot support herself reverts to the widow's father or closest male kin. Although, as said above, a widow has the right to take care of her minor children, it is their father's closest agnate who is their natural guardian and owes their maintenance.[30] This separation of care and guardianship in principle lightens the burden of widows in taking care of their children; in practice, however, the maintenance paid is seldom sufficient. The widow and her children are reduced to poverty, and if she remarries the widow will lose her children.[31]

An insurance for the maintenance of a woman who becomes widowed or divorced was foreseen in the Quranic rules about giving women upon marriage a *mahr*. This bridewealth or dower was henceforward to be paid by the groom to the bride and not to her father and thus increased the individual economic security of women. It can be and still often is partly paid upon dissolution of the marriage. For poor widows especially – who will not inherit much and have few relatives to support them – this sum can be crucial for survival.

Other verses concerning widows were less positive and the conditions and persons that gave rise to them are less known. One verse regulates the obligatory waiting period before widows can remarry as four months and ten days or, in the case that they are pregnant, until forty days after giving birth, the 'idda. Sûra 2:234 reads: 'Widows shall wait, keeping themselves apart from men, for four months and ten days after their husbands' death. When they have reached the end of their waiting period, it shall be no offence for you to let them do whatever they choose for themselves, provided that it is decent.' This rule is said to be based on the traditional mourning period of widows in pre-Islamic times, which in some tribes lasted a full year, during which the widow would live secluded in a small tent and not wear jewellery, make-up or colourful clothes. For widows the 'idda thus meant the reduction of the mourning period. It probably served also as a model for the introduction of a waiting period for divorcées (lasting three months) which before had not existed.[32]

The verse on the waiting period was in later jurisprudence combined with the verse on maintenance in order to reduce the right to maintenance to four months and ten days instead of one year. After that, maintenance reverts to the widow's father or closest male kin if she has no means of her own. The verse, however, can also be interpreted more positively as allowing widows to do whatever they choose for themselves after this period as long as it is decent. Thus, although widows still cannot formally contract their own marriage because all women need a marriage guardian (*walî an-nikâh*) to do so, they were given considerably more say in whether or whom to remarry. More than other women they are able to resist the rights of their male kin to arrange their marriage. The old Arabian literature shows that some distinguished ladies married according to their own choice and without any assistance from their male relatives.[33] While widows could take over some of these freedoms, those of other marriageable women were restricted.

Another verse, intended to solve the problem of girl orphans and widows, had even more serious consequences for other women, as it became the justification for polygyny: 'If you fear that you cannot treat orphans with fairness, then you may marry other women who seem good to you: two, three, or four of them' (Sûra 4:3). It reflects Muhammed's concern: he married several widows himself. Apart from Khadîja, who had such a forceful character that he married no other woman until she died, there was Sawda, the second woman he married,[34] Hafsa, a 20-year-old who had lost her husband in a recent battle,[35] Zainab, who died several months after the marriage;[36] and the Jewish Rayhana, whose husband was executed by the Muslims. This verse always served to defend polygyny and it is significant that in that case it is quoted without the first part of the sentence. Male dominance in the interpretative process prevented an interpretation that polygyny was only allowed in order to provide for orphans and widows. Despite an increase in polygyny after some wars, it is unlikely that many widows and girl orphans profited from this protective measure as most men preferred a young maiden for a second wife. The case of polygyny best illustrates the point that improving the dire fate of some widows in Muhammed's time, by allowing limited polygyny, cannot be seen as benefiting other women, either in that period or in other times and places. This type of protection of widows was already at that time detrimental to the other wives, who now had to share both the husband and the inheritance. At present, in modern states that can provide social security and pensions to widows it is not even a feasible solution for widows. This male privilege is disadvantageous to women and should, according to women's organizations in many Muslim states, be taken away.

Fired by previous successes women also asked Muhammed to intervene on their behalf for the right to fight with arms in order to get a share in war booty, in those days an important source of income. In this respect they were less successful.[37] But that is not where women's influence in theological and political matters ended. This brings us to another exemplary widow: 'Aisha. She was the Prophet's favourite wife. It was in her bed that he fell sick, it was in her arms that he died, and in her house that he was buried.

'Aisha

'Aisha bint Abi Bakr, born in AD 613, was married to the Prophet when she was 6 years old and he about 50. The marriage was consummated when she was 9. The extreme difference in age made it likely that she would survive him, and so it happened. When he died in AD 632 'Aisha became a widow at the youthful age of 18. Although she was young and had no children, she never remarried. 'Aisha and eight other women who remained with Muhammed at the end of his life were given a position of considerable honour in the community and the honorific title 'mothers of the believers' was bestowed on them, but it came to be understood that they were not to marry any Muslim after Muhammed's death.[38] 'Aisha remained an important and well-known person in the history of Islam for several reasons.

Firstly, there were her military activities. She participated without doubt in the revolt against caliph 'Uthman and later actively supported the insurrection against her arch-enemy 'Ali, the Prophet's son-in-law, when he was elected caliph. She aligned herself with Talha and Al-Zubair in the Battle of the Camel, fought in AD 656 against 'Ali. The battle is called after the camel that was given to her for the expedition by the greatest sponsor of the battle. Seventy men perished in the defence of 'Aisha and her camel, but they lost, the camel was killed and 'Aisha was taken prisoner by 'Ali and later sent home. 'Aisha was not the only woman of her time to engage in military activities, although she is the most famous example. A famous woman warrior among the adversaries was the widow Umm Qirfa, daughter of Rabi'a, under whose orders the caravan of Zayd, Muhammed's adopted son was attacked. Later, Zayd took revenge, surprised her troops, slew and scattered them and put her to a cruel death.[39]

Secondly, and more important than 'Aisha's martial behaviour, there was her contribution to the corpus of traditions. As his favourite wife, 'Aisha had much occasion to watch and listen to the Prophet, and a long life left to remember her beloved husband. She transmitted 1210 traditions.[40] Though not equally canonical with the

Quran, traditions nevertheless exerted a great influence on the development of Islamic thought and the formulation of Islamic law.

In the period after Muhammed's death a large number of traditions surfaced, among which were quite doubtful ones intended to justify certain practices rather than to give faithful accounts. 'Aisha became very active in refuting many of these, as is shown by Imam Zarkashi who, in the fourteenth century, collected 'Aisha's refutations in a book. The author says in his preface that this book deals with her special contribution in this field, especially with those points where she differed from others, where she added information and where she totally disagreed with the learned men of her time. She refuted especially many *hadîth*-s of Abu Huraira, one of the greatest producers of traditions who remembered more than 5300 events. 'Aisha said of him that he could not listen very well and that when he was asked something, he gave the wrong answers.[41] 'Aisha was often consulted about theological or juridical subjects. According to one tradition the Prophet said: 'Get a part of your religious knowledge from the little red haired woman.'[42] She was admired for her many talents, as she could read and write, and not only knew much about the *fiqh* (Muslim law), but also about poetry and medicine.[43]

How is it that 'Aisha managed to maintain a position of power, even after the Prophet's death, when this was not true of his other wives? The fact that her father Abu Bakr became the first orthodox caliph of Islam and reigned for two years of course helped to maintain her position. But most important, besides her obvious personal magnetism and a reputation as the Prophet's favourite wife, was her learning and intelligence. In particular, her role in establishing traditions gave her an intellectual position in the new community of Islam which few women could rival.[44]

Historians, biographers and contemporaries have not always been very positive about the way 'Aisha filled in her widowhood. Whereas she was by many respected as favourite wife, as 'mother of the believers' and intelligent contributor to the important traditions, she was reviled by others. Some called her a murderess and an agitator, according to her biographer Said Al-Afghani,[45] and she was held responsible for the massacre during the Battle of the Camel which purportedly cost 15,000 lives and which caused the split in the Muslim community into Sunnites and Shiites. For Al-Afghani she personified the evil of women in politics and a warning for Arab countries not to follow western countries in giving political rights to women because it would lead to broken families and much shedding of blood. The widow 'Aisha was simultaneously seen as the best and the worst among women.

Both Khadîja and 'Aisha had considerable power and were influential in the economic, religious, juridical as well as political domains. Other widows too, especially those whose husbands gave their life for the Muslim cause, were influential in the establishment of Quranic norms to their benefit. As such they may inspire Muslim feminists who look for powerful examples of female strength, knowledgeability and independence combined with religious propriety. Insight into these strong female characters in the early days of Islam offers a view of women as actors and participants. At the same time, their stories show that they were exceptions compared with the large mass of women, and that an ethic of care for widows and orphans had to be laid down and enforced precisely because the majority of widows and orphans were destitute and not cared for. As I have shown elsewhere,[46] widows were not only among the most powerful, but also among the most powerless in society. They were prominent as actors, but no less so as victims. And, as we saw in the case of 'Aisha, these opposite characteristics could be combined in one person. As such, widows were in a different position from married women. Moreover, what could be beneficial to widows at a certain time was not necessarily beneficial to other women, as the example of polygyny clearly shows.

A WIDOW OF THE PRESENT: ALGERIAN AMINA

To what extent can an insight into the position of some widows in the early Islamic era on the Arabian peninsula, and into Quranic norms about widows, inform us about the positions of present-day widows in other Muslim regions? Unfortunately, not very much. Some religious rules have been incorporated in Islamic jurisprudence and later national laws, and thus survived the ages. These can also influence a widow's life today. Other elements of her life, however, can only be understood in their specific historical context. To illustrate this I will give the example of Amina, one of the widows I met in an Algerian town in 1982 when studying their plight.[47]

Amina was born in 1940 and became a widow when she was 17. Her husband was murdered in the first days of the Algerian War of Independence against France, when he brought money to the resistance fighters. She stayed behind with a 15-day-old baby girl, whom she named Shahîda ('woman martyr'). Because her husband died in the resistance Amina was given the status of 'widow of a martyr' (*mart shahîd*) after the war. This was a privileged status in post-war Algeria as it gave a widow rights to a job, a pension,[48] a house – half the rent of which was paid by the state – free public transport, provision of tuition and special privileges in university entrance exams, and free school meals and school clothes for the children. Widows of martyrs seldom freely gave up such privileges and thus rarely remarried. Also Amina, although young and very attractive, and with only one child that could easily have been taken care of by her mother, never remarried.

The first years after her husband's death were difficult, since it was wartime. Amina maintained herself and her child by doing cleaning jobs in other people's homes. She still felt ashamed of having done this degrading work, and never told me about it herself. In 1959 she managed to find employment as a seamstress at the hospital, at that time controlled by the French, where she is still working. In the evening, she earns an extra income by sewing privately for other people.

Amina was never maintained by her family of birth after becoming a widow, nor was her child maintained by its paternal kin, although this would have been her legal and moral right. Keeping the child meant working for an income. Moreover, in her case, the state took over the duty of maintenance from the two families. This state support, originally intended only for widows of martyrs, has flooded over onto other widows. A fixed percentage of all places in public service is reserved for war veterans (both male and female) and widows of martyrs. Yet those women eligible and interested in a job have long found work, so it is common for offices and factories to fill this quota by hiring other widows. This state protection of some widows led to a decline in the willingness of families to support widows in general. Many families expect widows, especially younger ones and those with children, to find employment and provide for themselves. Due to the extreme pressures on the labour market this is not always possible, despite the preferential treatment by the state sector. Widows find it much more difficult to find work than their families claim it is. Moreover, norms of seclusion of women are so strong that at the same time the widow is criticized for working in public and sexually exposing herself. This stigmatization and the double burden of work and maintaining at least the appearance of seclusion frequently leads to a cool or a broken relationship between the widow and her family.

Given the negligible property of Amina's deceased husband she is not a good example for the understanding of inheritance practice in Algeria. So we have to look at other widows. Here we find that the precise description of inheritance rights of widows in the Quran, and the extensive elaboration of these norms in Islamic law, have not prevented the widespread practice in Algeria, as in many Muslim countries and especially when landed property is concerned, of actually disinheriting women. As this was difficult to do legally, recourse was taken to pressurizing women who inherited from their fathers into 'freely' giving up their rightful share to their brothers. Women who inherited from their husband did the same in favour of their sons. Or use was made of legal loopholes such as the system of making religious endowments to religious institutions whereby inheritors were left with usufruct rather than the property. Although this system could be used to treat female and male inheritors more equally or give the widow an extra stipend, in North Africa it more often had the effect that women were actually disinherited.[49] The moral exhortation in the Quran to give widows their share in the property is for most Algerian widows in practice an empty phrase. Most widows refrain from taking legal action as it would alienate them from their family. Only if they are totally deserted by their in-laws and kin can they and do they claim their inheritance rights in court. Moreover, women are well aware of their legal rights to inheritance. If a woman gives up her share she knows that this puts a moral obligation on the brothers or sons to maintain her if she loses her husband and she will often use their indebtedness to her to gain negotiating power in the family.

Another solution to the economic deprivation of widowhood, apart from work, could be remarriage. The presentation of polygyny as a solution for destitute orphans and widows is not unknown in Algeria. After the War of Independence (1957–62) in which Amina became a widow, men were encouraged to take a second wife for this reason. It is suggested that this policy may have influenced the increase of polygynists in those years. Between 1962 and 1966 their number rose from 27,000 to 40,000.[50] We have already seen that for Amina remarriage would have entailed the loss of many privileges. But most of the half-million widows in Algeria who enjoy fewer privileges do not remarry either. Those with pensions would lose an income, those with a job would lose their freedom, and those with children would be frowned upon for leaving them. Older widows are not attractive as marriage partners, or have grown-up children who can take care of them. Remarriage usually entails a loss of status for widows: they must accept a man who is much older, a widower with children or an already-married man. Of the few widows who do remarry, 46 per cent become a second wife, often to the brother of their late husband.[51] Most polygynists, on the other hand, prefer a virgin as a second wife.[52] We may conclude that, although polygyny after the war was still legitimized by referring to widows, actually few widows profited from it. Rather, the possibility of polygyny had the negative effect for widows that married women now consider them as a threat to their marriage, thus widening the gap and dissolving the solidarity between married women and widows.

The public perception of Amina, and other widows, as a threat to the sexual order is enhanced by her autonomy. Compared with married women Amina enjoys many freedoms. Whereas most women in town live secluded and only go out veiled, Amina leaves the house unveiled and travels extensively within and outside the country. On our first meeting she had just returned from a vacation in Spain. Her wages combined with her pension and her irregular earnings make her economically not just independent, but even well-off. Her pension alone is higher than the legal minimum wage, while her living and travel expenses are very low. She lives in a villa left by its French owners after Independence and has created her own family. She has taken in her mother and two adopted children: her sister's daughter who is 11 years old and does nearly all the household chores, and an abandoned boy of 9. Her daughter, with a husband and child, also moved in with Amina.

The marriage arrangements of her daughter Shahîda are informative about the special position of widows and their daughters. Shahîda told me that her husband had paid no *mahr* (bridewealth or dower) for her because they married 'out of love'. This contrasted sharply with her dowry, given to her by her mother, which amounted to '45 million'. (That is local idiom for DA 450,000, which at that time was equal to about $94,500). Even if we allow for some exaggeration, which is usual when talking about marriage payments,[53] her dowry was enormous and its value was far above the average in the area. It was visible in the gold jewellery she showed, as well as in the two gold-stitched velvet dresses she owned. These cost DA 7000 apiece and only wealthy families can afford one such dress for a daughter. Apparently all the savings of the mother, as well as the wages of the daughter as a typist, had gone into the dowry. Given this wealth and the beauty of the daughter one would have expected her to be able to make a good match, and a good match is normally symbolized by a high price paid by the groom. But not in this case, nor in the case of many other daughters of widows.

The Quranic injunction to give women their *mahr* was ignored here. Remember that the *mahr* was meant to be an insurance for the woman if she became widowed or divorced. Legally one cannot even contract a marriage without payment of bridewealth, so at least a symbolic amount must have been given. Normally the father of the bride and her male kin commands a *mahr* congruent with the prestige of the family. They expect the groom to give a gift to the bride which can match in size the gift the bride receives from her own family. The *mahr* expresses the respect the groom and his kin have for the bride and her kin. In this case, literally, no respect was paid. The girl's next male kin, her father's brother, a politician living in Oran, neither supported her nor defended her customary rights as he should have as a marriage guardian. When asked about his role she said about him: 'We see his brother very little. I have very little contact with the family of my father, but a lot with the family of my mother. Last year I saw him at a feast, but I did not even embrace him. I hadn't seen him for three years. No, he never showed any interest in us.' Other orphans, whose paternal kin did intervene at the time of their marriage, often complained that they only did so to put part of the bridewealth in their own pocket. This is accepted practice when done by a father, because of all the money he has invested in his daughter's dowry, but it is resented when done by an uncle who has neither provided maintenance nor put up a dowry for the girl. Widows who have provided for and brought up their children cannot marry them, as only men can be contractual partners in marriage and negotiate the bridewealth. Children of widows find it more difficult to marry (most marriages are still arranged), but, and that is the other side of the coin, can also more often make their own choice. This can lead to frustrating situations. In one case a 26-year-old daughter of a widow, a university graduate who held an excellent position as a personnel manager, and who had for years supported her mother and her empty-headed younger brother and his family and taken all the decisions for them, had to let herself be married by the same mindless brother, although she had chosen her own partner.

Shahîda does not realize that her case forms part of a pattern in which daughters of widows are deprived of their *mahr*. She cannot but accept that her husband is unwilling to pay and gladly takes over his use of western notions of love as an excuse. Shahîda: 'If one marries out of love one need not give many presents. It is idiocy to give a woman so much gold. It is better not to have gold but use it for nice furniture, as in Europe.' This is not a principled argument, however, as it might be among Algeria's urban, educated élite, where both partners can have a career and can afford to be independent of relatives. Shahîda would have preferred gold; why else has she saved so much gold for herself? She would also have liked the social respect and status that come with a high *mahr*, as her eagerness in showing her jewels publicly shows. Moreover, she needs the husband's marriage gift as an insurance against hard times. She forgets that her husband has unilateral and nearly absolute rights to divorce her, that she has no state support when she becomes a widow, and that it will be very hard to find suitable work when she loses him. She is excusing his indifference towards her, while he is unscrupulous when it comes to accepting and spending her dowry. Shahîda is deprived of her *mahr*, and in this she differs from some of her contemporaries who freely give up the dower out of feminist motives. In Algeria a growing group of young, educated, urban women object to the groom's gift because not they but their father negotiates the level, receives it and often takes a cut, which makes them feel as if they are sold, as if women are turned by males into sexual commodities. Yet for most young women a high dower still means respect and economic independence, and for many daughters of widows it hurts when they are deprived of it.

The living arrangements of the couple are also indicative of the position of the widow and her daughter. Patrilocality is the dominant pattern of post-marital residence in Algeria and consistent with the Quranic norm that a man should provide his bride with lodging, food and clothes. Despite the severe housing shortage in Algeria, which forces many young people to postpone marriage, matrilocality is rare. It is considered degrading to have to depend on your wife's family, as it means that the man can or will not provide properly for his wife. Shahîda and her husband only lived for three months with his family before moving in with her mother. Amina's house is also too small to house another family, but she gave up her spatial privileges in favour of her son-in-law. He soon became the master of the house: the widow has to leave the living room when he is there. The daughter's husband appropriated both the widow's property and her space, without exchanging it for respect.

These violations of the Algerian cultural codes can take place because Amina is a widow; they are abuses she shares with many other widows. Her decent income, her savings, her property and her independence are not enough to give her a good social status and negotiating power. Wealth, however convenient, is in itself not sufficient as a basis for social prestige. Female wealth is suspected, is associated with easy virtue or outright prostitution. Bragging about the size of the dowry is therefore dangerous, as it might arouse suspicions about both the widow's and her daughter's sexual behaviour, while bragging about the groom's gift could have brought prestige and social status. Shahîda's high dowry is more of a liability than an asset, but she has nothing else to brag about. Widows have to fend for themselves, in all domains. This can give them significant de facto decision-making power over their own life and that of their children. Strong characters can blossom in widowhood. Yet these remarkable power opportunities on the one hand meet severe restrictions and stigmatization on the other hand. Occasionally they get frustrated by the dejure restriction of their decision-making power in matters of marriage or use of space. Widows may find themselves dependent on unsympathetic affines when they want to marry their children, or on the permission of a son when they want to travel abroad. Worst of all is the social control of their behaviour, the accusations of sexual libertarianism, the stigmatization because no man controls their sexuality. Widows are both powerful and not respected.

CONCLUSION

I have tried to show that the coming about of specific rules for widows in the early Islamic sources can only be understood in their historical context and by taking into account the impact of real widows on this process. The influence widows and other women could exert in the earliest days of Islam soon withered, but never completely died out. The case of Amina, the modern Algerian widow, was added to see what effect the old rules had under new and different circumstances. Here too, the widow's position could only be understood in the Algerian context, in which the War of Independence and the resulting state responsibility for widows played a large role.

The cases presented here, Khadîja, 'Aisha, Amina, all concern strong characters with substantial economic, political and social resources. They stand out among a crowd of widows whose scale has tipped the other way, towards poverty, destitution and lack of protection. The ambiguous situation in which they find themselves after the death of the husband, and in which they have to make their own decisions and defend their own rights because nobody else does, enables some to unleash all their strength while others go under in the stream of unfamiliar responsibilities and problems.

In specific contexts, the interest of widows was not necessarily the interest of all women. For instance, many widows and other women profited from economic security offered by the *mahr* although some women's organizations now denounce it as anti-emancipatory and degrading to women. Widows and many other women have also profited from gaining a share in the inheritance, whether they actually obtained it or not. But for present-day activists this Quranic injunction, which was innovative at the time of the revelations, perpetuates inequality between women and men in Islam in the modern context. The benefits for women in general of the protection extended to widows through polygyny are even more doubtful. The interest of widows in specific contexts does not always converge with the interest of women in general.

What the widows discussed here have in common, other than a few interesting but hardly enforceable religious rules, is that widow-hood enabled them to become remarkable women. Only as widows did they gain access to resources they would normally not have had access to, or over which they could not have gained control. Widows have, compared to married women, more decision-making power over their own lives and that of their children. They provide for the family, they manage their own property, have more freedom in the use of space. This potentially enables them to gain powerful pos-itions. Many powerful women in the history of Islam – and also in world history – have reached this position as a widow or through widowhood if they manage the economic, political or spiritual inheritance of an important man as both Khadîja and 'Aisha, but also Amina, did.

This potential can also turn the other way, especially if the husband was not influential but poor, and left them with a number of children. Then they might find themselves at the bottom of the economy, carrying the double load of poorly paid jobs and housework, while suffering from severe social control and stigmatization. The ex-ceptional position of widows means that they can rise high but also fall low.

Widowhood is an ambiguous state for women. They are women and subjected to what is expected of women, but at the same time exceptions are being made for them and options opened to them which are not available to other women. It is easier for them to run a business or to be employed than for married women. It is also easier for them to claim special rights. But at the same time they are disrespected for doing so. 'Aisha's political activities are condemned, Amina's riches make people think of prostitution rather than economic acumen and therefore do not bring respect to her and her daughter. Widows are examples, to show the best in women (for feminists) and to show the worst in women (for mysogynists). The ambiguous position of widows in Islam, compared for instance with married women, is not so much a consequence, but rather a cause, of the special Islamic rules for them.[54]

NOTES

1 The results of this research on widows and other unmarried women are published in W. Jansen, *Women without Men: Gender and Marginality in an Algerian Town* (Leiden, 1987).

2 A. A. Engineer, *The Rights of Women in Islam* (London, 1992) 32.

3 H.A.R. Gibb and J.H. Kramers (eds), *Shorter Encyclopaedia of Islam* (Leiden, 1974) 231.

4 Gibb and Kramers, *Shorter Encyclopaedia*.

5 W.M. Watt, *Muhammed: Prophet and Statesman* (London, 1961) 12–22.

6 Watt, *Muhammed*, 35.

7 Engineer, *The Rights of Women in Islam*, 31.

8 M. Rodinson, *Mohammed* (Harmondsworth, 1971) 229–32.

9 Abû al-Faraj al-Isfahânî, *Kitâb al-Aghânî* (Bulaq, 1863) analysed in M. Smith, *Râbi'a the Mystic and her Fellow-Saints in Islâm*, 1928[1] (Cambridge, 1984) 112.

10 G.A. Wilken, *Het matriarchaat bij de oude Arabieren* (Amsterdam, 1884); W. Robertson Smith, *Kinship and Marriage in Early Arabia*, 1903[1] (Boston, 1983) 267–73.

11 J. Wellhausen, *Die Ehe bei den Arabern* (Göttingen, 1893) 474; Smith, *Râbi'a the Mystic*, 112.

12 J. Bamberger, 'The Myth of Matriarchy: Why Men Rule in Primitive Society', in M.Z. Rosaldo and L. Lamphere (eds), *Woman, Culture and Society* (Palo Alto, 1974) 263–80.

13 Rodinson, *Mohammed*, 229–31.

14 E.A. Doumato, 'Hearing Other Voices: Christian Women and the Coming of Islam', *International Journal of Middle East Studies* 23 (1991, 177–99) 177, 178.

15 Ph. K. Hitti, *History of the Arabs* (London, 1970) 113. According to Watt, *Muhammed*, 36f., the first converts were mainly young men from the strata of society immediately below the topmost stratum of powerful merchants. Yet he also indicates a category of young men originating from outside the clan system, including former slaves and confederates.

226

He gives no information about the women who figure on the list of about fifty names of those who converted early to Islam.

16 Gibb and Kramers, *Shorter Encyclopaedia*, 503 (Sawda), 125 (Hafsa).

17 Smith, *Râbi'a the Mystic*, 124f.

18 Sûra 33:35. F. Mernissi, *Le harem politique: Le Prophète et les femmes* (Paris, 1987), tr. in Dutch as *De politieke harem* (Breda, 1991) 139. Here and in the following page references to the Dutch translation are used.

19 Mernissi, *Le harem politique*; Engineer, *The Rights of Women in Islam*.

20 The Muslim commentators added that it was the custom in the pre-Islamic period that only capable men, those who defended with the sword what was theirs, could inherit to the exclusion of women and children. Mernissi, *Le harem politique*, 144.

21 For this and all following Quranic texts the translation by N.J. Dawood, *The Koran* (London, 1990[5]), following the traditional sequence of sûras and with parallel Arabic text, is used.

22 Th.W. Juynboll, *Handleiding tot de kennis van de Mohammedaansche wet volgens de leer der Sjâfi'itische school* (Leiden, 1925), who gives more information on this tradition than Mernissi and from him we learn that the widow's husband was killed in the battle of Uhud. The relevant Sûra 4:12 reads regarding widows: 'Your wives shall inherit one quarter of your estate if you die childless. If you leave children, they shall inherit one-eighth, after payment of any legacy you may have bequeathed or any debt you may have owed.'

23 See Hitti, *History of the Arabs*, 117.

24 Engineer, *The Rights of Women in Islam*, 71, who refers to Fakhruddin al-Razi, *Tafsir Kabir* V (Beirut, n.d.) 210.

25 For its benevolence to orphans, see the Quran 2:83, 177, 215, 220; 4:2–3, 5–6, 8–10, 36, 127; 6:152; 8:41; 17:34; 18:82; 59:17; 76:8; 89:17; 90:15; 93:6–9; 107:2.

26 L. Peirce, 'Matriarchs and Slaves: Gender and Political Power in the Ottoman Empire', paper presented at the 8th Berkshire Conference on the History of Women 'Crossing Boundaries in Feminist History' 8–10 June 1990, Douglass College, Rutgers, New Brunswick, USA; cf. also Juynboll, *Handleiding*, 236.

27 Robertson Smith, *Kinship and Marriage*, 105.

28 Mernissi, *Le harem politique*, 151.

29 E.g. A. Moors, *Women and Property: A Historical-Anthropological Study of Women's Access to Property Through Inheritance, the Dower and Labour in Jabal Nablus, Palestine* (Dissertation, Amsterdam, 1992).

30 Over time, different law schools have changed the rules concerning the period of *hadâna* or the obligation of maintenance. See, e.g., for Hanafi law: J. Anderson, 'The Development of Islamic Family Law in the Legal System of Jordan', *The International and Comparative Law Quarterly* 37 (1988) 868–86; L. Welchman, 'Recent Developments in Shari'a Law: V. The Dissolution of Marriage', *The Muslim World* 42 (1952) 190–206. N. Coulson and D. Hinchcliffe, 'Women and Law Reform in Contemporary Islam', in L. Beck and N. Keddie (eds) *Women in the Muslim World* (Cambridge, 1979) 37–51, show how the general Quranic norms and injunctions, especially those geared to protect or improve women's

status and position in the family, suffered progressive dilution during the more than two centuries of juristic development in which the classical formulation of Islamic law according to the different Sunni and Shiite schools took place. Most Muslim countries in turn have adapted classical Islamic law to suit their own national laws (e.g. by combining rulings from different law schools or making specific interpretations); see E. H. White, 'Legal Reform as an Indicator of Women's Status in Muslim Nations', in Beck and Keddie, *Women in the Muslim World*, 52–68. A discussion of these kinds of changes lies outside the scope of this chapter.

31 At present, a widow who wants to keep her children usually has to provide their maintenance herself through paid work. If she cannot find work, her own relatives, who have to maintain her, are seldom also prepared to contribute to the maintenance of her children. If she remarries she loses her children, cf. Jansen, *Women Without Men*; Moors, *Women and Property*, 63.

32 Juynboll, *Handleiding*, 188.

33 Juynboll, *Handleiding*, 174, n. 1. For a description of the freedom some noble ladies permitted themselves, see also Smith, *Râbi'a the Mystic*, 112–25.

34 Gibb and Kramers, *Shorter Encyclopaedia*, 503; L. Ahmed, *Women and Gender in Islam* (New Haven, 1992) 49. On women, including widows, in early Islam see I. Lichtenstadter, *Women in the Aiyam al-'Arab* (London, 1935); G.H. Stern, 'The First Women Converts in Early Islam', *Islamic Culture* 13 (1939) 291–303, and 'Muhammad's Bond with the Women', *Bulletin of the School of Oriental and African Studies* 10 (1940–2) 185–97; N. Abbott, 'Women and the State in Early Islam', *Journal of Near Eastern Studies* 1 (1942) 106–26, 341–68; J. Smith, 'Women, Religion and Social Change in Early Islam', in Y.Y. Haddad and E.B. Findly (eds) *Women, Religion and Social Change* (New York, 1985) 19–35.

35 Rodinson, *Mohammed*, 176.

36 E.W. Fernea and B.Q. Bezirgan, "A'ishah bint Abi Bakr: Wife of the Prophet Muhammed,' in Fernea and Bezirgan (eds), *Middle Eastern Muslim Women Speak* (Austin, 1977, 27–36) 28.

37 Mernissi, *Le harem politique*, 153–9.

38 Watt, *Muhammed*, 226, very recently, D.A. Spellberg, *Politics, Gender and the Islamic Past: The Legacy of 'A'isha Bint Abi Bakr* (New York, 1994).

39 Smith, *Râbi'a the Mystic*, 139 ('Aisha), 121 (Umm Qirfa). Smith cites contemporary and secondary sources who talk of heroic women in those early days who went into battle, both on the side of the Muslims and that of their adversaries. One was Nusayba, daughter of Ka'b, who fought and was wounded on the day of Yamâma and in the battle of Uhud (AD 625) or Hind, daughter of 'Utba. Among the first Muslims to wage war by sea was a woman, Umm Harâm, who was killed in Cyprus when thrown off by her mule.

40 Gibb and Kramers, *Shorter Encyclopaedia*, 26. A figure of 2210 traditions attributed to 'Aisha is given in Hitti, *History of the Arabs*, 394. The lower figure, however, is probably true, as it is also given in Mernissi, *Le harem politique*, 95, who derived it from Imam Zarkashi.

41 Mernissi, *Le harem politique*, 95.
42 Ibid., 96.
43 Gibb and Kramers, *Shorter Encyclopaedia*, 26.
44 Fernea and Bezirgan, "A'ishah bint Abi Bakr,' 34.
45 According to 'Aisha's biographer Said Al-Afghani cited by Mernissi, *Le harem politique*, 14–16.
46 Jansen, *Women Without Men, passim.*
47 Ibid.
48 At the time of research in 1982 the pension amounted to 1500 Algerian Dinars a month, which according to the official rate equalled about $315 or £180. The pension was higher than the guaranteed minimum wage of qualified personnel (DA 1300).
49 This system is called *waqf* or *habous*, cf. F. Peltier and G.H. Bousquet, *Les successions agnatiques mitigées* (Paris, 1935) 147–9, 176–8; L. M. Lefèvre, *Recherches sur la condition de la femme kabyle* (Algiers, 1939) 126–32; G. Tillion, *Le harem et les cousins* (Paris, 1966); J.L. Esposito, *Women in Muslim Family Law* (Syracuse, 1982) 65–72; M. Gast (ed.), *Hériter en pays musulman: Habus, lait vivant, manyahuli* (Paris, 1987).
50 M. Borrmans, 'Perspectives algériennes en matière de droit familial', *Studia Islamica* 37 (1973, 129–53) 151.
51 Ibid., 133; M. Virolle and B. Souibbs, 'Enquête introductive à l'étude de quelques aspects sociaux de la vieillesse dans une ville moyenne: Tizi-Ouzou', *Bulletin du CRAPE* 11 (1980, 135–83) 157.
52 In 1979, 58% of the already-married grooms married young girls, 19% married widows and 22% divorcées: *Annuaire Statistique de l'Algérie 1981* (Algiers, 1981) 33.
53 W. Jansen, 'A Bride for Three Million: Symbolic Dominance in Algerian Marriage Gifts,' in A. Blok and H. Driessen (eds), *Cultural Dominance in the Mediterranean Area* (Nimwegen, 1984) 4–36.
54 I thank Marjo Buitelaar for her helpful suggestions.

11

WIDOWS HIDDEN FROM VIEW

The disappearance of mourning dress among Dutch widows in the twentieth century[1]

Geertje van Os

> For mourning a vast array of special clothing developed over the centuries, to be worn by the bereaved and particularly by widows. The study of fashionable European mourning dress provides us with an extraordinarily revealing insight into the function of dress and the social position of women.[2]

Women in black are highly identifiable. Of all the ways in which a woman can express her identity as a widow, mourning dress is the most conspicuous. By means of colour and clothes a widow can distinguish herself from other women. In her mourning clothes she shows her status as a widow to the outside world and will be treated accordingly.[3]

In the Netherlands, mourning dress fell into disuse within a relatively short period after the Second World War. Dutch widows no longer distinguish themselves from other women in any visible way. What is the meaning of mourning dress and what made widows in the Netherlands give up their black mourning clothes in modern times? In this chapter I will first describe how significant clothes are for people's identity. Next, I will discuss the functions of mourning dress in general as well as present a brief review of the historical development of mourning dress in Western Europe, illustrated by some examples from the Netherlands. And finally, I will suggest various reasons for the disappearance of mourning dress in modern Dutch society.

CLOTHES AND IDENTITY

> Through clothes, the individual puts on the 'façade' required
> by the role and, in doing so, displays his own role-identity.
> Since role helps bring order to an otherwise chaotic world,
> clothes may also be said to do the same.[4]

Clothes provide people with an identity and say something about
their values and their place in society. Clothing confirms and eluci-
dates social relations, it is an expression of social identity and
value.[5] Clothes are often compared with words. Both language and
garments can be modern, old-fashioned, foreign, common, charming,
solemn or childish. Clothing as well as language has its own vocabu-
lary.[6] Language and style of dress are the outward face of people's
social roles.

Research has shown that people are able to judge other people in
as little as thirty seconds as to their sex, age, nationality, profession
and class. Besides, they can tell in which state of mind the other
person is: kind, reliable, shy or authoritarian.[7] Two important
indicators for this impression are the clothes one wears and the
language one speaks. By wearing clothes you bare part of yourself.[8]
Many people face the same problem every morning: what shall I wear
today? Choosing clothing, in a shop or at home from the wardrobe,
is a delicate or even oppressive daily affair to them.[9] Dress is a means
to construct identity. Some follow the style of the times they live in
or the group to which they belong, others develop a more individual
form of expression.[10] People's identity can be guessed by their
clothes. Man lives in different worlds and plays many roles. In every
world another language is spoken and other clothes are worn. To
each role belongs a specific speech and dress.

For the American anthropologist Sahlins the production of clothes
is the realization of a system of symbols.[11] The article of dress which
reaches the market is in point of fact a materialized social category
and consequently helps to consolidate this category in society. Every
garment possesses a combination of three elementary units; fabric,
cut and colour, and is suitable for a certain age, sex, class, activity,
time, place or other dimension of the cultural order. Apparently
minor distinctions can point to a significant difference in social
meaning. For instance, if the buttons of a shirt are on the left, the
shirt is worn by women; if they are on the right it is worn by men.
This results from the ancient idea that the left side of the body is
female and the right side is male. Consequently, according to Sahlins,

capitalism is wholly rational. 'It is a definite form of cultural order; or a cultural order acting in a particular form.'[12]

Anthropologists generally assume that clothing the body and covering the genitals originally had little to do with a sense of shame. Apart from utilitarian aspects like protection against cold, in the first instance clothes met the needs of adornment and the related intention to make oneself sexually attractive.[13] By adorning oneself, that part of the body which is decorated remains secret. It is precisely by concealing it that attention is attracted and its charm is accentuated. Which parts of the human body need to be covered to avoid exceeding the limit is of little concern. Sexual interest is always evoked by the edge of what is still visible. 'Victorian poets were enthusiastic about ankles; Renaissance poets about breasts; Arab poets about eyes.'[14] The most exciting part of the female body is that which can just or just not be seen.[15]

Clothing as well as language is a means to communication. Both are expedients to elucidate relations between people. Goffman has called this 'the art of impression management'.[16] The manner in which people 'guide' the image by which they present themselves to others indicates how they see themselves in relation to others and different social contexts. Dress is part of our material self and helps to create as well as to confirm the image of ourselves. A self-image is not static or unequivocal, it is continuously moving and changing. 'Clothes and other forms of adornment are part of the identity kits that we all use to manage the impression we present to others.'[17] Whether the social roles we play are assigned to us or acquired by us, clothes help to identify ourselves to a certain extent with our role. From people who play an imposed role, we expect a corresponding mode of acting and dressing. Uniform identifies its wearers as members of a group and often places them in a hierarchy.[18] For its wearers uniform also helps identify them with their social role. Uniform 'makes' the social role. The fact that uniform is worn testifies that social institutions also function by means of symbolic categories.

MOURNING CLOTHES

In the human life-cycle one way of dressing is sometimes ritually exchanged for another. In this way role alteration is officially displayed. At significant ceremonial moments in human life, like baptism, communion, marriage or burial, ritual dress is worn. One enters into a new social category. To make this known and to identify with the new status, a different dress is assumed after the ritual. Someone who adopts the clothing of another social category cannot easily dispose of it.[19]

A woman whose husband has died undergoes a *rite de passage*. She turns from a married woman into a widow and moves into another social category. The bride who enters marriage is dressed in white and wears a veil. The widow who leaves marriage is shrouded in black and is veiled too: 'all grand forms of feminine life show the woman veiled; the bride, the widow, the nun are bearers of the same symbol'.[20] The black, veiled appearance of a widow makes a mysterious sight.

The period of time during which a widow wore mourning dress could extend for many years, perhaps a lifetime. By means of her mourning dress she presented herself to the outside world as a respectable woman, whose husband had died, but who wanted to remain true to him and see herself attached to him. Her mourning dress identified her clearly as belonging to a social category. Her cultural identity as widow was obvious to everybody, whereas her identity as mother, middle-aged woman, chairperson of the women's association or as shopkeeper was less visible and seemed to be subordinate to this cultural state.

Origin of mourning dress

'In not a single respect is man as conservative as in his care of, and deference to, the dead', wrote Fahrenfort and Van de Graft. These Dutch scholars, the former an ethnologist, the latter a historian, described various funeral customs in the Netherlands whose origins could likely be traced back to the pre-Christian period, although their meaning had gradually changed over time. For example, eyes and mouth were closed for fear that the soul would leave the body, but nowadays this is done out of aesthetic considerations.[21] Similarly, the soul was believed to remain attached to the body for three days, and in Holland today the dead are still not buried or cremated until three days have gone by. Most likely, the wearing of mourning dress originally also had another meaning. One much-mentioned explanation of the wearing of mourning dress is the concealment from the dead person's soul,[22] since the spirit of the dead was not well disposed towards his relatives. To distract the attention of the departing soul the mourners wore the opposite of their usual wear.

If they were used to dark clothes, they would now wear bright colours instead. They even attempted to disguise themselves as ghosts, since a ghost never appears where other ghosts are present.

A widow had to observe the rules of mourning most diligently, since she ran the largest risk of being dragged down into death through her husband's jealousy or desire. Her veil kept her deceased husband's soul away and made her unrecognizable.[23] According to the authors mentioned above, mourning dress acquired another meaning in the first centuries of Christianity. It now became an expression of respect for the deceased, a gesture of grief, seclusion and abandonment of pleasure. Mourning dress made the modesty, integrity and chastity of the widow perceptible.[24]

There is a parallel between widows and nuns. In earlier Christian times, when the first convents were founded, many a widow retired from the world to a convent, where she had to take the nun's gown.[25] Like nuns, widows had left ordinary life, had forsworn sexuality and did not take an interest in elegant and stylish garments. Nuns were dressed in black, grey or brown, but they also wore white, as a token of their purity and humility. Widows wore black and grey to give evidence of their sorrow and rejection of all amusement. The feminine figure of the nun was kept secret underneath her formless habit. The face and figure of the widow disappeared behind veils and wide, old-fashioned robes.[26] Nuns and widows did not keep up with fashion. Nuns dressed conservatively for longer than widows and their habit remained unaltered for centuries. Widows were more easily seduced by fashions, though this was a long-drawn-out process: not until the end of the Victorian Age was mourning dress allowed to be fashionable.[27]

In the Victorian Age there was, so to speak, a boom in European mourning display, particularly in England. The rules of mourning etiquette and mourning dress became far-reaching and refined, almost pathological. It is common knowledge that Queen Victoria disliked undressing, but it is less well known that for a period of forty years she did not take off her mourning dress.[28] Queen Victoria was 42 years old when she became a widow and was left with nine children. Until her death in 1901 she continued to wear mourning dress, becoming a leading figure in mourning etiquette and dress in the second half of the nineteenth century.[29]

At the outbreak of the First World War the extensive mourning and funeral etiquettes of the nineteenth century came to an end. 'The sight of millions of women of all ages shrouded in crape would have been too much to bear.'[30] Many women did not even have time or money to isolate themselves in mourning for a specific time, as the old mourning customs dictated. Besides, in wartime conditions women occupied all sorts of jobs and activities which were left vacant by the departing men. The fallen men left an army of widows: 'it was no longer socially realistic for them all to act as though their emotional and sexual life was over for good, which was the underlying message of the ritual mourning. And with the underlying message, the ritual too was discarded.'[31] When the war was over, the Victorian mourning etiquette was not revived.

In the Netherlands the (prolonged) wearing of mourning dress fell into disuse in the second half of the twentieth century. The First and Second World Wars contributed to this development, though the influence of the wars was far less than in England or France. However, the disappearance of mourning dress in the neighbouring countries may have contributed to its disappearance in the Netherlands.

The colours of mourning

White is an ancient colour of mourning and is still worn in China, Japan, India and in some parts of Europe. It is the colour of innocence, simplicity and purity of the soul.[32] White is also an aristocratic mourning colour. On 8 December 1962 the Dutch Queen Wilhelmina, following the example of her late husband Hendrik, was led to her grave in a white coach drawn by eight greys. At the funeral of Anwar Sadat, the assassinated president of Egypt, on 10 October 1981, 'Prince Charles was conspicuously evident in his white naval uniform.'[33]

Red has been a mourning colour as well. In the Christian church red symbolized the blood of Christ. Popes still wear red robes while celebrating Mass and are dressed in red on their death-bed. According to Taylor, purple was a mourning colour for royal rulers and emperors, since in the seventeenth century European kings wore purple when mourning.[34]

Black is the colour which is most characteristically associated with mourning. The symbolic meanings attributed to the colour black vary from time to time and from place to place. In the Middle Ages the colours black and white were almost empty of symbolic meaning in everyday usage. Sometimes they were opposites, but nearly as frequently they were synonymous.[35] An indication of mourning was discarding colours, and for that reason mourning colours could be both black and white.[36]

The Christian church encouraged the wearing of black for mourn-ing.[37] In the Middle Ages, when colours were distrusted,[38] black was associated with the ascetic ideal of the good Christian. Until the sixteenth century all good dyes came from the Orient, where the dye specialists lived. Consequently, coloured cloth was considered a luxury article.[39] The monastic orders, especially the Benedictines, exerted great influence on 'blacking' colour by wearing garments of undyed wool, since Benedict had ordered his monks to dress soberly and to make use of local goods only. At the time, the natural colour of wool was black, for the simple reason that sheep were black in the Early Middle Ages.[40]

In sixteenth-century Europe colourful garments had become accessible to all strata of society and the élite began to dress in black to dissociate themselves from the great mass of the people.[41]

Nineteenth-century European dandies dressed in romantic, melan-cholic, refined black, and around ladies shrouded in black there emerged an air of danger and fatal attraction: 'a lady in black is not only dramatic and dignified but also dangerous'. Before the eighteenth century this aura of danger was absent from black worn by women, yet in later times it was never lacking, even during the exuberant use of black for mourning in the nineteenth century. Women in black mourning dress were a favourite theme in Romantic painting; senti-mental with a hint of eroticism. The blacker and severer the mourning, the more erotic the effect. By the end of the nineteenth century the reasons for wearing black had become more diverse. Widows lost their means of distinction and added a 'widow's peak' to their black figure to make themselves known as widows. A widow's peak was a hood or cap which ran into a peak on the forehead.[42]

Black mourning dress also helped to disguise widows. It was a means to set them apart from other persons.[43] In the twentieth century the colour black lost many of its symbolic meanings. 'All fashion is now aware of its history and of itself as personal, theatrical or dramatic costume, so that to wear black clothing is to refer to a variety of earlier manifestations for black clothes – earlier styles, former meanings, obsolete conventions.'[44]

THE DISAPPEARANCE OF MOURNING DRESS

Becoming a widow is a tragic event in a woman's life for which she is often not prepared. Women who become widows enter a new phase of their life, which can signify a dramatic, sudden change of identity. In order to adopt a different identity attributes and ritual are needed.[45] To change her style of dress is likely to help both herself and others in acquiring the new role. Her mourning clothes help identify herself with her new status. In everyday social life it is important for others to know in which stage of life we are. We have to identify ourselves for our surroundings.[46] The mourning dress of the widow was beyond all doubt in this respect. Moreover, there were distinct degrees of mourning dress which indicated in which stage of mourning she was. So allowance could be made for her condition and awkward situations could be avoided. Above all, mourning dress created clarity. In modern Dutch society, though, widows are no longer recognizable by their clothes. Why did they give up their mourning dress?

The self-image of women in black

A recent Dutch dissertation on older Dutch widows observes: 'It is no wonder that many widows are frightened by the bleakness of their future.' The status of widow is socially vulnerable, in that it is an ambiguous status containing elements of the status of an unmarried and married woman. 'Widows have trouble moving out of bereavement because there is no identity readily accessible to them beyond widowhood: they have "no place to go" in a society which socializes women primarily to be wives and mothers.'[47]

People tend to distinguish themselves from others in a positive way. According to Tajfel and Turner's social identity theory, society is composed of *groups* of individuals that differ from one another particularly in power and status.[48] People evaluate themselves in relation to other individuals. They also try to structure the similarities and differences between social groups. The need for positive distinctiveness is the primary motivation behind social comparison. Individuals can improve their self-image if the social group (or one of the groups) to which they belong is rising in status. However, if comparisons with other groups are unfavourable, then group membership comes to be associated with low status, which results in a less positive social identity.[49]

Women in general do not derive a positive social identity from their gender group membership. Due to the negative qualities which are attributed to the category 'women' and the low status relative to the other gender group 'men', women can find it difficult to identify with their own gender group.[50] They tend to dissociate themselves psychologically from their own category by trying to identify with a group of higher social status or by reducing the status differences between the two gender categories.[51] However, women do not constitute a homogeneous social group, since there exist great differences in age, marital status, class, schooling or profession. It is true that, by their clothes, they are all almost inmediately recognizable as women.[52] Their identity as woman is just one part of their total identity, but it has a considerable influence on practically all fields of life from which a person derives identity.[53]

To a great extent self-images are constructed by means of interaction with other people. Individuals are continuously moulding an image of themselves. They do not have a coherent self-image at their disposal which is visible for other people, but they succeed in constructing an imaginary sense of completeness and personal continuity out of the actual inconsistent experiences of 'the self'. The key is in memory, which is able to recall experiences from the past which refer to someone's self-image, at every desirable moment. 'Individuals have a remarkable capacity to maintain an experience of wholeness in the face of contradictions, by keeping only one frame of reference in mind at any particular moment.'[54]

Women in general find it hard to derive a positive self-image from their social category. Widows equally do not feel happy about their social identity as widows. By shrouding themselves in black they place themselves unambiguously in this category. After the Second World War, widows abandoned their black dress, but war was not the only reason. Previously, mourning dress seemed not to have this negative influence on a widow's self-image. 'They submitted, usually with enthusiasm, to the dictatorial rules, wearing depressing, dull, black clothes, sometimes for years on end.'[55] Widows in the past met the requirements of mourning etiquette, since the wearing of mourning was appreciated by their surroundings. Mourning dress voiced their integrity and chastity, proved their alliance with their deceased husband and perhaps protected them. How could the wearing of mourning become a matter of little honour for present-day Dutch widows?

Women of dead men

There is nothing which makes you grow more lonely than 'acting normal' in a world of eroding norms.[56]

In the years after the Second World War various significant social changes rapidly took place in Dutch society. I cannot discuss these transformations in detail, but I will briefly sketch two major social developments which are highly relevant to our subject. The first transformation concerns changing attitudes towards death.[57] Mourning can be seen as an official acknowledgement of death and an affirmation of the surviving importance of the deceased. Until the mourning rites are completed, death is less absolute, since the deceased still has living needs.[58] Moreover, mourning is comforting; as long as there is something one can do for the deceased, there remains, as it were, a living bond.[59] The period in which a widow was in mourning could even last for her whole life.

In 1955 Geoffrey Gorer observed that death and mourning in Great Britain had gone more and more backstage and developed into a taboo. Death seemed to have taken the place of sexuality as an illicit theme.[60] This flying from death should not be attributed to indifference, quite the opposite. According to Ariès, the pioneer of research into the history of death, the origin of this taboo is the hunger for happiness which characterizes present-day life.[61] People are no longer able to experience death as a trusted end of life.[62]

The mourning process thus turned from a public into a private matter. People no longer believed in a hereafter, the dead could not be helped. For the privatization of family life, showing grief or personal misfortune became out of place and pointed to a lack of self-control.[63] This privatization of mourning is leading to an institutionalization; nowadays, widows end up with their problems and sorrow in talk groups: 'mourning assimilation'. A recent interview with a widow about her life after the death of her partner well illustrates this problem. After having followed a training in welfare work after the death of her husband, she decided to obtain an additional qualification as well – as an undertaker. 'I discovered that death is not properly dealt with: not by ourselves, nor by professionals . . . I would like to bring back many things to the relatives.'[64] Equally, wearing mourning dress is no longer an indication of chastity and integrity. The result of this development is a solitary and humiliating experience of mourning and sorrow. As a Dutch author and widow writes in one of her autobiographical novels: 'I do not know which process is more painful, what gnaws more at man's heart: the grief of mourning or the cold without.'[65]

From this point of view it is understandable that women whose husbands have died do not want to dress in black. Women in black are considered bearers of death and death at present has become 'unmentionable', to quote Ariès. However, this is not the only reason that widows shook off their black shadows of death. The second social development which contributed to a changing appreciation of the social category 'widows' is the changing relation between men and women.

Widows not only dislike being associated with death, they prefer not to be identified with the category 'widows' at all. Even though men and women are still not treated equally, one could speak of a certain, general ideology in the Netherlands which advocates equality. Women find it hard to derive a positive image of themselves from their status as spouse.[66] Women who derive their identity to a great extent from matters outside the domestic sphere have a higher status and a more positive self-image than women who identify with a husband and children.[67] As a result of modern welfare facilities especially, women have become financially less dependent on their husbands. In modern Dutch society women seem to derive more identity from being-a-mother or being-at-work than from being-a-spouse.

CONCLUSION

Women in mourning dress clearly signal that they feel closely allied with their husbands and, what is more, with their dead husbands. Within present-day ideology these widows are assigned a cultural identity which will damage their self-image. Though widows are not a homogeneous group, if they are shrouded in black their widow-hood manifests itself in every other role they play.

Widows in the Netherlands gave up not only their black mourning dress, but also almost all other means which set them perceptibly in the social category 'widows'. There are few situations left in which widows present themselves socially as widows. For instance it is rare, on doorplates, letterheads, addresses or in the telephone directory, to see the abbreviation 'Wdw' in front of a name; and widows no longer want to be addressed as such, as the image evoked by the term 'widow' has become unfavourable. This disappearance of the widow is well illustrated by the decree of the Dutch government that changes the denomination 'Widows and Orphans' Act' into 'Rela-tives' Act' and adjusts the widows' pension accordingly.

The black mourning dress gave widows an identity which was almost literally written on the body. The refusal to dress in black marked a step in the direction of the dismantling of widowhood as a cultural identity. Widows in modern life are hidden from view.

NOTES

1 The present chapter is a revised version of a paper presented at the seminar on Cultural Identity organized by Willy Jansen at the Graduate School of the Social Sciences in Amsterdam, 1991. I wish to thank Willy Jansen and the participants of that seminar for their helpful comments, and Anton Blok for his careful reading and useful suggestions. I am grateful to Jan Bremmer and Lourens van den Bosch for their scrupulous editing and to Dave Quail and Steve Alan Trott for correcting my English.

2 L. Taylor, *Mourning Dress: A Costume and Social History* (London, 1983) 20.

3 In this chapter I am concentrating on the meaning of mourning dress for widows. Women who are not in mourning for their dead husbands are set aside. Men in mourning are left out of consideration as well. Rules regarding mourning and remarriage for widowers were usually less rigid. Within the scope of this chapter it is not possible to go further into this.

4 B. Lönnqvist, 'Symbolic Values in Clothing', *Ethnologia Scandinavica* 9 (1979) 92–105, especially 102.

5 J. Schneider, 'The Anthropology of Cloth', *Annual Review of Anthropology* 16 (1987) 409–48, especially 412–16.

6 This idea is developed further by A. Lurie, *The Language of Clothes* (Feltham, 1981).

7 M. Sahlins, *Culture and Practical Reason* (Chicago, 1976) 203.

8 Lurie, *Language of Clothes*, 3.

9 Lurie, 36.

10 A. Rugh, *Reveal and Conceal: Dress in Contemporary Egypt* (Cairo, 1987) 148 writes that people in modern Egypt don't bother themselves about originality or individuality of their clothes; 'People in Egypt receive their strength from primary groups and thus have no reluctance to show their identification with them.'

11 Sahlins, *Culture and Practical Reason*, 179–204.

12 Ibid., 185. About the more general meaning of minor differences, see: P. Bourdieu, *La Distinction: Critique sociale du jugement* (Paris, 1979).

13 There are some cases known of peoples who go naked, among whom only prostitutes wear clothes, cf. G. Simmel, *On Women, Sexuality and Love* (New Haven and London, 1984) 136.

14 E. Leach, 'Levels of Communication and Problems of Taboo in the Appreciation of Primitive Art', in A. Forge (ed.) *Primitive Art and Society* (London and New York, 1973) 221–34, especially 226.

15 In Egypt women in particular have to dress themselves modestly, because women are able to dishonour their family by their actual or presumed lack of virtue. However, the meaning of modest clothing is twofold, cf. Rugh (see note 10 above), 142: 'Modesty garments are symbolic in the sense that they mark people's intentions about moral issues. They are not covers intended to make women unrecognizable or unfeminine. On the contrary, they emphasize femininity, and by covering the imperfections allow the imagination free rein to conjure up the most alluring possibilities underneath.'

16 See E. Goffman, *The Presentation of Self in Everyday Life* (New York, 1959) 208–338.

17 S. Kaiser, *The Social Psychology of Clothing and Personal Adornment* (New York, 1985) 152.

18 Lurie, *Language of Clothes*, 18f.

19 In this connection Lönnqvist refers to a study of gypsies in Finland. He who turns his back on his gypsy origin first of all parts with his gypsy clothes. Once that has happened, there is no way back. Lönnqvist 'Symbolic Values', 100f.

20 G. von Le Fort, *De eeuwige vrouw* (Antwerp, 1953) 25f.

21 J. Fahrenfort and C. van de Graft, *Dodenbezorging en cultuur* (Amsterdam, 1947) pt II, 83f.

22 Cf. H. Goossens, 'Oude gebruiken bij ziekte, dood en begrafenis' in *Feestbundel voor A. H. J. van Delft, pastoor te St. Anthonis: Bij zijn gouden priesterjubileum aangeboden door zijn vrienden* (Heerlen, 1955) 50–7; A. van Hageland, 'De magische kring om de dood', *De Brabantse Folklore* 144 (1959) 489–535, especially 519–24; H. Kok, *De geschiedenis van de laatste eer in Nederland* (Lochem, 1970) 240–3; *Rendezvous met Magere Hein: Doods- en rouwgebruiken in de negentiende eeuw* (Catalogue, Museum voor Volkskunde Gent, 1986) 31. In the Dutch provinces of Brabant, Gelderland and Limburg, other customs, which were intended to deceive the spirit of the deceased, like closing the shutters, turning the mirrors and stopping the clocks, were observed till the Second World War.

23 H. Grolman, 'Volksgebruiken bij sterven en begraven in Nederland', *Tijdschrift voor het Koninklijk Nederlandsch Aardrijkskundig Genootschap*, 2nd series pt XL (1923) 359–96, especially 387–91.

24 Perhaps mourning dress had this meaning in pre-Christian times as well.

25 According to Taylor, *Mourning Dress*, 66 this is the origin of the widow's mourning dress.

26 A remarkable garment which was worn by women in mourning in the Dutch province of Brabant till the Second World War was the *falie*. A *falie* was a rectangular piece of black wool or silk of approximately three metres in length and one metre in breadth. A *falie* covered the head and body of a woman, hiding practically her entire figure. The outward appearance of a widow in *falie* and a nun in habit was virtually the same. Elsewhere in the Netherlands the *falie* was worn too; according to the region it was called *reekleed, regenkleed, regensprei, dwaal* or *dweel*. Cf. Kok *De geschiedenis* 246f.; Van Hageland 'De magische kring', 523f. In Flanders in the thirties the *falie* was already only worn during funerals. The woman who announced the death in the neighbourhood also distributed the necessary *falies*. Usually this was done by the dry-nurse, the woman who was responsible for both the first and last cares of man. See P. Sterckens-Cieters, *Volksklederdrachten in Vlaanderen* (Antwerp, 1935) 33f.

27 Taylor, *Mourning Dress*, 66–73.

28 H. Franke, 'Het heengaan van de dood: Over de veranderende inhoud van overlijdensadvertenties (1794–1983)', *Sociologisch Tijdschrift* 11 (1984) 286–326, especially 303.

29 Taylor, *Mourning Dress*, 154f. In the Victorian period, a widow who remarried wore grey at her wedding, since grey stood midway between joy and regret: a second marriage could never be as worthy as a first marriage. It was a public acknowledgement that a respectable woman would not sleep with two men (Taylor, 256f.).

30 Taylor, *Mourning Dress*, 276.

31 G. Gorer, *Death, Grief and Mourning* (London, 1965). Some women showed in a different way that they were mourning, for example by wearing a purple band round their left arm, a symbol of the patriotic death of their husband – perhaps an effort to make the bereavement endurable, a token that the life of the beloved is not lost, cf. Taylor, *Mourning Dress*, 268–70.

32 In Austria, Hungary, Romania, Switzerland and other European countries children were buried in white. Sometimes young single women were buried as brides, cf. G. Kligman, *The Wedding of the Dead: Ritual, Poetics and Popular Culture in Transylvania* (Berkeley and Los Angeles, 1988) and E. Venbrux, 'A Death-Marriage in a Swiss Mountain Village', *Ethnologia Europaea* 21 (1991) 193–205.

33 Taylor, *Mourning Dress*, 250.

34 Taylor, *Mourning Dress*, 259–62. According to V. Turner, *The Forest of Symbols: Aspects of Ndembu Ritual* (Ithaca and London, 1967) 59–93, the colours red, white and black make a fundamental triplet. In many societies these colours have symbolic meanings referring to products of the human body. (White = sperm or milk: life giving; red = blood: life; black = excrements, dirt: dead.) People make classifications by their own physical experiences, which have a direct association with colour.

35 R. van Uytven, 'Rood-wit-zwart: kleurensymboliek en kleurensignalen in de middeleeuwen', *Tijdschrift voor geschiedenis* 97 (1984) 447–69, especially 457.

36 W. Brückner, 'Farbe als Zeichen: Kulturtraditionen im Alltag', *Zeitschrift für Volkskunde* 78 (1982) 14–27, especially 22. Black and white are not regarded as colours.

37 Taylor, *Mourning Dress*, 251f.

38 The word 'coloured' still has a negative connotation in several languages, for instance: 'tainted'. Fixatives were also called *menstruae*, a word with a connotation of distrust because it refers to menstrual blood; see J. Schneider, 'Peacocks and Penguins: The Political Economy of European Cloth and Colors', *American Ethnologist* 5 (1978) 413–48, especially 422.

39 Schneider, 'Peacocks and Penguins', 420.

40 Schneider, 'Peacocks and Penguins', 423. Mediterranean Europe was in more direct contact with the Orient than Europe north of the Alps. More and more dye-specialists established themselves in the towns along the merchant routes and provided the rest of Europe with colour. A well-known example is Florence. According to Schneider, sheep became white in the course of the Middle Ages because the black sheep were removed from the flocks, for black wool is hard to dye. Subsequently the monks were forced to dye their habits black (ibid., 423f).
     In Schneider's view the propagation of black by medieval monastic orders was an economic boycott of the import of luxury goods.

Therefore, north-western Europe was able to develop autonomously, because black cloth, in contrast to colourful textile, could be perfected by their own artisans with their own raw materials. The Flemish textile industry specialized in black and was very successful in that, because of the abundance of natural raw material which is needed to dye cloth black: 'Flemish black was the best in Europe' (ibid., 425). For that reason the symbolic meaning of black contributed indirectly to the economic development of north-western Europe.

41 A. Hollander, *Seeing Through Clothes* (New York, 1975) 374, 365–90 (a historical description of the wearing of black from about the sixteenth century).

42 Ibid., 376f. (quotation, dandies, erotic effect); 382f. (widow's peak).

43 Black dress may also have helped to marginalize or to isolate widows from society.

44 Hollander, *Seeing Through Clothes*, 388.

45 See, for instance, R. Huntington and P. Metcalf, *Celebrations of Death: The Anthropology of Mortuary Ritual* (Cambridge, 1979). Rituals mark identity and can be used to establish a new identity. In this connection one could make a comparison with the communist countries, where an attempt was made to impose upon the collective population a new, socialist identity. One of the most important means for this purpose was the introduction of new celebrations and rituals. However, the latter were not accepted, neither partly nor in altered form, cf. K. Roth and J. Roth, 'The System of Socialist Holidays and Rituals in Bulgaria', *Ethnologia Europea* 20 (1990) 107–20.

46 A.L. Strauss, *Mirrors and Masks: The Search for Identity* (London, 1977) 126f.

47 Nan Stevens, *Well-Being in Widowhood: A Question of Balance* (Dissertation, Nimwegen, 1989) 22f.

48 H. Tajfel and J. Turner, 'An Integrative Theory of Intergroup Conflict', in W. Austin and S. Worchel (eds), *The Social Psychology of Intergroup Relations* (Monterey, 1979). Behaviour can be conceived as lying on a continuum – from group/intergroup to personal/interpersonal. At the group end, actions are determined by 'social identity' (identification with social groups or categories). At the interpersonal end, actions are determined by 'personal identity' (personality, peculiar aspects of the self), cf. D. Abrams, 'Differential Association: Social Developments in Gender Identity and Intergroup Relations during Adolescence', in S. Skevington and D. Baker (eds), *The Social Identity of Women* (London, 1989) 59–83, especially 60–2.

49 D. Baker, 'Social Identity in the Transition to Motherhood', in Skevington and Baker (eds), *The Social Identity of Women*, 84–105, especially 85f.

50 Abrams, 'Differential Association', 59–83.

51 Baker, 'Social Identity', 86f.

52 In this context it is remarkable that women's clothes changed substantially at about the same time as the mourning dress disappeared, cf. A. Lurie, *Language of Clothes*, 225f. in western Europe and the United States: 'It was not until the 1920s that women and girls began to wear

slacks and even shorts for sports and lounging. The new style was greeted with disapproval and ridicule. . . . Nevertheless the fashion spread, and by the mid-1930s a woman could go on picnic, play tennis or dig in the garden in clothes that did not handicap her. This freedom, however, was limited to the private and informal side of life. . . . In the late 1960s trousers for women finally became elegant as well as respectable.'

53 In fact the same holds for 'age'. The general attitude towards the elderly in our society does not provide the members of this group with a positive social identity, cf. B. Myerhoff, 'Rites and Signs of Ripening: The Intertwining of Ritual, Time and Growing Older', in D. Kertzer and J. Keith (eds), *Age and Anthropological Theory* (London and Ithaca, 1984) 305–30: 'Often the less future, the less to lose, from the point of view of the individual, and from the point of view of society; often old people are dispensable, their conduct a matter of little consequence, their controls a matter of diminished importance' (310). This has consequences not only for their identity as elderly persons, but also for all the other roles they play.

54 K.P. Ewing, 'The Illusion of Wholeness: Culture, Self, and the Experience of Inconsistency', *Ethos* 8 (1990) 251–79, especially 266f., 274 (quotation).

55 Taylor, *Mourning Dress*, 286f.

56 Annie Romein-Verschoor, widow of the well-known Dutch historian Jan Romein, quoted by J. Forceville-van Rossum, *Oud Blauw: Dagen van voortbestaan* (Baarn, 1990) 75.

57 The changing attitude towards death in western Europe was first described by the French historian Philippe Ariès, *Western Attitudes toward Death, from the Middle Ages to the Present* (Baltimore, 1974) and *The Hour of Our Death* (New York, 1981). In the Netherlands it was, among others, Herman Franke who paid attention to this phenomenon; see his 'Het heengaan van de dood' (see note 28 above) and *De dood in het leven van alledag: Rouwadvertenties en openbare strafvoltrekkingen in Nederland* (The Hague, 1985).

58 Cf. B. Myerhoff, 'Rites of Passage: Process and Paradox', in V. Turner (ed.) *Celebration: Studies in Festivity and Ritual* (Washington, 1982) 109–35. In many places simple biological death is no death at all: 'Ceremonies must transform the corpse into a properly deceased person' (109).

59 Cf. P. Marris, *Widows and their Families* (London, 1958) 31, 33; L.M. Danforth, *The Death Rituals of Rural Greece* (Princeton, 1982) 139–52.

60 Geoffrey Gorer said this in his pioneering article 'The Pornography of Death', *Encounter* (October 1955) and in *Death, Grief and Mourning* (London, 1967) 192–9.

61 Ariès, *Western Attitudes*, 93f.

62 According to C. Wouters, 'Sterven en voortleven in Nederland vanaf 1930; de regulering van macht en emoties aan het levenseinde', *Sociologisch Tijdschrift* 16 (1989) pt 3, 3–30, death in the Netherlands is no longer repressed. He reproaches Philippe Ariès, and Norbert Elias too, for having contributed to an idealization of the past. Wouters thinks that in our time dying persons are no longer lonely. Since the beginning of

the 1970s we have been in a phase of stabilization and resignation. Death can be mentioned again. Wouters investigates changes in the prevailing relationships between dying persons and their surroundings. His conclusions are based on literature by and for doctors and nurses, in view of their professional contact with the dying.

63   Marris, *Widows and their Families*, 87.
64   Ella Weisbrod, 'Alleen verder', *Opzij* (Dutch feminist monthly), 17 (October 1989) pt 10, 14.
65   Forceville-van Rossum, *Oud Blauw*, 53.
66   They have adopted, and made others accept, new forms of address, e.g. *mevrouw*, which removed the distinction between married and unmarried women.
67   Except for, as described by Baker (see note 49 above), women who have opted for a life which is for the most part enacted within the domestic sphere and who are admitted in a network of like-minded women. Even though their relative status will remain lower, their self-image will be more favourable.

12

WIDOWS IN WESTERN HISTORY
A select bibliography

Frouke Veenstra and
Kirsten van der Ploeg

What follows is a personal sampling of the vast literature on widows. The subject is, of course, endless and we have therefore mainly concentrated on books and articles with a historical analysis of widowhood in Europe and, to a somewhat lesser extent, North America. Naturally we have profited from previous bibliographies, in particular the one by Ida Blom. We thank Jan Bremmer for various suggestions.

BIBLIOGRAPHIES

Barrett C.J., 'Women in Widowhood (1960s–1970s)', *Signs* 2 (1977) 856–68.
Blom I., 'The History of Widowhood: A Bibliographic Overview', *Journal of Family History* 16 (1991) 191–210.

ANTIQUITY

Beaucamp, J., 'La reference au veuvage dans les papyrus byzantins', *Pallas* 32 (1985) 149–57.
Bopp, L., *Das Witwentum als organische Gliedschaft im Gemeinschaftsleben der alten Kirche* (Mannheim, 1950).
—— *Das Witwentum der alten Kirche* (Regensburg, 1960).
Johnston, H.W., 'Widows in the First and the Seventeenth Centuries', *Classical World* 25 (1931) 48.
Latorre, A., '*Uxor praegnans relicta*', *Labeo* 1 (1955) 195–201.
Mayer-Maly, Th., 'Trauerzeit und Wiederheirat', *Kirche und Recht* 4 (1963) 314–30.
Nazzaro, A.V., 'La vedovanza del cristianesimo antico', *Annali della Facoltà di Lettere e Filosofia dell' Univ. di Napoli* 26 (1983–4) 103–22.

Penta, M., 'La viduitas nella condizione della donna romana', *Atti della Academia di Scienze Morali e Politiche di Napoli* 91 (1980) 341–51.

Rosambert, A., *La veuve en droit canon* (Paris, 1923).

Tibiletti, C., 'Le vedove nei papiri greci d'Egitto', *Atti del XVII Congresso Int. di Papirologia* (Naples, 1984) 985–94.

Viteau, J., 'L'institution des diaconesses et des veuves', *Revue d'Histoire Ecclesiastique* 22 (1926) 513–37.

Walcot, P., 'On Widows and Their Reputation in Antiquity', *Symbolae Osloenses* 66 (1991) 5–26.

MIDDLE AGES

Brownlee, K. and W. Stephens (eds), *Discourse of Authority in Medieval and Renaissance Literature* (Hanover, 1989).

Emery, R.W., 'Les veuves juives de Perpignan (1317–1416)', in *La famille juive au Moyen Age: Provence Languedoc* (special issue) *Provence Historique* 37 (1987), 559–70.

Gauthier, B., 'Les veuves Lyonnaises au XVe siècle', *Cahiers d'Histoire* 26 (1981) 353–63.

Klapisch-Zuber, C., 'La Mère cruelle: maternité, veuvage et dot dans la Florence des XIVe–XVe siècles', *Annales* 38 (1981) 1097–1109.

Lorcin, M.T., 'Veuve noble et veuve paysanne en Lyonnais d'après les testaments des XIVe et XVe siècles', *Annales de démographie historique* (1981), 273–88.

Mirror, L. (ed.), *Upon My Husband's Death: Widows in the Literature and Histories of Medieval Europe* (Ann Arbor, 1992).

Ramis, G., 'La benedicion de las virgenes y las viudas en la liturgia celtica', *Ephemerides Liturgicae* 101 (1987) 145–9.

——— 'La benedicion de las viudas en las liturgias occidentales', *Ephemerides Liturgicae* 104 (1990) 159–75.

Walker, Sue Sheridan (ed.), *Wife and Widow in Medieval England* (Ann Arbor, 1993).

Wurtele, D.J., 'Chaucer's Wife of Bath and the Problem of the Fifth Husband', *Chaucer Review* 23 (1988) 117–28.

EARLY MODERN EUROPE

Aubry, Y., 'Pour une étude du veuvage feminin à l'époque moderne', *Histoire, Economie et Société* 8 (1989) 223–36.

Bacon, J.L., 'Wives, Widows and Writings in Restoration Comedy', *Studies in English Literature, 1500–1900* 31 (1991) 427–43.

Bellettini, A., 'Les remarriages dans la ville et dans la campagne de Bologne au dix-neuvième siècle', in E. Dupâquier *et al.*, *Marriage and Remarriage in Populations of the Past* (London, 1981) 259–72.

Bethke, R.D., 'Chester County Widow Wills (1714–1800): a folklife source', *Pennsylvania Folk Life* 18 (1968) 16–29.

Bideau, A., 'A Demographic and Social Analysis of Widowhood and

Remarriage: The Example of the Castellany of Thoissey-en-Dombes, 1670–1840', *Journal of Family History* 5 (1980) 28–43.

Boulton, J., 'London Widowhood Revisited: The Decline of Female Remarriage in the Seventeenth and Early Eighteenth Centuries', *Continuity and Change* 5 (1990) 323–55.

Carlton, C. 'The Widow's Tales: Male Myths and Female Reality in 16th and 17th century England', *Albion* 10 (1978) 118–29.

Diefendorf, B.B., 'Widowhood and Remarriage in Sixteenth-Century Paris', *Journal of Family History* 7 (1982) 379–95.

Dooghe, G. and Vanderleyden, L., 'Loneliness of Old Widows and Married Women', in G. Dooghe and J. Helander (eds), *Family Life in Old Age* (The Hague, Boston and London, 1979).

Hallissy, M., 'Widow to be: May in Chaucer's "The Merchant's Tale"', *Studies in Short Fiction* 26 (1989), 295–304.

Juneja, R., 'Widowhood and Sexuality in Chapman's "The Widow's Tears"', *Philological Quarterly* 67 (1988) 157–75.

Keysser, A., 'Widowhood in 18th Century Massachusetts: A Problem in the History of the Family', *Perspectives in American History* 8 (1974) 83–119.

Knodel, J. and K.A. Lynch, 'The Decline of Remarriage: Evidence from German Village Populations in the Eighteenth and Nineteenth Centuries', *Journal of Family History* 10 (1985) 34–59.

Lafouge, J.P., 'Sincerité et veuvage: Corneille, Racine, La Fontaine, Mme de Villedieu, Mme de Lafayette', *Cahiers du Dix-septième: An Interdisciplinary Journal* 4 (1990) 151–66.

Mikesell, M.L., 'Catholic and Protestant Widows in *The Duchess of Malfi*', *Renaissance and Reformation* 7 (1983) 265–79.

Palazzi, M., 'Female Solitude and Patrilineage: Unmarried Women and Widows during the Eighteenth and Nineteenth Centuries', *Journal of Family History* 15 (1990) 443–59.

Pitchon, M., '"Widows"' Wills for Philadelphia Country, 1750–1784: A Study of Pennsylvania German Folklife', *Pennsylvania Folklife* 26 (1976–77) 19–26.

Ricketson, W.F., 'To be Young, Poor, and Alone: The Experience of Widowhood in the Massachusetts Bay Colony, 1675–76', *New England Quarterly* 64 (1991) 113–27.

Rigaud, N.J., *Femme mythifiée, femme de raison: la veuve dans la comédie anglaise au temps de Shakespeare, 1600–1625* (Aix en Provence, 1986).

Riley, J.C., 'That Your Widows may Be Rich: Providing for Widowhood in Old Regime Europe', *Economisch- en Sociaal-Historisch Jaarboek* 45 (1982) 58–76.

Speth, L.E., 'More than Their "Thirds": Wives and Widows in Colonial Virginia', *Women and History* 4 (1982) 5–41.

Thomas, R.P., 'Twice Victims: Virtuous Widows in the Eighteenth-Century French Novel', *Studies on Voltaire and the Eighteenth Century*, no. 266 (1989) 433–49.

Thompson, J.A., *Wives, Widows, Witches and Bitches: Women in Seventeenth-Century Devon* (New York, 1993).

Waciega, L.W., 'A "Man of Business": The Widow of Means in Southeastern

Pennsylvania 1750–1850', *William and Mary Quarterly* series III, 44 (1987) 40–64.

Wintjes, S.M., 'Survivors and Status: Widowhood and Family in the Early Modern Netherlands', *Journal of Family History* 7 (1982) 396–405.

Woloch, I., 'War-Widows Pensions: Social Policy in Revolutionary and Napoleonic France', *Societas* 6 (1976) 235–54

MODERN PERIOD

Basler, R. 'And for His Widow and Orphans', *Quarterly Journal of the Library of Congress* 27 (1970) 291–4.

Borchart, B., *Clara Schumann: die Witwe als Herausgeberin* (Stuttgart, 1991).

Bradbury, B., 'Surviving as a Widow in 19th-Century Montreal', *Urban History Review* 17 (1989) 148–60.

Dardy, C., 'Les nouveaux veufs ou à la recherche de la veuve et l'orphelin', *Les Temps Modernes* 42 (1986) 94–103.

Gertzog, I.N., 'The Matrimonial Connection: The Nomination of Congressmen's Widows for the House of Representatives', *Journal of Politics* 42 (1980) 820–33.

Kincaid, D.D., 'Over his Dead Body: A Positive Perspective on Widows in the U.S. Congress', *Western Political Quarterly* 31 (1978) 96–104.

Lopata, H.Z., 'Social Relations of Black and White Widowed Women in a Northern Metropolis', *American Journal of Sociology* 78 (1973) 1003–10.

—— 'Widowhood in Polonia', *Polish American Studies* 34 (1977) 7–23.

—— *Widows II: North America* (Durham, NC, 1987).

Lopata, H.Z. and H.P. Brehm, *Widows and Dependant Wives: From Social Problem to Federal Program* (New York, 1986).

Marris, P., *Widows and Their Families* (London, 1958).

Menchik, P.L., 'Is the Family Wealth Squandered? A Test of the Merry-Widow Model', *Journal of Economic History* 44 (1984) 835–8.

Palmore, E., 'Cross-Cultural Perspectives on Widowhood', *Journal of Cross-Cultural Gerontology* 2 (1987) 93–105.

Pitt-Rivers, J., 'La veuve andalouse', in *Femmes et patrimoine dans les sociétés rurales de l'Europe méditerranéenne* (Paris, 1987) 261–8.

Proffer, C.R., *The Widows of Russia and other Writings* (Ann Arbor, 1987).

Scadron, A., *On Their Own: Widows and Widowhood in the American Southwest, 1849–1939* (Urbana, 1988).

APPENDIX: HINDUISM

Bosch, L.P. van den, this vol., ch. 8.

Caroll, L. 'Law, Custom and Statutory Social Reform: The Hindu Widow's Remarriage Act of 1856', *Indian Economic and Social History Review* 20 (1983) 363–88.

Copley, A., 'The Debate on Widow Remarriage and Polygamy: Aspects of Moral Change in Nineteenth Century Bengal and Yorubaland', *Journal of Imperial and Commonwealth History* 7 (1979) 128–48.

Mazumbar, V., 'Comment on Suttee', *Signs* 2 (1979) 269–73.

Vasta, R.S., 'The Remarriage and Rehabilitation of the Hindu Widows in India 1856–1914', *Journal of Indian History* 54 (1976) 713–30.

Yang, A.A., 'Whose Sati? Widow burning in early 19th century India', *Journal of Women's History* 1 (1989) 8–33.

INDEX